Becoming an
Interior Designer

D1089375

Other Titles in the Series

A GUIDE TO CAREERS IN DESIGN

Becoming an Interior Designer

Christine Piotrowski, ASID, IIDA

WILEY

JOHN WILEY & SONS, INC.

Wiley also publishes its books in a variety of electronic formats. Some content that appears in print may not be available in electronic books. For more information about Wiley products, visit our web site at www.wiley.com.

Library of Congress Cataloging-in-Publication Data:

Piotrowski, Christine M.,
 Becoming an interior designer : a visual career guide / by Christine M. Piotrowski.
   p. cm.
Includes bibliographical
   references and index.
 ISBN 0-471-23286-6 (Paper)
1. Interior decoration—
   Vocational guidance.
   I. Title.
 NK2116.P56 2004
 747'.023'73—dc21
        2003007940

Printed in the United States of America

10 9 8 7 6 5 4 3 2 1

Disclaimer

To Martha and Casmier,

looking down from above.

With love,

Christine

A truly committed decision is the force

that changes your life.
—*Anonymous*

Contents

Preface

THIS BOOK IS ABOUT the profession of interior design and the professional interior designer. If you are a student in high school or a postsecondary student who is considering interior design as a career, this book will help you understand what the profession is about. Maybe you have lost interest in your current career and are looking for a way to express your creative side. This book can assist you in understanding how interior design may help you achieve that goal. It will not, however, explain how to establish a practice or actually teach you how to do interior design.

The interior design profession has two broad segments of specialization. Residential interior design, primarily the design of private residences, is the area most familiar to the public. Commercial interior design is the other large segment of the profession. This specialty involves the interior design of businesses such as offices, hotels, stores, restaurants—even airports, sports stadiums, and prisons. Within each of these broad areas, designers might focus on one or more subareas—condominiums or retail stores, for example.

The profession has changed significantly over the last forty years or so. Here are just three ways in which it is different:

(1) building and safety codes are emphasized; (2) the growing complexity of projects and the design process means interior designers must be better educated and trained; and (3) licensing and legal responsibilities focus added attention on project management and contract administration. Thus, educational preparation, technical skills, knowledge requirements, and the measurement of professional competency via testing have raised the profession to a higher level than that of the stereotypical decorator. Interior design in the twenty-first century is much more than selecting colors and arranging furniture.

This book will help you better understand this exciting, creative profession by describing interior design as a career. Chapter 1 provides an overview of the profession of interior design through a brief look at its history, licensing, and other general topics. Chapter 2 describes the activities that occur between the inception of a project and its completion. It also discusses working relationships with allied professionals and project management. Chapter 3 offers insights into the opportunities for specialization within the field through interviews with practitioners currently working in many of the specialties. Chapter 4 discusses the various environments in which interior designers work. For example, some designers work by themselves from home offices while others work as team members in large design firms—and everything in between. Chapter 5 presents an overview of the business side of the profession. This chapter discusses how interior designers find clients through marketing activities, the importance of contracts in defining proposed services, and how interior designers earn revenue. The educational requirements of interior designers are discussed in Chapter 6. Information about finding a job in interior design appears in several chapters.

An exciting element of this book is the inclusion of quotes and comments by practicing professionals. Numerous interior designers in many specialties have provided their insights to help you discover what this profession is like. Their comments in response to specific questions can be found at the end of each chapter. This feature is unique among career books and will help you understand what interior design is like from people doing professional work every day.

You will note initials that follow the names of many interior designers. These represent the appellations of professional organizations in which the designers hold membership and are included because attaining professional association membership is an important milestone for professional interior designers—or any design professional. Here is how to interpret this important alphabet soup:

AIA—American Institute of Architects
ARIDO—Association of Registered Interior Designers of Ontario
ASID—American Society of Interior Designers
CID—Certified Interior Designer
CMG—Color Marketing Group
IDC—Interior Designers of Canada
IDEC—Interior Design Educators Council
IFMA—International Facility Management Association
IIDA—International Interior Design Association
NKBA—National Kitchen and Bath Association
RIBA—Royal Institute of British Architects

If a designer's appellation begins with *F*, as in FASID, that individual has earned the highest national honor of his or her association—a fellowship.

References at the end of the book point you to more detailed information on the topics covered in the text. The appendix provides contact information for the organizations mentioned.

I hope you will find *Becoming an Interior Designer* a valuable source for learning about the exciting career of a professional interior designer. This multidisciplinary creative profession is a satisfying way to express creativity while providing functional and aesthetic solutions to the client's projects. Because the field offers so many avenues of work, it is quite likely that you can find a niche that will be as exciting and rewarding to you as it has for the thousands who have come before you. These are exciting times for the interior design profession. I welcome you into it!

Acknowledgments

I WOULD LIKE TO THANK the many interior designers, educators, and other design professionals who have shared their insights, experiences, and passions about the profession as well as their project photos and drawings for this book. Their names appear in the appendix. Lauren LaFrance of John Wiley & Sons also deserves much thanks for assistance above and beyond the call as well as Monique Calello at Wiley for guiding this book through the production process. Of course, special thanks go to Amanda Miller (also of John Wiley & Sons), my long-time editor and friend, for encouraging me to do this book and for patiently seeing it to completion.

Chapter One

An Introduction to the Interior Design Profession

We spend over 90 percent of our day in interior spaces.
Despite this, most of us take interiors for granted,
barely noticing the furniture, colors, textures, and
other elements—let alone the form of the space—of
which they are made. Sometimes, of course, the design
of the interior does catch our attention. Maybe it's the
pulsing excitement of a casino, the rich paneling of an
expensive restaurant, or the soothing background of a
religious facility.

As you are reading this book, you obviously have an interest in interiors and interior design. It might be because you have always enjoyed rearranging the furniture in your home. Maybe you like to draw imaginative floor plans for houses. It could be that a relative or friend is a contractor and you have been involved in the actual construction of a building in some way.

Interior design professionals provide the owners of homes and many kinds of businesses with functionally successful and aesthetically attractive interior spaces. An interior designer might specialize in working with private residences or with commercial interiors such as hotels, hospitals, retail stores, offices, and dozens of other private and public facilities. In many ways, the interior design profession benefits society by focusing on how space—and interior environment—should look and function. By planning the arrangement of partition walls, considering how the design affects the health, safety, and welfare of occupants, selecting furniture and other goods, and specifying aesthetic embellishments for the space, the designer brings the interior to life. A set of functional and aesthetic requirements expressed by the client becomes reality.

The interior design profession is much more than selecting colors and fabrics and rearranging furniture. The professional interior designer must consider building and life safety codes, address environmental issues, and understand the basic construction and mechanical systems of buildings. He or she must effectively communicate design concepts through precisely scaled drawings and other documents used in the industry. The professional interior designer space-plans the rooms and the furniture that goes into them, determining location of partition walls, selecting colors, materials, and products so that what is supposed to occur in the spaces actually can. Another critical responsibility concerns how to manage all the tasks that must be accomplished to complete a project as large as a 1,000-room casino hotel or as small as someone's home. The interior designer must also have the business skills to complete projects within budget for the client while making a profit for the design firm.

The National Council for Interior Design Qualification (NCIDQ)—an independent agency whose purpose is to administer an examination testing the competency of interior designers for professional licensing and association membership—offers the following definition of the interior design profession. It was developed with the cooperation of practicing interior designers and educators:

> The professional interior designer is qualified by education, experience and examination to enhance the function and quality of interior spaces.
>
> For the purpose of improving the quality of life, increasing productivity and protecting the health, safety and welfare of the public, the professional interior designer:
>
> - analyzes the client's needs, goals and life safety requirements;
> - integrates findings with knowledge of interior design;
> - develops and presents final design recommendations through appropriate presentation media;
> - prepares working drawings and specifications for non-load bearing interior construction, materials, finishes, space planning, furnishings, fixtures and equipment;
> - collaborates with licensed practitioners who offer professional services in the technical areas of mechanical, electrical and load-bearing design as required for regulatory approval;
> - prepares and administers bids and contract documents as the client's agent;
> - reviews and evaluates design solutions during implementation and upon completion.[1]

Professional interior designers are not interior decorators and interior decorators are not professional interior designers, although the public generally does not see any difference. "Interior design is *not* the same as decoration. Decoration is the furnishing or adorning a space with fashionable or beautiful things. Decoration, although a valuable and important element of an interior, is not solely concerned with human interaction or human behavior. Interior design is *all* about human behavior and human interaction."[2]

Although a professional interior designer might provide interior decoration services, an interior decorator does not have the education and experience to perform the many other services of a professional interior designer. A decorator is primarily concerned with the aesthetic embellishment of the interior and rarely has the expertise, for example, to produce the necessary drawings for the construction of non–load-bearing walls and certain mechanical systems that are routinely produced by a professional interior designer.

History

COMPARED TO MANY other professions, the interior design profession has a relatively short history. Architects, artisans, and craftspeople completed interiors before interior decorators began offering their services. Architects created the design of a building's structure and often the interiors. They would engage craftspeople to create and produce the furnishings needed to complete the interior. Other artisans lent their expertise with decorative embellishments and the production of handmade pieces for the interior. Of course, all this was accomplished for the world of the wealthy and the mighty—not the average person.

Many historians have credited Elsie de Wolfe (1865–1950) as the first person to successfully engage in interior decoration as a career separate from architecture. At about the turn of the twentieth century, de Wolfe established a career by offering "interior decoration" services to her society friends in New York City.

"She was an actress and a society figure before she began to remodel her own home, transforming typically Victorian rooms with stylish simplicity by using white paint, cheerful colors, and flowery printed chintzes."[3] Her friends recognized her alternative decor, which was a great contrast to the dark, deep colors and woods of Victorian interiors. She is also believed to be among the first decorators to charge for her services rather than be paid only a commission on the goods she sold to clients.[4]

The door opened for this profession at the turn of the twentieth century for several reasons. One was the development of new technologies during the nineteenth-century Industrial Revolution that helped make possible machine-made furnishings and other products.

These mass-produced items were cheaper and more available to the average consumer. As demand for these goods grew, department stores—a new concept in the nineteenth century—began displaying the new products in

Ethical Standards

The consequences of unethical behavior by politicians, business leaders, sports figures, and many others are widely discussed in the media. Ethical behavior by all members of our society is expected, though not always forthcoming.

Ethical standards help those engaged in a specific profession understand what is considered right and wrong in the performance of the work of the profession. In the case of interior design, ethical standards are guidelines for the practitioner's work relationships with clients, other interior design professionals, employers, the profession in general, and the public.

Interior design professionals who affiliate with a professional association are required to abide by that organization's written code of ethical standards. When they do not, the association may take action against them—and it does not take ethics charges lightly. Designers who remain independent are also expected to conduct their business in an ethical manner, although they cannot be charged with ethics violations. Many unethical actions have legal consequences as well.

Behaving ethically is not hard. What is hard is facing the consequences when one behaves in an unethical manner, regardless of whether or not one is affiliated with an interior design professional association.

their stores, attracting the average consumer. This exposure to new products helped generate interest in the decoration of residences by trained decorators.

The success of the early decorators encouraged many women to seek this avenue of professional and career enrichment. It was, after all, one of the few respectable ways for women to work in the early part of the twentieth century. Educational programs were developed to train the early decorators in period styles and to provide the educational background needed to plan interiors. One of the first schools to offer effective training in interior decoration was the New York School of Applied and Fine Arts, now known as Parsons School of Design.

As the profession continued to grow in the major cities, "decorators clubs" were formed in order for the decorators to meet, share ideas, and learn more about their profession. The first national decorators association was formed in 1931 and was called the American Institute of Interior Decorators (AIID)—later to be called the American Institute of Interior Designers (AID). In 1975, the two largest groups of professionals at the time—AID and the National Society of Interior Designers (NSID) merged to form the American Society of Interior Designers (ASID).

By the 1940s, due to changes in the profession and the built-environment industry in general, many individuals working in the field began to call themselves *interior designers* instead of *interior decorators* and to refer to their profession as *interior design* rather *decorating*. The distinction reflected in these new terms was first applied to those few interior designers working with business clients. In addition, many kinds of new business clients appeared, slowly providing other opportunities for the gradual growth of the commercial interior design profession. Dorothy Draper (1889–1969) is well known for her design of commercial interiors such as hotel lobbies, clubs, and stores. Her influence grew in the 1940s, and she is often identified by historians as one of the first interior designers to specialize in commercial interiors rather than residences.

Of course, numerous influential interior decorators and designers contributed to the development of the profession as we know it today. The names Eleanor McMillen, Ruby Ross Wood, Mrs. Henry Parish II, Dorothy Draper, Billy Baldwin, Florence Schust Knoll, and T. H. Robsjohn-Gibbings are familiar to many practitioners in the field. Architects Frank Lloyd Wright, Mies van der Rohe, and Richard Meier along with designers David Hicks, Mark Hampton, Michael Graves, and Warren Platner are just a few of the fine professionals whose talent immeasurably contributed to the growth of the interior design profession in the twentieth century. If you would like to learn about the history of the profession in greater detail, you may wish to read one of the books listed in the references.

Getting In

Getting a job in interior design today requires an appropriate education and mastering skills from drafting and drawing to effective communication. It involves learning technical areas of construction, mechanical systems, and codes as well as showing you have the interest and enthusiasm to work in the profession. Getting in also means knowing what kind of job you want and whether you want to work in a residential or commercial specialty. You also need to consider if you would work best in a small studio, a large multidisciplinary firm, or an intermediate-size practice.

When it comes time to look for a job, be sure to do your homework on the companies in which you are interested. If you know something about the company before the interview, you will make a far better impression *at* the interview. Investigate the style and type of interior design work the firm does by researching trade magazines and local print media. Look for the firm's website and carefully examine as much of it as you can. Talk to professors who know something about the company. Your college placement office might be able to help as well.

You can also find out about possible jobs and about a specific company by researching:

- Chamber of Commerce articles and reports
- local magazines and newspapers
- Dun & Bradstreet Reference Book
- Registrar of Contractors
- Board of Technical Registration
- Yellow Pages directory
- professional association chapters
- family and friends

You may need two or more versions of your résumé, each specific to a type of design work you are interested in obtaining. For example, you should organize your résumé differently when you apply for a position with a firm primarily engaged in residential design work versus one that specializes in hospitality interior design. The résumé also should be somewhat different if you are applying to a large multidisciplinary firm versus a small firm. The same goes for your portfolio. Showing a commercial firm a portfolio of residential projects could be a waste of time all around. Résumés and portfolios are discussed in other sections of this book.

Looking for a job in interior design—whether your first one as you finish school or when you move from one firm to another—is a job in itself. It is important that you go about it in a sensible and organized fashion. The more prepared you are, the more homework you do before you even start your search, the greater your chances of gaining that ideal position.

High-End Residential, Construction Remodeling

DONNA VINING, FASID
President, Vining Design Associates, Inc., Houston, Texas

What has been your greatest challenge as an interior designer?
Interpreting clients' wishes and giving them what they want and need.

How important is interior design education in today's industry?
It is monumental. If we are to be a profession, we must have a consistent, quality educational program, ever changing and evolving as today's advances move faster and faster.

What led you to enter your design specialty?
My mother was a huge influence. She was my very own Sister Parish, always decorating our home. When I was a teenager, she opened her own antique shop in a small house on the same property as our home.

What are your primary responsibilities and duties?
Everything!! When you are the owner, you have all the financial and managerial type of responsibilities and duties as well as being the lead interior designer. In residential, clients want you, and even though my staff teams on all projects, I am heavily involved in most of them.

What is the most satisfying part of your job?
Hearing the clients say they love our work!

What is the least satisfying part of your job?
Depending on others for my end product—so many people are involved, and it is hard to make things happen just like I want them.

Private residence: master suite. Donna Vining, FASID, Vining Design Associates, Inc., Houston, Texas. Photographer: Rob Muir.

What is the most important quality or skill of a designer in your specialty?
Listening skills and teaching clients what is best for them and their lifestyle.

What advice would you give someone who wants to be an interior designer?
Take business and psychology classes and realize that the actual design portion is a small part of the business.

Who or what experience has been a major influence on your career?
My mother was a huge influence. And once I was in the field, the ability to make things beautiful but always functional and durable.

Private residence: living room. Donna Vining, FASID, Vining Design Associates, Inc., Houston, Texas. Photographer: Rob Muir.

Private residence: dining room. Donna Vining, FASID, Vining Design Associates, Inc., Houston, Texas. Photographer: Rob Muir.

Professional Associations

SEVERAL ASSOCIATIONS SERVE members of the interior design profession in the United States and Canada. Some, such as the American Society of Interior Designers (ASID), serve broad segments of the profession. Others, such as the Institute of Store Planners (ISP), represent specialty designers. The two largest associations in the United States are ASID, with over 33,000 members, and the International Interior Design Association (IIDA), with over 10,000 members. In Canada, the Interior Designers of Canada (IDC) is the national professional association. Eight Canadian provinces also have provincial associations that support local interior designers.

When you become a member of a professional association, you join a network of colleagues with similar interests. Many interior designers are sole practitioners, working by themselves from home offices or small studios. Chapter and national activities of associations give sole practitioners and designers working in larger firms opportunities to obtain and exchange information and gain from peer relationships. Becoming involved in chapter and national committees gives members another opportunity to hone leadership and management skills as well as form extended networks that develop into valuable resources for both personal and professional growth. Members of associations are able to take advantage of the services offered by a headquarters staff who analyze and disseminate large amounts of information that the nonaffiliated designer may not have access to, let alone time to read and absorb. Professional associations also serve as a filter and source of information to help members address issues related to interior design practice, thus helping them remain effective practitioners of interior design.

Association members obtain information via newsletters, mailings, national

Canadian Interior Design Professional Associations

National Association
- Interior Designers of Canada (IDC)

Provincial Associations
- Registered Interior Designers of Alberta
- Interior Designers Institute of British Columbia
- Professional Interior Designers Institute of Manitoba
- Association of Registered Interior Designers of New Brunswick
- Association of Interior Designers of Nova Scotia
- Association of Registered Interior Designers of Ontario
- Société des Designeurs d'Intérieur de Québec
- Interior Designers Association of Saskatchewan

Private residence: kitchen remodel. Sally Howard D'Angelo, ASID, S. H. Designs, Windham, New Hampshire. Photographer: Bill Fish.

and regional conferences, and email news flashes. Of course, association websites also provide a great deal of important information to interior designers, some of it only available to members. In addition, local chapters throughout the United States and Canada hold member meetings on the local level and provide information via chapter newsletters, educational seminars, and electronic communications.

In addition, association membership conveys a meaningful credential that proves important in marketing to potential clients. Acceptance into an association, especially at the highest level of membership, means you have met stringent criteria related to education, experience, and competency testing. It also means you are bound to abide by stated ethical standards. The prestige this offers helps you compete against individuals who have not obtained the education and other competency qualifications of association members.

An important responsibility of the associations is to function on behalf of members in relation to government regulation and to national and even international issues. Professional associations have staff departments that research governmental regulations that might affect the professional practice of interior design and the health, safety, and welfare of the public. This information is forwarded so individual state or provincial chapters can inform local members about impending legislation, regulation, and other issues that affect the profession.

Which association is best for you? You alone can answer that question by

becoming involved in one, initially as a student member while attending university or college programs and then advancing to the first level of practitioner membership on graduation. Although each association provides similar services, the activities of the local chapter often differ; this commonly influences the individual's choice of organization. Attending a few local chapter meetings and getting to know people in the chapters will help you determine which association is right for you.

So you may have an understanding of the qualifications of membership in a professional association, Exhibit 1-1 provides a brief overview of membership qualification for ASID and IIDA. These associations were selected because they are the biggest, in terms of membership, in the United States. Membership qualifications in other associations may vary. Exhibit 1-2 gives short descriptions of a few other professional interior design associations. Addresses for all these associations are in the Appendix.

Exhibit 1-1

Membership Qualifications

American Society of Interior Designers (ASID)

Professional
- graduation from recognized program of study in interior design
- educational requirement must meet NCIDQ requirements
- minimum two years' work experience in interior design
- completed NCIDQ examination
- appellation usage: Jane Doe, ASID

Allied
- graduation from recognized program of study in interior design
- minimum two years' work experience in interior design
- appellation usage: Jane Doe, Allied Member ASID

Other membership categories exist for individuals who are not interior design practitioners.

International Interior Design Association (IIDA)

Professional
- graduation from recognized program of study in interior design
- educational requirement must meet NCIDQ requirements
- minimum two years' work experience in interior design
- completed NCIDQ examination
- Ten hours (1.0) continuing education units (CEU) credits every two years
- appellation usage: John Smith, IIDA

Associate
- graduation from recognized program of study in interior design
- minimum two years' work experience in interior design
- Ten hours (1.0) CEU credits every two years
- Appellation usage: Associate Member, IIDA

Other membership categories exist for individuals who are not interior design practitioners.

Note: NCIDQ requires a minimum of six years of education and work experience in order to qualify to take the examination. The minimum educational requirement by NCIDQ is a two-year certificate in interior design.

Exhibit 1-2

Other Professional Associations

American Institute of Architects (AIA)
Represents the interests of professional architects. Interior designers may be eligible for affiliate membership in a local AIA chapter.

Building Office and Management Association (BOMA)
Members are primarily owners or managers of office buildings. Interior designers who work for firms specializing in large corporate office facilities often belong to BOMA.

Interior Designers of Canada (IDC)
The national association of Canadian interior designers. It deals with issues of national and international interest on behalf of the members of the provincial associations (see Box, page 10).

International Facility Management Association (IFMA)
Members are primarily those responsible for the management and/or planning of corporate facilities. IFMA members may work for a corporation such as a large banking institution, IBM, or public utility such as AT&T, or be independent facility planners/space planners.

Institute of Store Planners (ISP)
Represents interior designers who specialize in retail stores and department stores.

National Kitchen and Bath Association (NKBA)
Represents interior designers who specialize in kitchen and/or bath design or are retailers of products for kitchens and baths such as cabinet makers.

U.S. Green Building Council (USGBC)
Represents individuals from across the built-environment industry working to promote buildings that are environmentally healthy to live and work.

Note: Many other specialty associations may be of benefit to interior designers, depending on their specialty practice. Some are listed in the Appendix; others may be found in interior design trade magazines such as *Interior Design*, *Contract*, and *Interiors and Sources*.

Corporate Headquarters, Offices, and Retail Spaces

FREDERICK MESSNER, IIDA

Principal, Phoenix Design One, Inc.
Phoenix, Arizona

What has been your greatest challenge as an interior designer?
There is a fine balance between the activity of design and the need to handle all the business activities that go into the normal day. They are both necessities and constantly in competition for the ten hours per day we seem to feel are required.

Corporate headquarters: entry. Fred Messner, IIDA, Phoenix Design One, Inc., Phoenix, Arizona. Photographer: Christiaan Blok.

What led you to enter your design specialty?
From a young age, I was always interested in how things go together and in drawing. As I learned more about the tools of our trade, I became more interested in how I could manipulate space to affect people. My interest is in commercial design because I believe it has the potential to have great impact.

What are your primary responsibilities and duties?
Design mentor, financial control, strategic planning for the design firm, human resources, design and project management, marketing, and father confessor.

Corporate headquarters: reception area. Fred Messner, IIDA, Phoenix Design One, Inc., Phoenix, Arizona. Photographer: Christiaan Blok.

What is the most satisfying part of your job?

Teaching the many aspects of design as well as practicing the same is the reward that is most enjoyed.

What is the least satisfying part of your job?

The challenge of dissatisfied clients due to any number of reasons is a part of the job that can be, at times, very difficult.

What is the most important quality or skill of a designer in your specialty?

The ability to listen and interpret wants and needs with the best possible solution is the mark of a good commercial designer. In the design of office space, it takes knowledge of competing space and construction methods and understanding of the client's sophistication, budget, and taste as well as timelines. The best solution most often is a compromise that blends the most positive aspects of all.

How important is interior design education in today's industry?

It all starts here. This is the opportunity to start building a base that will last a lifetime. Interests and habits that start in school will carry designers into the profession.

Who or what experience has been a major influence on your career?

My involvement with IBD and then IIDA was a link to my colleagues and the profession. It allowed me to gain insight into everyday occurrences with a different perspective. I have also built valuable friendships.

Corporate headquarters: board room. Fred Messner, IIDA, Phoenix Design One, Inc., Phoenix, Arizona. Photographer: Christiaan Blok.

Commercial—College and University Buildings

LINDA KRESS, ASID
Director of Interior Design
Lotti, Krishan & Short Architects
Tulsa, Oklahoma

University: University of Northern Iowa, cappuccino bar. Linda Kress, ASID, Lotti, Krishan & Short, Inc., Tulsa, Oklahoma. Photographer: Shimer@Hedrich Blessing.

What has been your greatest challenge as an interior designer?
Greatest challenge number 1: Keeping a marketing focus at all times. It's my opinion that many if not most universities fail to prepare design students enough for the importance of the business angle and the marketing of a firm—even if you are not the owner!

Greatest challenge number 2: Accepting that in our type of work, no project is ever perfect. In our field (commercial design), we nearly always have to settle for projects that are less than perfect—primarily to keep budgets under control, but occasionally as a compromise with the client. I feel that having total control over projects while in school is fun and tells the instructor whether or not you've got what it takes; but it doesn't prepare you for the necessary art of compromise.

What led you to enter your design specialty?
I think each individual designer has to try things until he or she finds a niche. One mostly applies for any design-related job at first—which often determines how one acquires a specialty. After several years in residential design, I felt very restless. In order to make the move to a commercial firm, I had to be willing to get comfortable with AutoCAD very fast. Luckily, I found an architectural firm willing to give me time to learn several programs in exchange for my immediate experience and expertise in the area of finishes and furnishings.

University:
University of Northern Iowa, bistro. Linda Kress, ASID, Lotti, Krishan & Short, Inc., Tulsa, Oklahoma. Photographer: Shimer@Hedrich Blessing.

What are your primary responsibilities and duties?
As director, I now have the opportunity to look over projects that may be done by a younger designer before they go to the client. I also handle problems as they come up—diplomatically, of course. And I represent our firm in a marketing capacity, calling on clients. I am often part of a presentation team after our firm has made a short list and is going for the contract.

What is the most satisfying part of your job?
Most satisfying: Working every day with talented, creative people—on most commercial projects one is part of a team. I find this generally exciting and fun. Second most satisfying: The walk-through when a project is newly finished, the furniture is installed, and the client is excited and happy.

What is the least satisfying part of your job?
Least satisfying: Not getting a project that I worked and marketed hard to get! Second least satisfying: Working on a project where the client does not allow me to do the professional job I know should be done, which results in a finished work that is far from what it could have been.

What is the most important quality or skill of a designer in your specialty?

One must be a good listener—whatever your design specialty—be very organized, and be able to work under pressure. Naturally, you should be a good designer and constantly keep abreast of developments in the field.

University: University of Northern Iowa, pizza bar. Linda Kress, ASID, Lotti, Krishan & Short, Inc., Tulsa, Oklahoma. Photographer: Shimer@Hedrich Blessing.

Who or what experience has been a major influence on your career?

Several of my professors at the University of Missouri, but particularly Dr. Ronn Phillips, who first introduced me to the real depth and power of this profession. In class, he taught us about design and behavior. In and out of class, he taught us that what we do should always be *useful*; that we absolutely must be able to think a thing through; that a career as a designer should be interesting, challenging, rewarding, and exciting—but it would be up to us to make it so.

My three employers (architects John Lotti, Garret Krishan, and David Short) have constantly challenged me with projects and tasks that always seem a step above my capability. In doing this, and in expecting me to get the job done, they have helped me stretch and grow. It's not always comfortable, but it's always interesting!

Interior Design Registration and Licensing

BEGINNING IN 1982, states began passing legislation to license or register professionals working in interior design. Of course, attempts to regulate interior design practice had been made before. Alabama was the first state to successfully enact legislation affecting interior design. As of 2002, 24 jurisdictions in the United States and Puerto Rico had legislation that required specific educational, work experience, and testing requirements in order for individuals to work as or call themselves an interior designer. Exhibit 1-3 lists the states that have legislation pertaining to interior design work and the type of legislation that has been enacted. Canadian provinces with provincial associations all have some form of legislation.

Legislation can take many forms. In some states, it restricts who may call himself or herself an interior designer. In this case, the legislation is commonly referred to as *title registration*. It does not limit who may practice interior design but rather limits the title one may use as a practitioner. Some states have a state certification regulation. This is similar to a title act, but in this case practitioners can call themselves *certified interior designer*.

Where such legislation exists, individuals cannot advertise themselves as a "registered interior designer" or *certified interior designer* unless they meet the education, experience, and examination requirements defined by the jurisdiction. This type of legislation is currently the norm in the Canadian provinces.

Some jurisdictions have gone one step further and passed legislation that limits who may practice interior design services as described by a state board of technical registration. If designers do not pursue and meet the requirements set by the state to practice the profession, then they are prohibited from performing the professional services of an interior designer as defined by the state. This type of legislation is called a *practice act*. Generally, interior designers working where a practice act has been established are called *registered interior designers* or *interior designer* depending on the exact language of the law in the jurisdiction. As of 2002, only Florida, Alabama, Louisiana, Nevada, Washington, D.C., and Puerto Rico had enacted practice act legislation.

Within selected jurisdictions, licensing or other registration assures the consumer of interior design services that the person hired for the project has the training, experience, and competence to render professional interior design services. With licensure, problems occurring in the interior design phase are the responsibility of the interior designer, and the client has the opportunity to file a complaint with the state board, which can discipline the designer. This protection does not exist where licensing is not in effect. Interior designers use a combination of skills, knowledge, and experience

Exhibit 1-3

Interior Design Registration Laws
in the United States

Alabama	Title and Practice
Arkansas	Title
California	Self-certification
Colorado	Interior Design Permitting Statute
Connecticut	Title
Florida	Title and Practice
Georgia	Title
Illinois	Title
Kentucky	Title
Louisiana	Title and Practice
Maine	Title
Maryland	Title
Minnesota	Title
Missouri	Title
Nevada	Title and Practice
New Mexico	Title

to creatively solve functional and aesthetic problems and meet the needs of the consumer. This is true whether the consumer owns a home or a business facility. It can be argued that no other profession involves as wide a range of technical, aesthetic, planning, and health, safety, and welfare issues as interior design.

ENDNOTES

1. National Council for Interior Design Qualification. 2000. *NCIDQ Examination Study Guide*. Washington, DC: NCIDQ, pp. 22–23.

2. Charlotte S. Jensen. September 2001. "Design Versus Decoration." *Interiors and Sources*, p. 91.

3. John Pile. 2000. *A History of Interior Design*. New York: John Wiley and Sons, p. 255.

4. Nina Campbell and Caroline Seebohm. 1992. *Elsie de Wolfe: A Decorative Life*. New York: Clarkson N. Potter, p. 70.

Allied Professions

The interior designer or client, to provide expertise in specific areas of an interiors project, may hire professionals and consultants in allied fields.

- **Architecture:** The profession of designing and supervising the construction of buildings of all types.
- **Engineering:** The planning and design of various technical aspects of a building or its interior. Types of engineers that might be involved in an interior project include mechanical, electrical, plumbing, heating and ventilation, and structural engineers.
- **Facility planning:** Synonymous with *space planning*. Facility planners often work for client corporations.
- **Graphic design:** The design and development of a wide variety of graphic media for print, film, advertising, books, and other areas of commercial art.
- **Interior architecture:** Many consider this profession synonymous with interior design; however, most state boards of technical registration require that the term *interior architect* be used only by individuals who have graduated from a school of architecture or been certified as an architect.
- **Kitchen and bath design:** The specialty design of residential and commercial kitchens and/or baths.
- **Lighting design:** The specialty design of artificial and natural lighting treatments to enhance the design and function of an interior or exterior space.
- **Space planning:** The planning of interior spaces, especially in commercial facilities. Generally, the space planner has less responsibility for the decorative aspects of the interior than the interior designer.

"How Important Is Certification by Examination and Licensing of Interior Designers Today?"

As a former regulatory board member and president of NCIDQ, I feel certification by examination and the licensure through the states' regulatory processes is critical to the protection of the public health, safety, and welfare. This ensures that the public can rely on those individuals with certification and licensure as having obtained a certain standard of education and professional experience.
— Linda Elliott Smith, FASID

California licenses interior designers and I think it's very important for the profession.
— Jain Malkin, CID

Critical.
— Nila Leiserowitz, FASID

I would like to see Interior Designers certified by examination and licensing of professional qualification to represent the rigorous education that we must have. We need to overcome the image that Interior Designers are nothing more than furniture salesman by the public.
— Sandra Evans, ASID

It becomes more important with each passing year. I believe that in the next couple of decades certification and licensing will become as important and ubiquitous as the CPA exam. And, because of increased liability related to interior design issues (ADA, mold/air quality, ergonomics, etc.) the general public will begin demanding qualified designers.
— Jeffrey Rausch, IIDA

Passing a qualifying examination and becoming registered, or licensed, will be the minimum requirements for interior design in the very near future. Nearly half the states in the US and many of the Canadian provinces already have some legislation in place to regulate our profession. Another ten or so states are currently in the process of getting this type of legislation passed. These two things will become the minimum requirements for those wishing to practice or call themselves "interior designer" in the near future.
— Terri Maurer, FASID

Critical to continued advancement of the profession through regulation of activities undertaken under the heading of "interior design."
— Marilyn Farrow, FIIDA

Very important. As interior designers we work with lighting, building systems, finish materials and furnishings that impact the people living and working in the spaces we design. We need to show competence in designing and specifying for interiors spaces beyond the pure aesthetics. It is critical to be aware of the safety of a building's structural materials, the furnishings, and the finishes in respect to one's health and life safety.
—**Sally Thompson, ASID**

Monumental—the public needs to understand our profession. Examination and licensure assures the public that we are capable of protecting their health, safety, and welfare.
—**Donna Vining, FASID**

It is very important to set industry standards that require at least minimum standards of general knowledge. We owe it to ourselves and to our clients.
—**Michelle King, IIDA**

Very important because of the liabilities that exist in offering professional Interior Design services. A client is paying for professional service and expects the designer to be accountable for the results.
—**Leonard Alvarado**

Immensely!!!
—**Rosalyn Cama, FASID**

Medical office suite: multipurpose conference room. Terri Maurer, FASID, Maurer Design Group, Akron, Ohio.

"How Important Is Interior Design Education in Today's Industry?"

The knowledge gained through structured interior design education is invaluable as the basis for any practitioner.

However, because the interior design profession continues to evolve and expand, the interior design practitioner's education must not stop at graduation. With sources, processes, and code requirements in a constant state of evolution, the interior designer must make a commitment to lifelong education.
   —Linda Elliott Smith, FASID

Education is of the utmost importance. Competition is fierce, and the better prepared one is, the more successful one will be. Education is another ticket in the lottery. The more tickets you have, the better your chances are to win.
   —Charles Gandy, FASID, FIIDA

Critical. As technological data expands, so also does the client's need for professional expertise expand.
   —Marilyn Farrow, FIIDA

Interior design education is extremely important. This complicated profession has many aspects far beyond aesthetics; codes, materials, workflow systems, controlling costs, and just the actual process of implementing a design complicates the process far more than ever before. Therefore, a good design education is a critical foundation for any person's success as an interior designer today.
   —M. Arthur Gensler Jr., FAIA, FIIDA, RIBA

Interior design education is critical in today's industry. It is the first step on the way to becoming a professional in the field.
   —Terri Maurer, FASID

It's hard for me to imagine someone trying to enter this profession in a professional capacity and not have any formal education. I think it's critical.
   —Beth Harmon-Vaughn, FIIDA

It is monumental. If we are to be a profession, we must have a consistent, quality educational program, ever changing and evolving as today's advances move faster and faster.
   —Donna Vining, FASID

Educating designers is crucial to the evolution of our profession in the next generation of designers. We finally are licensed in many states and have begun on the true path to professionalism. But we must forever shut the door on the uneducated designer's ability to design projects, especially commercial projects. The health, welfare, and safety of the public are at stake daily in the decisions we make, and uneducated designers undermine the credibility of our profession.
   —Juliana Catlin, FASID

"Why Did You Become an Interior Designer?"

We all want to make a difference in someone's life and because interior design impacts so many, it was a good way for me to make that difference.
—Charles Gandy, FASID,FIIDA

I have always been interested in space and interior environments and grew up drawing and painting and naturally wanted to major in art in college. My college required that I select a specialty, so I selected interior design. I was still able to take art classes while learning a profession where I could find employment.
—Rita Carson Guest, FASID

I had always loved reading floor plans, even as a child; I had worked for several developers—one in the architectural department—and had always been interested in space planning. And then the social worker in me also liked the idea of working with people to create living environments that functioned well.
—Jan Bast, ASID, IIDA

My passion began as a desire to create better places for people to live and work. I believe that all interior designers share this basic passion. That passion has grown for me to include consideration for how we affect the natural environment in the process. I still focus on interiors, but the choices we make in the process have a significant effect on the larger environment we all share.
—Barbara Nugent, FASID

It provided an opportunity to use my artistic and analytical skills *and* make a living, which I didn't think I could do with an art career.
—Beth Harmon-Vaughn, FIIDA

I saw it as a problem-solving profession that had as its tools physical space, psychology, marketing, surface materials, furnishings, lighting, and so on.
—Bruce Goff, ASID

Couldn't live without the challenges of artistic problem solving.
—Marilyn Farrow, FIIDA

It was my childhood dream to improve interior environments. I described my desire to my grandfather, and he said I was describing a career in interior design.
—Roz Cama, FASID

Creating environments that impact people.
—Nila Leiserowitz, FASID

I envisioned interior design as an opportunity to apply my creativity in a practical way. I saw in it a way to fill my desire to improve our collective quality of life and to satisfy my interest in human behavior.
—Sari Graven, ASID

Believe it or not, I'd never heard of interior design as a profession until I was working my husband's way through college at a local university. I worked in the dean's office, where the interior design program was being developed, and the course curriculum came across my desk. I was so impressed with the interdisciplinary approach of the program through art, architecture, interior design, graphic design, and technology that I became interested in pursuing that new major. I

found it fascinating that many of the courses focused on various forms of creative problem solving.
—Terri Mauer, FASID

I found I had natural design skills that became evident as I was taking elective courses at university while studying for my BA in business and marketing. I then took a few more of these courses, and the rest followed.
—Jeffrey Rausch, IIDA

My love of art and design. I had a career as a graphic artist but found its one-dimensional aspect boring. I always found the presentation boards my fellow art students did for the interior design classes fascinating, so I decided to give it a try. Loved it ever since.
—Robin J. Wagner, ASID, IDEC

Love of beauty and order from chaos.
—Donna Vining, FASID

Actually fell into it working for a large design and furnishings firm after high school. I liked it and explored many avenues of industry.
—Michael Thomas, ASID

I began thinking about a career in interior design after many years of studying the fine

arts. I wanted to be able to develop my fine arts experience in a three-dimensional world.
—Linda Sorrento, ASID, IIDA

I liked the hardware store as a kid. While a business major in college, I decided to add fashion merchandising to make it more interesting and had to take a basic design course as well as textiles. I met a few interior students and figured if they could do it, so could I. So I switched majors and have been at it ever since.
—Melinda Sechrist, FASID

I was working in an architectural firm while in school and saw the potential for rapid advancement in commercial interior design. There was a lack of technical knowledge in the field at that time.
—Fred Messner, IIDA

Interior design is an extension of my creative nature and the fulfillment of my desire to be of service to persons who endeavor to enrich their lives through their physical environment.
—Sandra Evans, ASID

I became an interior designer because it was the closest degree I could find to a fine arts degree that my father would fund. At that time, I was interested in all the art classes, but as I began to take interior design labs, I enjoyed the challenge of interpreting a program combined with the complexity of transferring my ideas into a two- or three-dimensional format.
—Linda Santellanes, ASID

I'm a registered architect, not a professional interior designer. I suppose you could say I'm a professional interior architect who has a great deal of experience designing interiors.
—M. Arthur Gensler Jr., FAIA, FIIDA, RIBA

As a teenager I became interested in spaces, particularly my own personal space, and how, with some thought and manipulation of the elements within the space, that environment could take on a totally different feel.
—Linda E. Smith, FASID

I started out wanting to become an architect. Lucky for me, the closest architectural school to me was at the University of Manitoba, Canada (100 km away from my hometown). The program offers a masters in architecture and is regarded very highly. The undergraduate degrees offered are environmental studies (three years) and interior design (four years). I chose the interior design program. I knew I would have a solid profession to rely on if I did not continue studying for my masters. (The environmental studies program would provide an undergraduate with a very good foundation to proceed into architecture, but it would not provide a solid degree on its own.)

Once I graduated, I gave myself one year to work in the industry before going back to school for my masters. I have been practicing interior design for 15 years and have no intention of obtaining a masters in architecture.
—**Jennifer van der Put, BID, IDC, AEIDO, IFMA**

I started drawing in kindergarten. I was always fascinated with the details in the homes of friends while growing up.
—**Pat Campbell McLaughlin, ASID**

I was influenced by my uncle, who was a successful residential designer and had a propensity for the arts.
—**Leonard Alvarado**

At first it was because I wanted to fix up my own

house. Then others started asking for my interior design advice and urged me to take it up as a profession.
—**Greta Guelich, ASID**

I wanted a profession in which I could use my creative abilities while impacting the public in a positive manner. Interior designers have a great responsibility to the general public (corporate design, hospitality design, etc.). How a space functions, how people feel in that space, is the public safe while in that space, can all people utilize that space regardless of physical ability: these are all considerations I must make for every job. Interior designers have a great responsibility and a new challenge with every new client.
—**Christy Ryan, IIDA**

It was a blending of technical knowledge and the creativity of implementing design theories.
—**Linda Isley, IIDA**

My father was an engineer—too technical. I had a great art teacher mentor in junior high school and high school who encouraged me to pursue an artistic career. My uncle was an architect, so that seemed logical. I went to college for architecture but struggled through a pre-arch

major; then I was again encouraged to look at interior design by a professor. The short of it is that I fell into the profession and haven't looked back. It was the best educational/career decision I could ever have made.
—**David Stone, IIDA**

To provide functional, aesthetically pleasing environments for people to live and work.
—**Sally Nordahl, IIDA**

I always knew that I'd be involved with some type of design, but I had to take a number of art and design classes in college to decide which area was a good fit. I was steered into graphic design by a guidance counselor in college who didn't understand our profession at all. But when I took a job in college working with architectural models, I realized that architecture and design were where my true interests lay.
—**Suzanne Urban, IIDA, ASID**

I have always been intrigued by the built environment and how space, volume, and aesthetics impact our well-being and quality of life.
—**Robert Wright, ASID**

I didn't plan to become an interior designer. I started out with a degree in psychology and, later, through a circuitous route, discovered this field. This was way before Art Gensler had created the field of corporate office interiors. Health care design in those days didn't even exist. In fact, interior design as we know it was taught in only about three schools across the country. At most universities, it was in the home economics department, which was anything but commercial or institutional interior design. It's actually quite an interesting story how I got into the field, but it would take several paragraphs to even scratch the surface. It was, however, quite fortuitous, as I found I really enjoyed it and it brought together many of my talents and abilities. I always had a good head for business, was persuasive and also creative. Those are important prerequisites for this field, especially if one wants to be self-employed.
—**Jain Malkin, CID**

My mother told me I could never make money being an artist. I still like to create, and this seemed to be a good avenue for that.
—**Debra May Himes, ASID, IIDA**

On looking back, I can't say for sure that any one thing swayed me. I always knew that I wanted to be in an artistic profession, yet there was also the mechanical side and the what-makes-it-work? how-was-this-done? aspect. I think interior design found me. Once the decision was made, I have never regretted nor doubted the choice.
—**Derrell Parker, IIDA**

I considered interior design a perfect place to blend my artistic abilities with a desire for a professional career.
—**Juliana Catlin, FASID**

I wanted to focus on the effect of environment on personal success.
—**Neil Frankel, FIIDA, FAIA**

Healthcare: Rotunda with mural of Hygea and Panacea (Greek goddesses of prevention and treatment), Scripps Breast Care Center, La Jolla, California. Interior architecture and design, Jain Malkin, Inc., San Diego, California. Photographer: Glenn Cormier.

The plan has always fascinated me. As a very young child, I drew house plans for fun. And I had a high school art teacher who introduced rural kids to the world of applied art. Everybody assumed a college-bound rural kid would become a teacher or home economist. I enrolled in the College of Arts and Sciences as an art major! A couple of pre-architecture courses pointed me in the direction of architecture or interior design. Economics and circumstances put me in the interior design masters program at the University of Missouri, Columbia. I have never been sorry. The intimate relationship between an interior and the people who live and/or work there is fascinating. I truly believe that when an interior works, people live better, work better, learn better, and heal better.

—M. Joy Meeuwig, IIDA

I loved the idea of assisting people and business.

—Ellen McDowell, ASID

Growing up in the family carpet business, I learned to appreciate the construction of homes and of buildings. Over the years, I was exposed to how people worked and lived. In school, I was taught drafting at an early age. Art classes taught freedom of expression. I thought I wanted to become an architect or a home builder, and some day I might be. In college, I learned what an interior designer was. I realized I had several of the interests that make an interior designer. I believe I am a designer because the field of design found me.

—John Holmes, ASID, IIDA

I was already an architect for 20 years and could not separate the roles of architect and interior designer so I took the NCIDQ so I would be legit (South Carolina has no title or practice act for interior design).

—W. Daniel Shelley, AIA, ASID

To help people create beautiful and functional environments that promote healing and safety.

—Beth Kuzbek, ASID, IIDA, CMG

Engineering is too dry, and architecture is generally too focused on the massing and overall look. Interior design allows me to create the experience.

—Michelle King, IIDA

I enjoy helping people, the practical creativity of the profession, and that every day is different in the life of a designer.

—Stephanie Clemons, PhD, ASID, IDEC

I will give you the long version! This is the story I share with eighth-graders who are interested in interior design:

I grew up the daughter of an architect and engineer. My father designed our house and had it built in 1966. My parents always gave me great freedom in decorating my room—from painting in whatever color I wanted to allowing me to hang whatever I wanted on the walls. When I was in the seventh grade, I really wanted a loft. The ceilings in our contemporary house were very high. My father said if I drew a plan of what I wanted, he would build it. So I had this wonderful loft space in my room with my mattress up high. It was very cool for a 12-year-old!

I was in high school and not sure what I should study in college. I loved arts and crafts projects but didn't take art in high school. However, I did take mechanical drafting, and in the summer I worked a little bit in my father's office drafting elevations and floor plans. When I was in high school, I had a science teacher who said I should study forest engineering because it was a field with few women in it and I would make a lot of money. Sounded good to a 17-year-old—tromping around in the woods with a bunch of guys! I entered the University of Maine at Orono and promptly flunked out after one semester. While I was in Orono, however, I decorated my dorm room and won an honorable mention prize for my room. That prize got me to thinking that maybe I could make a living doing what I'd always enjoyed so much, so I entered Bauder College in Atlanta, Georgia, and received an AA in interior design in 1983. I graduated top of my class—proving that once I knew what I wanted to do I could excel at it.

I worked for an office furniture dealer (Herman Miller) for three years. Then, in 1986, when I asked for a raise (I was making $12,000) and was turned down, I decided to start my own company. At the age of 23, I started Lisa Whited Planning and Design, Inc. I kept the company until 2001.

In 1988, realizing I really needed to add to my design education, I entered the Boston Architectural Center, studying architecture. I studied for three years, commuting from Portland, Maine, to Boston (two hours each way) two nights per week. I did not get my degree—but the additional education was invaluable. I also took classes over the years at the Maine College of Art (color theory, etc.). In 2000, still wanting to add to my education, I entered

Antioch New England Graduate School and gained an MS in Organization and Management, graduating in fall 2002.

—**Lisa Whited, IIDA, ASID, IDEC**

I love buildings, the exterior blending with the interior, and bringing them together in a harmonious manner to create a special place to live, entertain your friends and family, work, and, especially, relax.

—**Kristen Anderson, ASID, CID, RID**

At the time I started interior design school in 1981, I was 30-year-old wife and mother, working in a furniture business my husband and I owned. I was good at helping the customers and thought it would be logical to finish my college degree in interior design rather than in journalism (which is what I was majoring in in the 1960s when I dropped out to get married, as many women did in those days).

As it happened, the FIDER-accredited program at the University of Missouri was powerful. I soon came to understand the true impact designers can have on environments and, therefore, on people (and I'm a people person). I loved every aspect of my education, but I especially loved the people part—the design and behavior

classes; the books *Designing Places for People, A Pattern Language, Humanscape, Environments for People,* and even *Human Dimension for Interior Space*—the ergonomics part even seemed interesting to me. (Weird, huh?)

Now my life has taken many turns away from the plans I had when I was 30! But I love my work—I love being a professional designer.

—**Linda Kress, ASID**

Strong interest in architecture, fine art, and construction.

—**William Peace, ASID**

Through growing up in Japan, I realized that life experiences shape who we are. Everything about my living environment—region, culture, interior dwellings, etc.—influenced the development of my character and how I feel about myself and living. In high school, I specifically realized that I wanted to influence others, as I knew so well how our environment can affect our motivation and zest for life. I decided to do this through interior design, where I could develop interior environments that enhance motivation and positive experiences for others.

—**Susan B. Higbee**

After reaching a previous career goal as a journalist early in life, I decided the only thing left to do was to write a book and quickly realized I didn't know much about anything other than journalism. I thought I should pursue another interest for the subject of the book and went back to college to study interior design. College led to practicing.
—Suzan Globus, ASID

As a child, I was influenced by my mother and grand-mother. Growing up in Miami, I spent a lot of time watching them renovate homes and boats. It was then I realized I could mentally visualize a space in three dimensions. Interior design just seemed to be the natural direction for me.
—Sally Thompson, ASID

I have always been inter-ested in art and architecture and decided to focus on the interior environment when I became familiar with this field in college.
—Janice Carleen Linster, ASID, IIDA, CID

I have always had a great interest in our history and culture as a society. The rooms we choose to inhabit are our interpretation of a personal history.

I grew up in a ranching family in Wyoming. The life-style and environment did not lend themselves toward much more than a practical exis-tence. As I was growing up, when I would visit a place or see a picture of a room that had been purposely composed and designed, it *felt* so enrich-ing. Rooms carry the spirit of their inhabitants, a well-designed room can excite the soul much the same as an exhilarating conversation.
—Cheri R. Gerou, AIA, ASID

This is my second career. I was a fashion designer for many years, but as I became caught up in the business side of the profession, I missed the creativity. Once a designer, always a designer. I switched professions from fashion designer to interior designer because (1) I wanted to design more all-encompassing projects calling for unique solutions in which I could deal directly with the end user, and (2) I wanted to move to a more entrepreneur-friendly field in which I could work alone or in a small team and still accom-plish great things.
—Sally D'Angelo, ASID

Corporate: office lobby. Susan Higbee, Group MacKenzie, Portland, Oregon. Photographer: Randy Shelton.

From a young age, I was always interested in design. I enjoyed art classes and visiting art museums with my parents. I would spend hours with large sheets of paper, drawing entire cities with buildings, houses, and roads. My cities were perfect places to race my matchbox cars. I enjoyed creating my own little world with Lincoln Logs and Legos. My Barbies always had the best-laid-out townhouse on the block. When asked what I wanted to be when I grew up, I would always answer, "an architect." I don't think I really knew what that meant, only that it had something to do with creating the built environment.

I took all the design and drafting classes I could in high school. I was fortunate to have the opportunity to participate in the Georgia Governor's Honors program in Design. My type of artistic talent—more technically oriented—seemed to be the perfect match for architectural design. I entered college determined to get into the School of Architecture and study interior design.
—**Kristi Barker, CID**

To design for the built environment.
—**David F. Cooke, FIIDA, CMG**

I want a career that utilizes both my technical capabilities and creative talents. Interior design is about balancing what is physical and tangible with aesthetic ideals. To me, form and function should be a happy marriage. I also enjoy having new challenges on a regular basis. Each new project offers a chance to approach things differently, to solve a new problem.
—**Kimberly M. Studzinski, ASID**

Institutional: commissioner's office, County Administration Building. Kim Studzinski, ASID. Buchart Horn, Inc./Basco Associates, York, Pennsylvania. Photographer: Bryson Leidich.

Art, architecture, and design were always of interest to me. I started out as an engineering major in college, mostly because I was familiar with it due to two of my sisters having engineering degrees. Quickly I knew engineering did not involve enough design and found myself coming home from class and sketching, drawing, doing anything that was artistic. I needed to get it out of my system. My first choice was to transfer to an architectural program, but the university I attended did not offer architecture and financially I could not transfer to other universities with quality programs. My university did offer environmental design as a degree program. I excelled in the program and mentally knew I had made the right decision.
—**Jennifer Tiernan, IIDA**

In high school, I was fascinated by the way a building's energy was embedded in its structure. I considered studying architecture, but at that time women were not encouraged to be architects, and I entered a liberal arts program instead. After graduation, I took a series of aptitude tests, and architecture looked like the best career choice, so I enrolled at the Boston Architectural Center. After two and a half years of going to school

Lodging: atrium, Millennium Hotel, St. Louis, Missouri. Jennifer Tiernan, Geppetto Studios, Inc.

nights and working days at anything I could get related to architecture, I burned out on school but continued to work. A recession and a move to Denver took me into retail management and human services work. In 1988, I moved back to Boston and got a job with an architect. A vocational counselor advised that, because I loved color and texture and was most interested in how people experienced and used interior spaces, I might study interior design. So back I went to the BAC's interior design program.
—**Corky Binggeli, ASID**

My dad was a contractor and, as a kid, I worked with him on some of his projects. I thought of becoming an architect but lacked the discipline to study, especially math, while I was in college. I was much more interested in following sports and finding a husband than getting an education. I ended up with an education and married later in my career.
—**Mary Fisher Knott, CID, RSPI, Allied Member ASID**

Chapter Two

The Design Process

The process to turn an empty interior into a functionally effective and aesthetically pleasing environment requires a number of tasks by the interior designer. They gather numerous pieces of information from a variety of sources. They make dozens, if not hundreds, of decisions. They develop drawings and documents to ensure the design concepts are properly turned into reality. They perform these tasks in an orderly fashion so as to avoid omitting any of the required tasks; in other words, their sequence of tasks defines the work. This sequence is called the *design process*.

The design process, regardless of the size of the project, falls into five phases. Each phase is important, as each builds on the previous step until the project is complete. The five phases are *programming, schematic design, design development, contract documents,* and *contract administration.* Exhibit 2-1 lists key tasks in each phase of interior design projects. Project development involves tasks required to prospect and secure projects before any actual design work is begun. Although vital to the whole of the process, it is generally not considered a part of the accepted project design process. A brief discussion on how projects are developed is presented to give you insight into this vital activity.

Of course, projects do not really fit into five neat little packages of activities with precise beginnings and endings that do not overlap. At certain times, activities of one phase are still going on as the work of the next phase commences. In addition, some designers argue, not all projects go through all the phases. However, every project, regardless of its complexity or its size, involves some of the activities of each design process phase.

This discussion will help you understand what is expected in the completion of a professional interior design project. The description of the design process in this chapter is presented as an overview of what is commonly done in either a residential or commercial design project. In many cases, many more tasks are necessary in any or all of the phases discussed. The design process discussed here is based on that defined by the National Council of Interior Design Qualification (NCIDQ), as the NCIDQ-defined phases are widely accepted. Sections of books listed in the references will provide further clarification of the design process.

Exhibit 2-1

Key Tasks in Interior Design Projects

1. Programming
- Determine specific client needs, goals, and project objectives.
- Check existing site conditions.
- Review existing or in-development floor plans.
- Review need for consultants.
- Research and review code issues.
- Evaluate existing furniture, furnishings, and equipment (FF&E).
- Finalize project program using graphics and/or written methods.

2. Schematic Design
- Begin initial space planning and furniture planning.
- Develop other conceptual sketches as needed.
- Develop preliminary materials and products specifications.
- Update programming information as needed.
- Prepare preliminary budgets.
- Ensure proposed design solutions comply with codes and regulations.
- Meet with any needed consultants such as architect, contractor, and engineers.
- Present preliminary concepts to client.

3 Design Development
- Refine space plan and furniture plan.
- Refine materials and products specifications.
- Refine budgets.
- Verify all code issues as related to refined plans.
- Prepare other design documents needed to clarify design concepts such as lighting plans, elevations, perspectives, and sample boards.
- Provide presentation of concepts to client.

4. Contract Documents
- Prepare working drawings and specifications of approved plans and concepts.
- Obtain required permits and/or approvals.
- Consult as needed with architect, contractor, engineer, etc.
- Prepare and distribute bid documents.
- Communicate with project stakeholders.
- Review contractor schedules.

5. Contract Administration
- Issue necessary addenda.
- Collect bids and make recommendations to client.
- Provide for client review and acceptance of work in progress.
- Issue purchase orders, invoices, and payments as client agent.
- Conduct periodic site inspections.
- Review submitted shop drawings and samples.
- Track orders of FF&E.
- Conduct final walkthrough.

Design Team Members

- **A&D community:** Stands for architecture and design community. People engaged in architectural and interior design practice.
- **Designer:** The job title usually associated with a mid-level interior designer. Depending on the firm, a "designer" has from three to ten years of experience.
- **Developer:** Provides financial resources to create building projects such as residential housing developments, large hotel properties, and shopping centers.
- **General contractor:** A company or individual licensed to supervise the actual construction of all phases of a building project.
- **Intern:** A student working for a limited period while completing academic course work. Interns are generally unpaid employees of a firm.
- **Junior designer:** An interior designer with limited experience in the profession. Also called a *design assistant*.
- **Principal:** The owner of an interior design practice. In some cases, a very senior-level interior designer with partial ownership of the design firm is also called a principal.
- **Project manager:** An experienced interior designer whose responsibilities primarily involve the supervision of a project rather than its creative design.
- **Senior designer:** Generally, an interior designer with ten or more years of experience in the profession.
- **Sole practitioner:** An individual who works independently as an interior designer. He or she may provide services in one or more design specialties.
- **Stakeholders:** All the parties who have a vested interest in the project, including the interior designer, the client, and vendors.
- **Subcontractor:** A firm or individual licensed to perform only specific portions of construction work, such as an electrical, flooring, wall covering, or finish carpentry.
- **Vendor:** An individual or company that sells goods or services to interior designers or the client. Also referred to as a *supplier*.

Other design team members are discussed in Chapter 1.

Project Development

THERE ARE MANY common activities—we shall call them *project development* activities—that are undertaken by designers before the design contract or other agreement between client and designer is finalized. Project development comprises many activities thought of as business practices. The activities of this project phase include marketing and prospecting for a new client, researching by the design firm into basic client/project needs in order to develop an understanding of what the project will involve, and the preparation of the actual agreement or contract that outlines the work to be performed.

The ways in which interior designers market their services and find new clients is discussed in Chapter 5. However, it is important to look at marketing briefly at this point. Clients learn about an interior design firm when the firm actively seeks them through public relations or another marketing method. Designers also obtain new clients from referrals provided by existing clients.

Once a contact is identified the interior designer sets out to determine if the project is one the firm should pursue. If it is, the interior designer will meet with or give a presentation to the client about the design firm. Part of this interview allows the designer to further investigate the client and project to determine its scope.

This is necessary so the interior designer can develop a proposal (or *design contract*) to present in a second meeting. At the least, the second meeting involves a discussion about how the client will be charged for interior design services. The interior designer should be careful not to offer free design concepts at this stage. It is unfortunate, but some clients interview several interior designers in order to obtain free ideas—and then hire none of them.

In commercial interior design, many clients use a process called *request for proposal* (RFP) to qualify several interior design firms for a potential project. The RFP is a document that explains many requirements of the project and the client's expectations of the interior designer. The RFP is sent to several design firms. If an interior design firm is interested in the project, it responds by preparing a proposal that addresses the client's stated needs. The client then decides which responding firms to interview.

As the interior design firm gains interest in a project, the designer must visit the project job site or review existing floor plans to get a handle on the site conditions of the potential project. When plans are not available, the interior designer will have to do a *site measure*. This involves measuring all the walls, door and window openings, and other features of the existing project spaces so a dimensioned floor plan can be prepared. In actual practice, some firms accomplish these activities in the next phase of the project rather than at this time.

During project development, the interior design firm assembles the team that will be responsible for the project. In a small firm or for a small project, the "team" may consist of a single interior designer. Complex projects require a multimember team headed by an experienced senior interior designer. Consultants may be hired for some projects; for example, a commercial kitchen designer may be needed to design the kitchen areas of a new restaurant.

When all the information needed to understand the conditions and requirements of the project and client is in order, the next step is to prepare a letter of agreement or design contract. This document describes such elements as the project process and how the design firm will charge for its services. Design agreements and contracts are discussed in Chapter 5. After the client returns the

University: University of Northern Iowa, central servery. Linda Kress, ASID, Lotti, Krishan & Short, Inc., Tulsa, Oklahoma. Photographer: Shimer@Hedrich Blessing.

signed documents, the designer is ready to begin the first phase of the project.

Programming

WHEN THE CLIENT has signed a contract with the interior designer, the project moves into the programming phase. It is easiest to think of this as the *information-gathering phase*. During programming, the interior designer goes about discovering exactly what the client wants to accomplish in the project and conducts necessary research. Some of this information was obtained during project development, as it is necessary to fully understand the project scope. In the programming phase, however, specific details about the project are clarified.

In many cases, this information is obtained when the interior designer interviews key client stakeholders (individuals or groups with a vested interest in the project) to determine specific needs such as space adjacencies, furniture, and color preferences. Alternatively, and for commercial projects, the designer may obtain this information via questionnaires rather than personal interviews. If scaled floor plans of the project space were not acquired during the project development, the interior designer obtains them during programming. The designer might also evaluate existing furniture to determine if any of it can be used in the new project.

Residential and Commercial

MELINDA SECHRIST, FASID

President, Sechrist Design Associates, Inc.,
Seattle, Washington

What led you to enter your design specialty?
The projects that came in the door when my firm was younger.
You get better and better at the same type of work, and then you
become known for it.

What has been your greatest challenge as an interior designer?
Managing a design business and the staff that goes with it.
Dealing with subcontractors and suppliers who don't follow
through on promises. Having to justify design fees.

**What is the most important
quality or skill of a designer
in your specialty?**
Communication of the design
to the client, contractors, and
so on by written, drawn, or
oral methods.

Apartment complex:
lounge/library. Melinda Sechrist,
FASID, Sechrist Design Associates,
Inc., Seattle, Washington.
Photographer: Stuart Hopkins.

Apartment complex: rotunda. Melinda Sechrist, FASID, Sechrist Design Associates, Inc., Seattle, Washington. Photographer: Stuart Hopkins.

How important is interior design education in today's industry?

Extremely important. Without it, you could not compete in the marketplace or provide the services expected of a professional designer.

What are your primary responsibilities and duties?

Procure all work; develop letters of agreement and scope of work for projects. Develop design concepts and ideas, meet with clients, and manage the projects and staff to support them.

What is the most satisfying part of your job?

Working with great clients and seeing a job that works well and is appreciated by the client and/or public.

What is the least satisfying part of your job?

Working with a difficult client who does not appreciate my work; having to justify design fees.

Who or what experience has been a major influence on your career?

Probably being a member of ASID. As a young designer, I met many designers who helped me out with information and encouragement, and then I was given many opportunities to grow as a leader that have helped me build my own firm. Still learning, too.

Corporate office: reception desk. Melinda Sechrist, FASID, Sechrist Design Associates, Inc., Seattle, Washington. Photographer: Stuart Hopkins.

An important part of programming involves the research of codes, which are legal regulations that influence both the way the interior project is space-planned and built and the finishes that may be used. In some jurisdictions, codes also regulate the furnishings that can be used in many commercial interior projects. Building, fire safety, life safety, mechanical, and accessibility codes are those that most affect the work of the interior designer. To some degree, all of these codes can affect the manner in which an interior project is planned as well as the furnishings and materials specified.

During programming, the interior designer determines if any consultants are needed. Some projects call for the services of an architect, electrical engineer, or mechanical engineer. Although laws vary by state, consultants are most often needed when a building permit is required, as interior designers generally are not allowed to prepare permit drawings under their own name. This type of consultative teamwork ensures the project is designed within the laws of the jurisdiction and in the best interests of the client.

All of these activities and others in this phase provide the interior designer with the information he or she needs to begin the actual design and preparation of drawings. A project cannot be executed successfully without careful attention to the gathering of information during programming.

Schematic Design

THE SECOND PHASE of the project, *schematic design*, is where the creative juices of the designer really start flowing. The interior designer produces rough sketches and makes preliminary decisions on materials and colors. Preliminary design concepts, drawings, and other documents are developed during this phase. An obviously important drawing developed during the schematic design phase is the floor plan. Sketches showing rough space plans (where the partition walls will be) and furniture layouts are a common communication tool in this phase for all interior designers regardless of design specialty (see Exhibit 2-2). Other preliminary sketches include bubble diagrams, adjacency matrices, block plans, thumbnail perspectives, and cross sections, which might be needed to help explain the design concepts.

The designer also develops preliminary selections for the many furniture and finish products that will be needed. Color and finish palettes are prepared to help the client visualize the completed spaces. Budgets are put together to help the client and designer clarify the costs involved in completing the design as it unfolds during this phase. If costs are too high, the client and interior designer must make compromises to be sure the client can afford the finished project (see Exhibit 2-3).

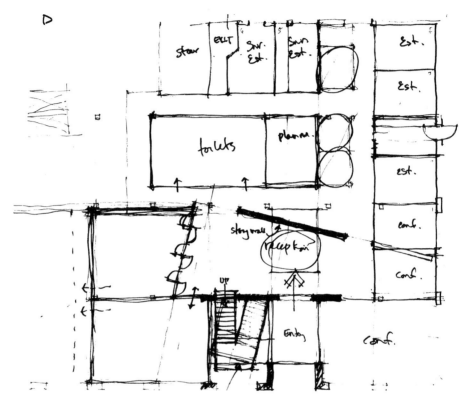

Exhibit 2-2. Floor plan detail is a typical sketch prepared in the schematic design phase. David Stone, IIDA. Associate. Sasaki Associates, Inc. Watertown, MA.

The design work prepared during the schematic phase is vital, as it sets the stage for the refinement of the project in the next phase. For the most part, drawings are done quickly and loosely, with the time spent on generating the concept, not in preparing highly refined drawings. When the client approves the concepts, the interior designer can confidently move the project to the next phase (see Exhibit 2-4).

Design Development

The design development phase of the project refines the concepts germinated in the schematic phase into the final approved plans and concepts. In this phase, the interior designer prepares drawings in a precise scale rather than

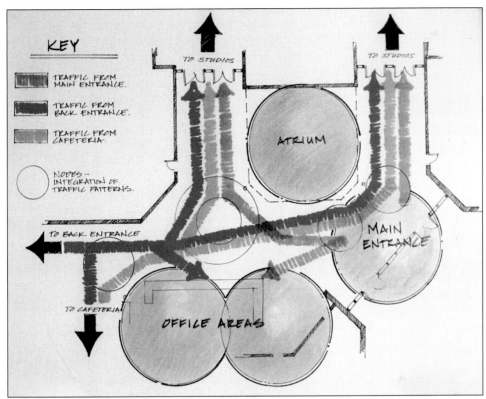

KEY

- TRAFFIC FROM MAIN ENTRANCE.
- TRAFFIC FROM BACK ENTRANCE.
- TRAFFIC FROM CAFETERIA.
- NODES — INTEGRATION OF TRAFFIC PATTERNS.

TO STUDIOS

TO STUDIOS

ATRIUM

TO BACK ENTRANCE

MAIN ENTRANCE

TO CAFETERIA

OFFICE AREAS

Exhibit 2-3. Traffic analysis sketch helps the interior designer understand expected traffic flow in large projects and acts as an aid in development of the floor plan. Robin J. Wagner, ASID, IDEC, RJ Wagner Designs, Clifton, VA.

sketches to ensure that the space plan and furniture plans actually fit the space (see Exhibit 2-9, p. 51). In today's practice, many interior designers prepare these drawings using computer-aided drafting (CAD) software. With CAD, needed changes are simple to achieve. CAD software also allows fully dimensioned drawings to be quickly produced, as the dimensions become another layer in the set of computer drawings. However, many small interior design firms prefer to use manual drafting techniques to prepare drawings. Thus, it is important for the prospective interior designer to learn both skills.

Other drawings at this phase might be lighting and electrical plans, elevations, and perspectives. Lighting plans (also called *reflected ceiling plans*) show the location of light fixtures for general and specific lighting. Appropriate lighting is important in both residential and commercial interior design projects to ensure

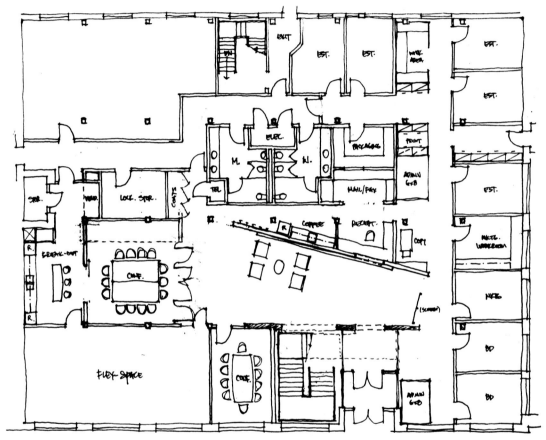

Exhibit 2-4. In commercial design, sketches of the floor plan showing furniture layouts is used to convey design ideas early in the project. Notice changes from Figure 2-2. David Stone, IIDA. Associate. Sasaki Associates, Inc. Watertown, MA.

functional use of the spaces. Electrical plans locate the outlets and switches that will control lighting fixtures and provide electrical service for all the other many electronics components of interiors. Electrical plans also identify locations for dedicated circuits for computers, networking of computers in commercial facilities, safety features such as fire alarms, and other high-tech applications that are becoming common in both residential and commercial interiors.

Elevations and perspectives are drawings that help explain design concepts in a form that clients can understand (see Exhibit 2-5). An elevation is a drawing that shows no depth but gives the idea of appearance by depicting heights and

Exhibit 2-5 Perspective drawing used as a concept drawing of proposed interior. Kimberly M. Studzinski, ASID. Buchart/Horn/Basco, Associates, York, PA.

widths. Some elevations are used for construction purposes and also provide dimensional information. Others are for presentation and may be highly detailed and even in color (see Exhibit 2-6). Perspective drawings provide a three-dimensional view of the interior. They are also called *orthographic projections* because they project a three-dimensional view on a two-dimensional plane (see Exhibit 2-7). In all cases, the drawings are based on true scale so the projection accurately depicts what the interior will look like when actually built or finished.

This phase of the project is where the interior designer establishes refined specifications and budgets for all the construction work and goods required for the project. The furniture, furnishings, and equipment (FF&E) specifications are finalized and approved by the client in this phase. The FF&E specifications clarify the products required for the interior. All projects in some way begin with an FF&E list of requirements.

When the interior designer has prepared all the drawings, specifications, and budgets needed for the project near the end of the design development phase, a presentation is made to the client. The goal of this important presentation is to obtain approval by and as few changes in the project as possible from the client in order to move on to the fourth phase of the project, contract documents.

Contract Documents

Contract documents consist of accurately scaled drawings called *construction drawings* and other written documents called *specifications* that explain what the interior is to look like and how the look is to be achieved. A set of construction drawings includes the dimensioned

VISITORS CAN CHOOSE A WINDOW SEAT, THE PATIENT CHAIR, OR THE DAY BED. THE DAY BED ALSO MEETS THE NEEDS OF OVERNIGHT FAMILY CAREGIVERS. THIS CORNER OF THE ROOM PROVIDES STORAGE FOR PATIENT BELONGINGS, A BUILT-IN FLOWER TABLE, AND DECORATIVE LIGHTING.

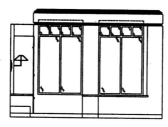

THE PATIENT HAS BED RAIL CONTROL OF TV PHONE, AND READING LIGHTS AS WELL AS NURSE CALL. LOW WINDOWS PROVIDE AMPLE DAYLIGHT. THE PATIENT'S FIELD OF VISION INCLUDES THE WINDOW VIEW, VISTOR SEATING, FRAMED ART, AND WOOD TRIM IN FURNITURE AND ARCHITECTURAL DETAILS.

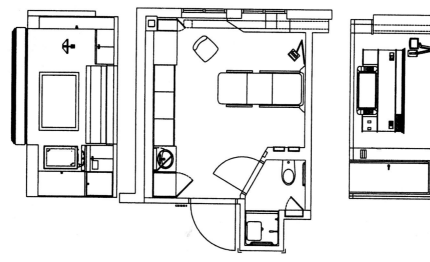

THE MIRRORED MEDICINE CABINET ABOVE THE SINK DISGUISES THE SOAP, PAPER TOWEL, AND CUP DISPENSERS. CONVENIENT STORAGE IS PROVIDED FOR CLEAN LINEN AND NURSING SUPPLIES AND FOR TRASH AND DIRTY LINEN DISPOSAL.

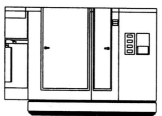

THE NURSING ZONE ON THE CORRIDOR SIDE OF THE PATIENT BED HAS CONVENIENT ACCESS TO ELECTRICAL POWER, MEDICAL GASES, LIGHTING CONTROLS, SHARPS CONTAINER, AND RECESSED GLOVE BOX HOLDERS.

PRIVATE PATIENT ROOM
TAHOE FOREST HOSPITAL

Exhibit 2-6. Floor plans are sometimes "exploded" showing both the floor plan and the walls in elevation. M. Joy Meeuwig, IIDA. Interior Design Consultation, Reno, NV.

Exhibit 2-7. Rendered perspective sketches are often used at the end of the design development stage to help clients understand important elements of the proposed design. Robin J. Wagner, ASID, IDEC. RJ Wagner Designs, Clifton, VA.

floor plan, a lighting plan, electrical, plumbing, and other mechanical drawings, and construction elevations for built-in cabinets or other features. Depending on the project, large-scale detail drawings may be prepared that show how something is to be built, furniture plans (sometimes called *equipment plans*), schedules to clarify wall, floor, and ceiling treatments, and any other specialized drawings required for the specific project.

The most commonly recognized part of the construction drawings is the dimensioned floor plan (see Exhibit 2-8). The dimensioned floor plan shows the partitions, built-in cabinets, dimensional information, and other notations needed by a contractor to build or finish the inte-

rior. The interior designer must prepare highly accurate drawings so the interior nonload-bearing structural elements are properly completed and the furniture and equipment plans work. For example, an error in drawing the size of an alcove that is to receive a piece of furniture could mean the furniture does not fit.

The specifications are the written instructions that accompany the drawings and give complete information on project requirements. Interiors projects often have two sets of specifications, one for the materials and construction methods related to partitions and non–load-bearing building features such as cabinets, the other for the FF&E.

In many small commercial and most residential projects, the client and the interior designer (or perhaps just the designer) purchase the needed goods and materials using the FF&E specification. For most large commercial projects, the interior designer must obtain prices (or *bids*) for the FF&E from more than one supplier. In this case, competitive bid specifications are prepared so the furniture and other movable products may be purchased from more than one company. Furniture specifications as competitive bids can be written so that a vendor (also referred to as a *supplier*) can offer to sell a product other than what was specified. If the vendor offers a different product, it must be similar to the original specification or the bid is not allowed. Competitive bid specifications are complicated but necessary for many commercial interior

design projects. The competitive bid specification process is not common in private residence projects for FF&E.

Construction documents are issued to qualified contractors and/or bidders. The interior designer often advises the client on the selection of contractors and vendors needed to complete the work. Some interior design firms prefer to hire these companies themselves, acting as an agent for the client. Separate contracts are needed to purchase furniture and other goods as well as to hire the contractors and subcontractors that will perform construction work. The best way to describe the "end" of this phase of the project is when the documents are issued in order to receive bids or prices on the goods and construction.

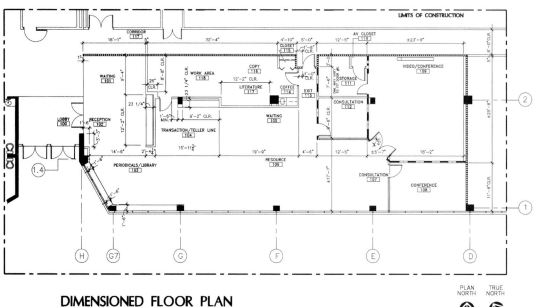

DIMENSIONED FLOOR PLAN
FIRST FLOOR
NTS

Exhibit 2-8. Dimensioned floor plan. Linda Santellanes, ASID. Santenalles Interiors, Inc. Tempe, AZ.

Contract Administration

The last phase of the project is called *contract administration*. In this phase, the actual construction and the actual ordering and installation of FF&E occurs (see Exhibit 2-9). As mentioned in the preceding section, the interior designer may be responsible for ordering the needed merchandise and hiring appropriate contractors to do the construction and installation work. For the design firm that does not sell FF&E, all this administration is done by some other entity—possibly the client or a consultative project manager. Selling the FF&E is an additional revenue source for many interior designers. However, the additional legal responsibilities that must be undertaken when selling the merchandise lead some firms to design and specify the project without also selling the merchandise.

Supervising construction and installation of nonmovable elements in an interior often requires special knowledge and certification. Depending on local laws, the interior designer might not be allowed to supervise this type of work. However, the interior designer is often on the job site to ensure the work is executed according to the requirements spelled out in the contract documents. Discrepancies are discussed with the client and contractor so changes can be made.

When the interior designer sells the required goods to the client, he or she is

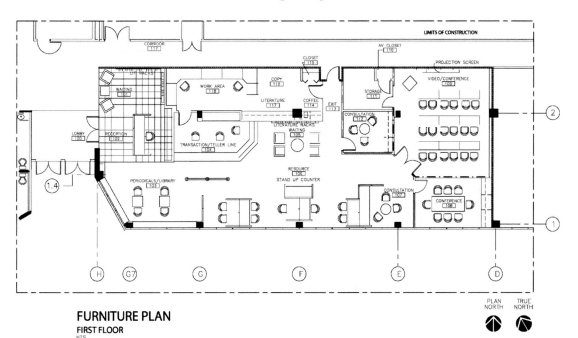

FURNITURE PLAN

FIRST FLOOR
NTS

Exhibit 2-9. Final furniture floor plan. Linda Santellanes, ASID. Santenalles Interiors, Inc. Tempe, AZ.

High-End Residential and Commercial Design: Custom Furniture and Product Design

DEBRA MAY HIMES, ASID, IIDA

Owner, Debra May Himes Interior Design & Associates, LLC, Mesa, Arizona

What has been your greatest challenge as an interior designer?
Becoming established—getting name recognition—finding the great jobs.

What led you to enter your design specialty?
I like to create and provide individual pieces for my clients.

What are your primary responsibilities and duties in your position?
I own the company—therefore I am responsible for everything, even taking out the trash.

What is the most satisfying part of your job?
Creating a space or product that makes my client say wow! is the best possible feeling.

Private residence: dining room.
Debra May Himes, ASID, IIDA,
Debra May Himes Interior Design &
Associates LLC, Mesa, Arizona.
Photographer: Dino Tonn.

Private residence: great room. Debra May Himes, ASID, IIDA, Debra May Himes Interior Design & Associates LLC, Mesa, Arizona. Photographer: Dino Tonn.

What is the least satisfying part of your job?
The paperwork is, of course, the least interesting for me.

What is the most important quality or skill of a designer in your specialty?
People skills and being a good listener. It is most important to make the client happy.

Who or what experience has been a major influence on your career?
My grandmother's work ethics probably influenced me the most.

Private residence: custom-designed wine room door. Debra May Himes, ASID, IIDA, Debra May Himes Interior Design & Associates LLC, Mesa, Arizona. Photographer: Dino Tonn.

Résumés

A résumé is a written summary of your work and personal experience relevant to employment in the interior design profession. Because it is a *summary*—often no more than one or two pages—information related to work experience, education, special skills, and certain personal information must be presented *concisely*.

Whether you are a student or a professional, your résumé will contain specific items:

- personal contact information
- career summary (for professionals)
- career objective (for students)
- education summary
- work experience summary

It is not a good idea to use your current work phone number or email address as your contact information. You should use personal phone numbers or email addresses for the job search. Other personal information such as marital status, service records, religion, and community service involvement should not be included, as this information can unwittingly allow an employer to discriminate against you.

A career summary has become common for professionals with previous work experience in interior design. The summary is a brief statement that explains what you have done and how you can be a benefit to the employer. It is a snapshot of the professional's experience. It is placed at the top of the résumé to catch the attention of the employer.

For entry-level designers, the career objective statement (also placed at the top) tries to entice the potential employer to read the rest of the résumé by using a few dynamic sentences to show how you can add to the firm or what you want to do in interior design. If the statement is too general, employers may feel you don't know what you want to do; if it is too specific, you may exclude yourself from consideration for a position.

Educational information should note the institution where you obtained your interior design education. Students may want to briefly list courses taken to help the employer understand the quality of your educational preparation. This is especially helpful if you are applying in a location where the employer may not be familiar with your school. Professionals should emphasize work experience over education and place the work experience section before education.

Résumés may be presented in one of three formats. For most job applicants, the work experience section is shown in reverse chronological order (the current or most recent position first). This format is called a *chronological résumé*. Each position generally is shown with the dates of work indicated, the name of the company, location, your job title, and a brief description of duties. This description should be a very short narrative that clarifies your accomplishments and responsibilities in the position. A *functional résumé* is one that deemphasizes chronological work experience and focuses instead on skills and qualifications. This type is used by applicants whose work history is somehow irregular. Other applicants use a *combination format* that combines some aspects of the chronological résumé with those of the functional résumé. For more details on how to construct your résumé, see the reference list at the end of this book and visit your local bookstore.

an agent for the client. When this is the case, the interior designer is responsible for managing a variety of documents so the proper goods are ordered and delivered. Purchase orders are required to actually place orders with a furniture factory. The factory sends an acknowledgement to the designer indicating they can supply the required goods. When the furniture is ready for shipment, the factory sends the interior designer an invoice (bill). The interior designer also sends invoices to the client for payment.

When the construction work is done and all the furniture and other items are delivered, the client and designer do a walkthrough to ensure the work is complete. This final project activity is done to note missing items or damaged goods. The interior designer or other appropriate company is then responsible for completing or repairing the work and ensuring that the missing items are delivered where required. Final payments of design fees to the interior designer and final payments to the contractors and vendors are also approved at this time to complete the interior design project.

Project Management

A major reason clients hire professional interior designers is their knowledge of how to professionally manage all the tasks required to complete the project. The person responsible for the orderly management of these many tasks is commonly referred to as the *project man-ager*. Project management is the orderly control of all the tasks required in order for the project to be completed as designed and at a reasonable profit for the design firm. For a small project such as a residence, the project manager and interior designer are often one and the same. Large-scale projects such as casinos can have both an interior design team and a project management team. Obviously, the more complex the project, the more staff members are involved in both the interior design tasks and the project management tasks.

The project manager has many duties and responsibilities. The smaller the interior design firm, the more these responsibilities fall on one person—often the lead interior designer, who may also be the owner of the firm. Some key tasks of project managers are serving as the primary liaison of the client, the design firm, and contractors and vendors; preparing and overseeing project schedules; supervising the design team; establishing budgets; overseeing the project files and documents; and preparing status reports for the client and other stakeholders.

Interior designers learn to be good project managers through the work experiences they gain after their academic training is complete. Only certain components of project management can be included in a curriculum. By observing senior designers, participating in meetings, and working as part of a design team, entry-level interior designers learn most project management skills on the job. Excellent project management also requires understanding the working relationships of the various stakeholders in a project. Let's take a brief look at that.

Hospitality and Residential

JULIANA CATLIN, FASID
President, Catlin Design Group, Inc.,
Jacksonville, Florida

What led you to enter your design specialty?
I worked for an architectural firm and found myself working on hotel projects. Then I was hired by a developer in the resort industry, and so began a career in hospitality design.

What are your primary responsibilities and duties?
As president of my own company, I basically do all the marketing and am involved in major client presentations. I have an excellent team of designers and support staff who do a lot of the day-to-day client contact—which allows me time to market and work on the big-picture part of our firm.

What is the most satisfying part of your job?
The most satisfying is seeing a completed project. There is nothing like the thrill of seeing your initial design concepts become a reality.

Hospitality: Restaurant interior. Juliana Catlin, FASID, Catlin Design Group, Inc., Jacksonville, Florida. Photographer: Dan Forer.

Hospitality: Restaurant interior. Juliana Catlin, FASID, Catlin Design Group, Inc., Jacksonville, Florida. Photographer: The Haskell Company.

What is the least satisfying part of your job?

The least satisfying is dealing with all the subcontractors to make sure the project is carried out. Dealing with suppliers and schedules is the least gratifying job—but one of the most important in making a project hassle-free to our clients.

What is the most important quality or skill of a designer in your specialty?

You need to have the ability to sell your concepts. We are, in many ways, salespeople because we have to convince our clients that our solutions are the answer to their problems. Many talented designers fail in our industry because they cannot communicate their ideas well.

What advice would you give to someone who wants to be an interior designer?

Get yourself to the best university that offers a FIDER-accredited interior design degree and plan on following the highest level of professionalism. I encourage all students of interior design to sit for the NCIDQ—the profession's two-day qualifying exam. Many states now require licensure to practice design, so make sure you have the proper education and experience.

Who or what experience has been a major influence in your career?

My professor and the head of the design department at the University of Florida had a huge impact on my career. He gave me confidence in my design ability and made me realize that my people skills would help me succeed in our profession. He saw beyond just design ability and really instilled in his students that ethics, communication, business skills, and being a well-rounded human being would greatly affect their success. He also taught us how to quickly sketch our concepts, and I use that skill every day. He was a great man for making us realize that we help clients solve their life issues through design. He passed away several years ago, but he will always be remembered by his students for his lifelong impact on us as designers and people.

Hospitality: Restaurant interior. Juliana Catlin, FASID, Catlin Design Group, Inc., Jacksonville, Florida. Photographer: Dan Forer.

Project Management Terms

Bidder: An interior designer or vendor who provides a price for goods and/or services required of the project.

Built-environment industry: All the professions and trades involved in the design, construction, and completion of a residence or commercial building project.

Contract documents: The drawings, specifications, and other documents, such as a design contract, needed for the completion of a project.

Construction drawings: Typical scaled drawings for an interior design or architecture project. Include dimensioned floor plans, elevations, sections, and detail drawings.

Furniture, furnishings, and equipment (FF&E): Projects that involve little construction work.

Load-bearing walls: Walls designed to carry the weight (or load) of the roof, ceiling, and other structural elements.

Partition walls: Walls that divide spaces into rooms or areas. A true partition wall is not a load-bearing wall.

Project management: The process of organizing and controlling the design project from beginning to end.

Space plans: Scaled drawings that show the layout of the rooms and other areas within the building. They usually do not show furniture.

Specifications: Written instructions that explain the quality and kinds of materials as well as the methods of construction related to the designs shown in construction drawings.

Walkthrough: A final inspection of the job site conducted by the client and interior designer to ensure that all required work has been completed and all specified products are in place.

Working Relationships

As is obvious from the previous discussion, interior designers frequently collaborate with other members of what is called the built-environment industry. Often, interior designers work alongside architects as plans for a building are being developed. While the architect focuses on the basic building and internal structural elements, the interior designer helps the client and architect with space planning of partition walls, furniture planning, and the specification of furniture and other decorative goods and treatments.

The interior designer also collaborates with building contractors, trade members, and vendors. The building contractor uses the plans developed by the architect and interior designer to construct the structural elements and fabricate the interior mechanical systems. One example of a trade member is a cabinetmaker who builds a custom cabinet. Vendors supply furniture, wallpaper, lighting fixtures, file cabinets, and other items necessary to complete an interior.

Good working relationships are essential, as dozens of vendors and other contributors are often needed for an interior design project to be completed. Thus, it is important for the interior designer to get along with not only the client but also all the others involved in the project. Managing this team is a critical responsibility in project management.

The interior designer's knowledge and skills of the design process, project management, and building systems helps blend the contributions of many individuals and groups into the final completed project. A successful project is not achieved solely by virtue of a great design created by an experienced interior design professional. A successful project also comes about because the interior designer knows how to orchestrate the vital working relationships that contribute to its achievement.

University: University of Northern Iowa, central servery. Linda Kress, ASID, Lotti, Krishan & Short, Inc., Tulsa, Oklahoma. Photographer: Shimer@Hedrich Blessing.

"What Is the Single Most Important Skill an Interior Designer Needs to Be Successful?"

A designer needs many important qualities and skills to be successful. Among them is the ability to be persuasive. Most clients have no idea what the design you've proposed is going to actually look like, and what they are buying is your enthusiasm and your ability to convince them that this is the right direction and that it will meet their goals and objectives.
—Jain Malkin, CID

Desire and hunger for design excellence.
—Nila Leiserowitz, FASID

Communication, good sense of color and proportion.
—Rita Carson Guest, FASID

The ability to listen to what is said and to understand the totality of the words is a skill the successful designers all seem to possess.
—Fred Messner, IIDA

I think different important skills apply to different designers in different job situations. As a sole practitioner, discipline and stick-to-itiveness are crucial to staying in business. However, perhaps teamwork is important in a large firm situation, or a high level of creativity could be important to an employee working in a firm doing high-end residential work. Different situations require different skills for success.
—Terri Maurer, FASID

Great interpersonal skills and great communication skills and great creativity.
—Beth Harmon-Vaughn, FIIDA

Besides talent, the ability to listen and interpret a client's needs and desires in a tasteful and efficient way is a critical skill.
—M. Arthur Gensler Jr., FAIA, FIIDA

I think the ability to convince or to sell your concept and ideas is a valuable part of your design abilities. Talent as a designer is important—but if you cannot convince your client of your abilities, you are unable to see them carried through. Many talented designers do not have successful careers because of their inability to verbalize their concepts—and, unfortunately, many untalented people do well in our industry because they can better convince clients to follow their advice.
—Juliana Catlin, FASID

Enjoying working with people. This is a people business, and if you don't enjoy being around and meeting new and interesting people, then this is not the business for you.
—Charles Gandy, FASID, FIIDA

Listening and really hearing what someone says.
—Donna Vining, FASID

Listening and communicating are at the top of the list to be successful in producing creative interiors and bringing order out of chaos.
—Sandra Evans, ASID

The most important skills an interior designer needs are to be passionate about design and inspired by the clients who occupy their spaces.
—Linda Sorrento, ASID, IIDA

All aspects of project management skills.
—Robert Wright, ASID

People skills; design skills can be learned.
—Jan Bast, ASID, IIDA

It is important that the practitioner have great listening skills combined with extraordinary people skills.
—Linda E. Smith, FASID

No single skill will make an interior designer successful; instead, an array of skills is needed. A successful designer is creative, knowledgeable, a good listener, dependable, and accountable.
—Linda Santellanes, ASID

Organizational skills, then attention to detail.
—Kristen Anderson, ASID, CID, RID

Concept selling—making themselves valuable to their customers by being skilled at creating the customers' need. Concept selling is hard. Why? Because the designer is fighting *the way it is* with *the way it could be.*
—Leonard Alvarado

To know his or her value as a designer. The expertise we have has value; thus we have the right to charge for it.
—Pat Campbell McLaughlin, ASID

The ability to connect the client's vision to the resources necessary to fulfill it. This seems obvious, but most designers don't really understand what the client wants, and more still lack the ability to source the necessary materials for the project. The Internet has made sourcing infinitely easier in the last few years.
—Jeffrey Rausch, IIDA

The ability to analyze projects and answer the problems with exciting designs.
—Robin J. Wagner, ASID, IDEC

Ability to put logical design solutions on paper and communicate those designs to the client.
—Melinda Sechrist, FASID

Presentation skills are vitally important to getting your idea across to the client.
—Greta Guelich, ASID

Big-picture thinking coupled with the communication skills necessary to allow implementation of the vision.
—Marilyn Farrow, FIIDA

The ability to listen and truly hear.
—W. Daniel Shelley, ASID, AIA

The ability to deliver the completed project.
—Suzan Globus, ASID

The ability to interview and interpret the findings into a three-dimensional solution that affects behavior.
—Rosalyn Cama, FASID

Continue your education. Stay on top of the latest technology. Be aware of what new tools and materials methods are available.
—Christy Ryan, IIDA

It is just being able to believe in the work and to communicate that to a client. Selling the concept is a must. Many great designs are not given the opportunity to come to life because the designer just isn't able to show the client that the solution is the best that can be created.
—Michael Thomas, ASID

Today, few offices will take on an entry-level designer without CAD capabilities. This applies to any career path—residential, commercial, retail, or healthcare.
—David Stone, IIDA

I think developing good people skills is extremely important.
—Sally Nordahl, IIDA

The desire to continually learn! The world is changing quickly, and it will continue to do so! As true professionals, we must all be committed to continuous learning. The issues, trends (and I don't mean fads), consequences, products, and methodologies touching our profession are changing; it is imperative that we stay informed. Our clients look to interior designers to help them make better decisions, and a large part of intelligent decision making is to understand the broad issues as well as the consequences of our choices.
—Barbara Nugent, FASID

The ability to make decisions.
—M. Joy Meeuwig, IIDA

People skills are very important.
—Debra May Himes, IIDA, ASID

Excellent listening skills.
—Lisa Whited, IIDA, ASID, IDEC

There isn't one single most important skill. That would simplify the profession too much. Important skills include eye for detail, creativity, hard work ethic, ability to communicate (graphically, orally, in writing). The latter could be one of the very top skills.
—Stephanie Clemons, PhD, ASID, IDEC

Being able to communicate—visually, orally, and through the written word.
—Michelle King, IIDA

To be a good listener.
—Beth Kuzbek, ASID, IIDA, CMG

Desire to be an interior designer. The passion to be a designer is tested on an ongoing basis. The business side of interior design will challenge the most creative designers, and it is the love of designing that drives them through the hard times.
—John Holmes, ASID, IIDA

To be able to listen, imagine, solve, and execute.
—Linda Isley, IIDA

Single most? People skills—you need to get along with clients who may have a different personality than you—and with vendors and so on.
—Ellen McDowell, ASID

Confidence and risk taking.
—Neil Frankel, FAIA, FIIDA

Without a doubt, I would say listening is the most important skill an interior designer needs to be successful. Every assignment or project begins with developing and understanding the client's goals. With the client, the designer establishes the design vision for the project. It's all about listening and developing the right vision for your client. The most successful results are produced when the project goals are thoroughly understood, ensuring solutions that meet the client's intent. Clients are not happy when they are not heard or when the designer persists in his or her personal design goals over those defined by the client.
—Susan Higbee

A no-static, open-minded personality.
—Derrell Parker, IIDA

Whether residential or commercial, an interior designer must be a good listener. Even commercial clients remark on whether or not the architect or designer really listens to them and responds to their needs.
—**Linda Kress, ASID**

In order to be successful, an interior designer needs to know that the profession is a business and that time is as much a commodity as design outcome itself.
—**Jennifer van der Put, BID, IDC, ARIDO, IFMA**

Communication, communication, communication.
—**Sari Graven, ASID**

Listening. Listen to your clients, observe their living and work patterns, and interpret your design around their needs and lifestyle.
—**Sally Thompson, ASID**

It is hard to limit this to one skill or trait. I might also suggest different skills depending on whether a designer chooses to focus more on the design or the management aspects of the project process. I would emphasize the importance of innate creative thinking and problem solving, honed visual and verbal communication skills, and a passion for the art and business of this industry.
—**Janice Carleen Linster, ASID, IIDA, CID**

Communication, both orally and through documentation of ideas and concepts.
—**William Peace, ASID**

This is a very tough one. You may be surprised by my answer. Having good design skills is, of course, an obvious choice, but I believe it is even more important that a designer display exemplary managerial skills, including the managing of clients, vendors, workrooms, and so on. If you were to ask me for the second most important skill, I would say orientation to detail.
—**Naomi Anderson**

The most important skills a designer needs are a desire to learn and a love of architecture, history, and art. Interior design is primarily the individual's interpretation of himself through his history, architecture, and art.
—**Cheri Gerou, AIA, ASID**

Chapter Three

Design Specialties

Most people think of interior design specialties in terms of two large categories: residential and commercial. Residential interior design focuses on private living places such as freestanding single-family dwellings, condominiums, and apartments. Commercial interior design addresses a large range of business- and government-owned facilities such as hospitals, hotels, schools, government office buildings, and corporate offices.

These two broad categories comprise a large number of targeted specialties. In fact, it is possible to say that any kind of specialty space can become a career niche. A niche is a highly specialized, even unique part of the total built-environment industry. For example, the design of family practice medical office suites is a niche within the commercial specialty of healthcare design.

It is important to point out that most interior designers and interior design firms do not focus narrowly on a single type of space. For example, many residential interior designers also occasionally design professional offices, a hospitality designer might design corporate offices, and an interior designer working for an office furnishings dealer might occasionally design an employee cafeteria. The interior designers and firms that are highly specialized and rarely design outside their area of expertise have a great deal of experience in that specialty and have totally focused their business practice on the specialty in order to remain successful in it. When the economy is robust, as it was in the late 1990s, it is more common for a design firm to tightly focus its practice on one design specialty. When the economy slows, the strategic thinking design firm often widens design practice into two or more similar specialties. Most of the professional interior designers you will read about in this chapter primarily design in one or two specialty areas; however, it is likely they have experience in a variety of types of interiors.

Commercial: corporate office break room. Bruce Goff, ASID, Domus Design Group, San Francisco, California. Photographer: John Sutton.

Residential Design

RESPONSIBILITY FOR designing the interiors of private residences is an interesting challenge. Residential interior designers bring their expertise and knowledge into the development of concepts that meet the family, social, and functional needs of the client as well as create beautiful spaces. The successful residential interior designer knows how to expertly examine the needs and wants of the client so as to help the client make the decisions that move the project to conclusion. A private residence is so special and personal a project that many clients have a difficult time making necessary decisions. Assisting them in making decisions is one aspect of residential interior design that attracts professionals to this specialty.

When specializing in residential interior design, the professional may work on projects involving the entire house, perhaps from the initial planning stage, in conjunction with the architect or custom home builder. Large residences can take several months, if not years, to complete. Less complex projects are remodeling or redecorating a residence. A remodeling project can involve moving non–load-bearing walls, replacing cabinets, relocating plumbing fixtures, and other mechanical elements. Remodeling might also lead to adding a room to the house. In some jurisdictions, these projects must be done with an architect. Redecorating involves changing architectural finishes on walls, flooring, and ceiling. It can also extend to replacing window treatments and planning new furniture items.

The interior designer is responsible for determining client preferences and the planning and specifications of the interior spaces to ensure the design meets the needs of the client. Depending on the size of the project, the interior designer may provide space planning options, furniture layouts, color palettes, and finish specifications for all interior architectural elements, accessories, and other elements outlined in the design process discussed in chapter 2. Local laws might allow the interior designer to prepare the construction drawings for the remodeling or require him or her to work with an architect to prepare the documents.

Exhibit 3-1 lists some of the many residential interior design specialties.

Exhibit 3-1

Residential Specialties

- single-family dwellings
- condominiums
- townhouses
- model homes
- kitchen and/or bathroom design
- home theaters
- residential historical restoration
- colorizer for homebuilders
- home office design

High-End Residential

CHARLES GANDY, FASID, FIIDA
President, Charles Gandy, Inc., Atlanta, Georgia

What has been your greatest challenge as an interior designer?
My greatest challenge as an interior designer has been to learn to listen to my clients, making sure I understand their needs and desires so I can help them achieve the best results.

What led you to enter your design specialty?
I saw the need for a businesslike approach to residential design. I enjoy people, and this seemed like the best place to use my skills in business and design.

Private residence: residential stairs. Charles Gandy, FASID, FIIDA, Charles Gandy, Inc., Atlanta, Georgia. Photographer: Ron Rizzo.

What are your primary responsibilities and duties?
Being the president of my company means I set the pace for design solutions and direct my associates to see that those solutions are carried out.

What is the most satisfying part of your job?
Seeing a happy client at the end—that special smile when they walk into a space.

What is the least satisfying part of your job?
The least satisfying is dealing with the day-to-day small problems that arise—but that's just being in business, I guess.

Private residence: dining room. Charles Gandy, FASID, FIIDA, Charles Gandy, Inc., Atlanta, Georgia. Photographer: Ron Rizzo.

Who or what experience has been a major influence on your career?
I have studied and written about the masters of design—those who came before. I have learned from them and been inspired from them. More recently, thirty years ago, Jack Lenor Larsen came to a school event and inspired me when he told us that he was successful because he "went to work!" I have tried to do that my entire career, starting each day with "What am I going to accomplish today?"

How important is certification by examination and the licensing of interior designers today?
Vitally! We have to make sure the public is protected. Qualified interior designers have a major impact on the health, safety, and welfare of those we come in contact with. We therefore should—must!—be examined and licensed.

Private residence: living room. Charles Gandy, FASID, FIIDA, Charles Gandy, Inc., Atlanta, Georgia. Photographer: Roger Wade.

High-End Residential—Primary and Secondary Resort

MICHAEL THOMAS, ASID

Principal, DESIGN Collective Group, Inc.
Jupiter, Florida

What has been your greatest challenge as an interior designer?
Trying to keep the balance of work, projects, income, and cash flow on an even keel.

What led you to enter your design specialty?
Moved to Florida, where this specialty exists.

What are your primary responsibilities and duties?
As principal, keeping the work flowing through the staff to accomplish the design specifications we've established for the project.

Private residence: master suite. Michael Thomas, ASID, DESIGN Collective Group, Inc., Jupiter, Florida. Photographer: Carlos Domenech.

What is the most satisfying part of your job?
I enjoy the work the most when I am presenting our solutions to a client and it all seems to be clicking with them.

What is the least satisfying part of your job?
Tracking down subcontractors who fail to show, do inferior work, won't return phone calls promptly; chasing around to make sure it all happens before the client kicks the bucket. Don't laugh. It happens.

What is the most important quality or skill of a designer in your specialty?
Much better than average communication skills, including the ability to sell the solution to the client.

Private residence: living room. Michael Thomas, ASID, DESIGN Collective Group, Inc., Jupiter, Florida. Photographer: Carlos Domenech.

Who or what experience has been a major influence on your career?
I guess nothing in particular stands out, but I have been provided with numerous opportunities to hone a number of skills, so I am broadly rather than narrowly experienced. This makes me deadly when I know a little something about everything I must ultimately be responsible for.

What advice would you give to someone who wants to be an interior designer?
Establish criteria in depth with the client. Believe that the solution you are offering is the right one for the criteria. Don't be afraid to sell the solution you believe in.

Can you describe the optimum job applicant?
Someone who has real-world experiences, and I find those people are over the age of thirty. In fact, for a long time I employed only people who were older than me. Now I'm older, and so are they. But I still like employing someone who is not just out of school—at any price.

Private residence: media room. Michael Thomas, ASID, DESIGN- Collective Group, Inc., Jupiter, Florida. Photographer: Carlos Domenech.

Commercial

ALL OF COMMERCIAL interior design, regardless of specialty, has certain common considerations. Commercial interior design projects must be executed with adherence to strict building, fire safety, and accessibility codes. Codes are "systematic bodies of law created by federal, state, and local jurisdictions to ensure the safety of the public."[1] These codes help the owner of the property, the architect, and the interior designer create safe places for employees to work and the public to enjoy.

Depending on the type of interior facility, the interior designer is challenged in meeting the needs of multiple groups. The owner of the property is always important in the design decision making, as the owner sets the budget and, often, the direction of the design project. Commercial facilities have employees, of course, and their satisfaction with the design of the space can be key to the success of a business enterprise. A third group that must be satisfied in one way or another comprises the customers, clients, guests, and other users of the space. A poorly designed restaurant will not succeed with some customers even if the food is very good.

Commercial interior design is an exciting area of the profession. It is also fast-paced and stressful. Commercial projects are far larger and often more complex than most residential projects. The responsibility for creating a safe environment for the general public who enters into a commercial space is considerable. Clients are generally budget-conscious, and the concept of "cheaper, better, faster" has certainly been true of commercial projects in the 1990s and today. However, it is a challenge that many in the profession accept. Exhibit 3-2 provides a partial list of specialty areas in commercial design. The rest of this chapter introduces you to many design specialties and includes comments by practitioners who have chosen to work in certain of these areas of professional interior design.

Corporate and Professional Offices

ACCORDING TO *Interior Design* magazine, the office design specialty led the way in revenue generation in the 2003 report on the 100 largest design firms, with the top ten firms earning $185,432,960 in interior design fees.[2] The corporate and professional office specialty is plainly the largest of the commercial interior design specialty areas.

An interior designer specializing in office design might design the office of the chief executive officer (CEO) of General Motors. Then again, he or she might be responsible for the offices of a group

Exhibit 3-2

Commercial Interior Design Specialties

corporate and executive offices
- any size office for any kind of business other than those listed below

professional offices
- law
- accounting
- stockbrokers
- real estate brokers

healthcare
- hospitals
- assisted living facilities
- medical and dental suites
- psychiatric facilities
- outpatient services
- medical laboratories
- veterinary clinics
- pediatric facilities

hospitality and entertainment/recreation
- hotels, motels, and resorts
- restaurants
- health clubs and spas
- park facilities
- country clubs
- museums and galleries
- sports complexes
- convention centers

retail facilities/merchandising
- malls and shopping centers
- department stores
- specialty stores
- gift shops
- visual merchandising for trade shows
- trade showrooms

institutional
- government offices and facilities
- financial institutions: banks, credit unions
- elementary and secondary schools
- universities
- day care centers
- churches and other religious facilities

industrial facilities
- manufacturing facilities
- training facilities

transportation
- airport terminals
- tour ships
- custom and commercial airplanes
- recreational vehicles

This is only a partial list of specialties. A commercial interior designer can specialize in any type of facility. However, if the specialty is too narrow, business may be insufficient to support the firm.

Corporate and Hospitality

BRUCE GOFF, ASID, IES
Principal, Domus Design Group
San Francisco, California

What has been your greatest challenge as an interior designer?
Keeping up with new products and solutions.

What led you to enter your design specialty?
Corporations and hospitality people understand and value the use of designers.

What are your primary responsibilities and duties?
As design director, I oversee all projects, set direction for concept, meet with clients, and supervise design staff.

Commercial: corporate office lunch room. Bruce Goff, ASID, Domus Design Group, San Francisco, California. Photographer: John Sutton.

What is the most satisfying part of your job?
Client interaction.

What is the least satisfying part of your job?
Managing people.

What is the important quality or skill of a designer in your specialty?
Communication skills: written, math, oral. Great ideas are only great if someone pays you for them.

How important is interior design education in today's industry?
Don't try this at home without an education—not unless you want to work for a small residential decorator or in a retail setting where selling, not tech skills, is the key.

Commercial: entrance to a hotel suite. Bruce Goff, ASID, Domus Design Group, San Francisco, California. Photographer: John Sutton.

Commercial: corporate office alternative office seating area. Bruce Goff, ASID, Domus Design Group, San Francisco, California. Photographer: John Sutton.

Office: media presentation room. Terri Maurer, FASID, Maurer Design Group, Akron, Ohio. Photographer: David Paternite Photography.

of employees in an advertising agency or even a neighborhood real estate office. A corporate interiors project might address the space planning and specification of office systems for thousands of employees at a corporate headquarters. Of course, the project might be for any size business that primarily uses office spaces to conduct business.

For the last thirty years or so, many office projects have employed office systems furniture consisting of freestanding panels and other components rather than private offices with standard desks. The use of office systems furniture—referred to as *open office furniture*—revolutionized office design in the 1960s. Designing with this product by correctly determining communication and work interaction patterns as well as space planning and component specification continues to be an important part of corporate design.

The design of corporate offices often involves considering the hierarchy of the office; it is common practice for higher-level employees to have larger and more elaborately designed offices than lower-level employees. This is true whether the office project is for the CEO of a technology industry giant or your neighborhood tax preparer. Status differences are indicated by the size and location of offices as well as the quality of the furniture items in them.

Office facilities are often mixed-use structures. Spaces for conferences and training, employee cafeterias, healthcare areas, retail stores, or even a nursery may be located in a large corporate building. Thus, the corporate interior design specialist must be familiar with design codes and constraints for many types of commercial spaces or hire consultants for assistance. The element of mixed use makes the corporate and professional office design specialty very exciting.

Law Office Design

RITA CARSON GUEST, FASID
President, Carson Guest Interior Design
Atlanta, Georgia

What is the most important quality or skill of a designer in your specialty?
The ability to communicate well and understand client needs along with design talent.

What has been your greatest challenge as an interior designer?
The greatest challenge has always been meeting unrealistic deadlines—the result of client needs and expectations—while still doing excellent design work.

What led you to enter your design specialty?
As a young designer, I worked for a firm and was assigned work on a law office. The design was successful, and my clients recommended us to other law firms. The repeat work led to many more law office design projects. Over the years, I started studying law office design and became an expert in the field. Law offices are set up differently than corporations. It has been fun to grow with the practice of law as technology continues to change it.

Law office: Alston & Bird LLP, elevator lobby. Rita Carson Guest, FASID, Carson Guest, Inc., Atlanta, Georgia. Photographer: Gabriel Benzur.

What are your primary responsibilities and duties?

I am president of my company and director of design. I work closely with our clients, set the design direction of our projects, make all major presentations, and maintain close contact with our clients from programming through the installation. I especially enjoy working with my clients on their art collections, selecting, framing, and supervising the installation of the artwork.

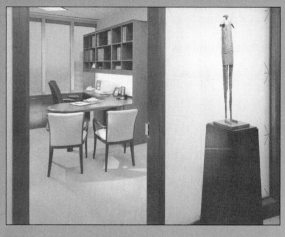

Law office: Alston & Bird LLP, office. Rita Carson Guest, FASID, Carson Guest, Inc., Atlanta, Georgia. Photographer: Gabriel Benzur.

What is the most satisfying part of your job?

The most satisfying part of my job is seeing space that we design built and see how their new environment makes our clients happy and adds to the success of their business.

What is the least satisfying part of your job?

The least satisfying part of my job is dealing with management problems with young designers.

Law office: Alston & Bird LLP, conference room. Rita Carson Guest, FASID, Carson Guest, Inc., Atlanta, Georgia. Photographer: Gabriel Benzur.

What advice would you give someone who wants to be an interior designer?

Understand that this is not a nine-to-five business. There are always deadlines to meet and after-hours installations to handle. If you want a nine-to-five job, select another profession.

Can you describe the optimum portfolio for a job applicant?

Provide a variety of work showing all your skills. Orient your portfolio to the type of work you want to do.

Who or what experience has been a major influence in your career?

My first boss taught me.

Hospitality

ONE BRANCH OF the hospitality design specialty is the interior design of food and beverage facilities. Restaurants, cafés, coffee shops, cocktail lounges and bars, fast food restaurants, and elegant dining rooms and lounges are the most common examples. The other main branch of hospitality design is lodging facilities. Examples are hotels, motels, resort facilities, bed-and-breakfast inns, and other places where guests stay for a few days to a few weeks. Hospitality facilities owned by large chains—Hyatt Hotels and Chili's Restaurants, for example—are usually designed by interior designers working at the corporate headquarters. The design of hospitality facilities starts with a carefully researched and developed design concept that clarifies both the problem presented by the client and the expected solutions, providing an overall idea that unites the project elements into a cohesive whole. The wrong design concept in the wrong location will fail—even if the actual design is well done. Design concepts, by the way, are common documents prepared by interior designers during programming for many kinds of commercial projects.

The interior planning and design of a restaurant or other food and beverage facility includes space planning for dining, locations of service areas, and support spaces. The design and specification of furniture items, architectural finishes, lighting design, and accessories are all important, even critical, to the success of a food and beverage facility. These items, in combination with the menu, fulfill the concept envisioned by the owners. Commercial kitchens are quite complex and are usually designed by individuals who specialize in kitchen design. The interior designer is responsible for areas customers will use and coordinates traffic flow issues with the kitchen designer.

Lodging: bar, Nine Zero Hotel. Trisha Wilson, Wilson & Associates, Dallas, Texas.

Residential and Restaurant Interiors

WILLIAM PEACE, ASID
President, Peace Design, Atlanta, Georgia

What has been your greatest challenge as an interior designer?
The education of clients with regard to the aesthetics of design and the value of our services.

What led you to enter your design specialty?
Personal relationships and the unique custom aspects of residential and restaurants.

What are your primary responsibilities and duties in your position?
Client contact, design vision on projects, custom furnishings, millwork design, project management, and all operations of a small business.

Restaurant: entry. William Peace, ASID, Peace Design, Atlanta, Georgia. Photographer: Chris A. Little.

Restaurant: bar. William Peace, ASID, Peace Design, Atlanta, Georgia. Photographer: Chris A. Little.

Restaurant: dining room. William Peace, ASID, Peace Design, Atlanta, Georgia. Photographer: Chris A. Little.

What is the most satisfying part of your job?
A delighted and satisfied client.

What is the least satisfying part of your job?
The distractions that take me away from design.

What is the most important quality or skill of a designer in your specialty?
Communication.

Who or what experience has been a major influence on your career?
Mentors . . . both from my formal education and my early years as a designer.

Restaurant: banquette. William Peace, ASID, Peace Design, Atlanta, Georgia. Photographer: Chris A. Little.

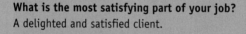

Commercial:
Office, Hospitality, Medical,
Elderly Care, Retail

DAVID F. COOKE, FIIDA, CMG

Principal, Design Collective Incorporated,
Columbus, Ohio

Restaurant: bar/lounge, The Ocean Club, New Albany, Ohio.
David Cooke, Design Collective, Inc., Columbus, Ohio.
Photographer: Michael Houghton, STUDIOHIO.

What has been your greatest challenge as an interior designer?
Planning for change in business (including economy, architectural community, and dealerships selling interior design services).

What led you to enter your design specialty?
A mentor/boss named Chuck Nitschke.

What are your primary responsibilities and duties in your position?
After 30 years...you name it! Marketing, design, planning, staff relations, forecaster.

What is the most satisfying part of your job?
I love the creation of a good idea into a real project and client interaction.

What is the least satisfying part of your job?
I dislike staff reviews!

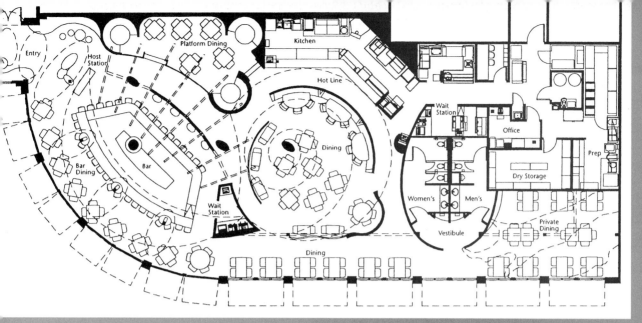

Restaurant: floor plan, The Ocean Club, New Albany, Ohio. David Cooke, Design Collective, Inc., Columbus, Ohio.

What is the most important quality or skill of a designer in your specialty?
Communication skills...can you talk *and* draw?

Who or what experience has been a major influence in your career?
Cannot think of one; some have been the great clients...IBD (now IIDA) national presidency... Industry participation (NCIDQ/FIDER/CMG)...trips to manufacturers, etc.

Restaurant: Mitchell's Steak House, Columbus, Ohio, dining room. David Cooke, Design Collective, Inc., Columbus, Ohio. Photographer: Michael Houghton, STUDIOHIO.

Restaurant: BluWater Café, Newburyport, Massachusetts. Corky Binggeli, ASID, Corky Binggeli Interior Design, Arlington, Massachusetts. Photographer: Douglas Stefanov.

Lodging facilities is the all-encompassing term for facilities where a guest stays for a short-term vacation, for a business conference or meeting, or while traveling. Some designers might include recreational facilities like golf clubhouses, spas, resorts, and casinos in this category because many of them include some form of lodging space. Interior designers who specialize in this type of facility are hired primarily to design the lobby, the ballroom and other meeting rooms, the guest registration area, the guest rooms, and the hotel offices.

Careful attention must be paid to the design of guest rooms, which constitute the primary revenue-producing area of the lodging facility. Of course, guest rooms must be attractive and meet expectations in terms of the price charged to stay there. Yet the planning and specification of products in the rooms is critical with respect to housekeeping and maintenance as well, because costs associated with these essential functions are large. A fragile fabric on chairs in the guest rooms of a family resort facility, for example, will present difficult, even expensive, maintenance problems. This kind of consideration—and similar ones related to other public areas of the lodging facility—is critical for the hospitality interior design professional.

A hotel is a mixed-use space as well. It commonly has food and beverage areas, retail stores, and perhaps service shops such as beauty salons. Other spaces may include specialty businesses, workout rooms, spas, and play areas for children, to name the most common. As with a corporate headquarters, one design firm may have the expertise to design all these spaces, or a team of designers may be involved.

Hospitality: Hotels, Restaurants, Clubs, Spas, Casinos

TRISHA WILSON, ASID
President, Wilson & Associates, Dallas, Texas

What has been your greatest challenge as an interior designer?
Managing employees.

What led you to enter your design specialty?
I studied design at the University of Texas in Austin. On graduation, I went to work for a department store chain in their home furnishings department. From there I started doing residential design, then moved on to restaurant design through a residential client. My first hotel design project was the Anatole Hotel in Dallas, which I landed by making a gutsy phone call to the developer.

Lodging: tea lounge, Yokohama Royal Park Hotel Nikko, Yokohama, Japan. Trisha Wilson, ASID, Wilson & Associates, Dallas, Texas. Photographer: Robert Miller.

What are your primary responsibilities and duties?

Overall management of the firm, which includes employees, clients, and vendors. I read financial reports, look over contracts, and talk on the phone endlessly. Our six offices span the globe and are in different time zones. Because of this, there is never an hour in the day when the office is closed. I do still work on the design of several projects each year.

What is the most satisfying part of your job?

The most satisfying is the accolades my team receives when we install a beautiful project. A satisfied client and appreciative public are really gratifying.

What is the most important quality or skill of a designer in your specialty?

Communication. Of course, a designer needs to have talent, but if you cannot communicate your ideas or vision, you are ineffective.

Lodging: guest suite, Las Ventanas al Paraiso, Los Cabos, Mexico. Trisha Wilson, ASID, Wilson & Associates, Dallas, Texas. Photographer: Peter Vitale.

Who or what experience has been a major influence on your career?

My first major influence was developer Trammel Crow in the early 1970s in Dallas, Texas. He took a huge risk in hiring me (an unknown designer) to design his hotel convention center, the Anatole. It was a daunting project, but with his support I just jumped right in and figured it out. A second influence was developer Sol Kerzner in South Africa in the early 1990s. He approached us to design his Palace of the Lost City hotel in Sun City, South Africa. It was another daunting project in a country that was extremely underdeveloped regarding the decorative arts and suppliers. With his encouragement and support (and a ton of hard work), we turned out a spectacular hotel.

Lodging: lobby, The Palace of the Lost City, Sun City, South Africa. Trisha Wilson, ASID, Wilson & Associates, Dallas, Texas. Photographer: Peter Vitale.

Lodging: bar, Nine Zero Hotel. Trisha Wilson, ASID, Wilson & Associates, Dallas, Texas. Photographer; Mike Wilson.

Hospitality/Healthcare/ Workplace Design

JENNIFER TIERNAN, IIDA

Principal, Geppetto Studios, Inc.
St. Louis, Missouri

Lodging: reception desk, Millennium Hotel, St. Louis, Missouri. Jennifer Tiernan, Geppetto Studios, Inc. St. Louis, Missouri. Photographer: Sam Fentress.

What has been your greatest challenge as an interior designer?

When I first ventured out into the "Real World" as it is called to those about to graduate from college, my biggest challenge was the adjustment to what was taught in class and what was expected in a design firm. There is much more business and non-design issues that need to be addressed than what was ever taught. Now my greatest challenge as an interior designer is not so much understanding the business end of the job, but making sure that all personalities of who I am designing for are satisfied. If your clients are dissatisfied, then you have failed as a designer.

What led you to enter your design specialty?

Healthcare: My first project that I worked on that had the greatest impact on me was a children's hospital. It was such a bittersweet process, but it made what I am doing so much more meaningful that I ever thought my job could be. We all knew that children are very resilient, but they need a nurturing, warm, fun, whimsical environment to escape to. This holds true for any healthcare project I am working on. Patients are affected by their surroundings greatly, so knowing that I am helping the healing process by designing warm, inviting, non-sterile environments makes what I do seem a little less stereotypical.

Hospitality: My first job was for a firm where most of the work was for the gaming and marine industry, so I was exposed immediately to the hospitality design market. There were contacts I made during this time that I still work with today.

What are your primary responsibilities and duties in your position?

Well, I am a partner in a new two-person firm, so you could call me the designer, librarian, accountant, human resources, and administrative assistant. Obviously my main responsibility is to be the designer and I would love for that to be all that I focused on, but that is not reality. My partner is the marketing arm and I am the design arm, but we are all of those things listed above every day. It definitely makes life a little more interesting.

Lodging: café, Millennium Hotel, St. Louis, Missouri. Jennifer Tiernan, Geppetto Studios, Inc. St. Louis, Missouri. Photographer: Sam Fentress.

What is the most satisfying part of your job?

Seeing a project being built is fascinating to me. I could spend hours at a job site because it is invaluable hands-on learning.

What is the least satisfying part of your job?

The least satisfying part would be the necessary "business" that has to take place in order to survive, such as generating contracts, invoices, timesheets, etc. When your passion is design and creativity these tasks can be trying at times.

What is the most important quality or skill of a designer in your specialty?

Knowing what materials and fixtures are appropriate and what are not. I have always thought if one can design healthcare projects, one could design anything. There are so many rules, regulations, codes, and new finish technologies a designer needs to be aware of in order to create a space that not only looks appealing, but will withstand the 24 hour use, needed maintenance, and pass all the necessary codes. A designer who is aware of the appropriateness of their designs is invaluable.

Who or what experience has been a major influence in your career?

I would have to say there is not one person or thing that has influenced me the most. There are a few architects that I have worked with in the past that I feel left a large impression on me as it relates to design. To this day, every once in a while there are days where I am entranced in the creative process and wonder what they would think about how I was approaching the design.

Lodging: waiting area, Millennium Hotel, St. Louis, Missouri. Jennifer Tiernan, Geppetto Studios, Inc. St. Louis, Missouri. Photographer: Sam Fentress.

"What Do You Look for in Hiring a New Designer?"

Passion, professionalism, talent, personality.
—Janice Carleen Linster, ASID, IIDA, CID

I look for designers with the innate ability to see the big picture and to make decisions within that framework. The pretty or different solution to the problem is not nearly as creative as the solution based on a balance of function, value, and aesthetics.
—M. Joy Meeuwig, IIDA

Education, people skills, and a good design eye. How well they will blend with the staff.
—Debra May Himes, IIDA, ASID

I look for someone with exceptional creative and technical skills. Someone who is willing to learn and can well represent my firm.
—Linda Santellanes, ASID

Children's area, W. T. Cozby Public Library, Coppell, Texas. Barbara Nugent, FASID, F&S Partners, Inc., Dallas, Texas. Photographer: J. F. Wilson.

For almost thirty years, I have been with design and/or architectural firms where a team approach has been the norm for projects. As a consequence, when hiring interior designers, I have always given consideration to the skills/experience of my existing staff and sought new hires who offered complementary skills so that we had a balanced team to work on projects. For example, if the current staff were detail-focused, then I might need a big-picture individual; if current staff was weighted on space-planning skills, then I might seek an individual with a gift with color/materials/finishes; if the current staff lacked good presentation/public speaking skills, then good verbal communication skills might be foremost in mind when interviewing. My focus was to have a well-rounded team whose members worked well together and could learn from one another.

Notwithstanding the need for a great team, competency in design, document execution, computer use, and problem solving are mandatory.
—Barbara Nugent, FASID

I automatically assume graduates of reputable schools know the process of design. Portfolios (of new graduates and practitioners) demonstrate their level of creativity relative to our firm's/client's expectations.

— Jennifer van der Put, BID, IDC, ARIDO, IFMA

Someone who has successfully completed design education. Some of the traits are talented, innovative, self-made, dedicated, energetic, communicative, bold, and disciplined. Often someone with an interesting background is also considered—for example, someone who is well traveled and has many types of interests.

— Alicia Loo, CID

Personality, ability to roll with the punches.

— Derrell Parker, IIDA

Basically, I look at their portfolio to see whether they have the skills.

— Ellen McDowell, ASID

I look first for design talent and technical skill; however, I look most for the willingness to learn and to be a team player.

— Beth Kuzbek, ASID, IIDA, CMG

I look for education first and foremost, involvement in a professional association, ability to market themselves, and someone on the path to take NCIDQ. Professional appearance and an organized and well-presented portfolio are also important. CAD knowledge and 3D design are getting more and more important.

— Juliana Catlin, FASID

Creativity, orientation to detail, and the ability to finish a project in a win-win situation. Each project takes months to complete. Misunderstandings will happen throughout the projects. How the situations are handled is very important to payment, future referrals, and the image of the company.

— John Holmes, ASID, IIDA

I haven't looked, but if I did I would want someone grounded personally, with a knowledge of building codes.

— W. Daniel Shelley, AIA, ASID

Common sense!! An ability to communicate well, a great attitude—positive—and a real focus on customer service. Presentation, polish, maturity—and a sense of humor!

— Lisa M. Whited, ASID, IIDA, IDEC

Ability to communicate graphically and verbally. Passion.

— Neil Frankel, FAIA, FIIDA

Good communication skills in the interview, a good portfolio, good intelligence, and competence in AutoCAD. Because I like to teach, I don't mind inexperience right now. But my firm hired me because I was older and had a lot of experience—they needed someone who could handle the client relationship thing—not just put together pretty finish boards (not that finish boards aren't important—we just received a nice compliment today from a commercial client who has truly enjoyed using the finish boards we prepared for them to promote the work they are about to do on their theological seminary!). And sometimes our firm is looking for a computer graphics expert—the verbal communication skills don't matter as much as a portfolio and competence. So the answer is, it depends on the needs of the firm at that time.

— Linda Kress, ASID

Basic CAD skills, personal and design presentation skills, a strong work ethic, technical knowledge, and enthusiasm. It is also good to see experience (internship) within the profession.

— Fred Messner, IIDA

University: University of Northern Iowa, bar. Linda Kress, ASID, Lotti, Krishan & Short, Inc., Tulsa, Oklahoma. Photographer: Shimer@Hedrich Blessing.

Communication skills, tech skills, design skills—in that order.
—Bruce Goff, ASID

Our firm is primarily an architectural firm. I look at the skill level of each new prospective employee. Design is important, but the realities of designing within the program of the project is more important. Anyone looking to make a serious future in the design profession should have a good background in the building environment—how a building is put together. It is also important to understand the history, ergonomics, and life safety factors behind any design problem. Last, I look for intelligence, common sense, and a love of the profession.
—Cheri Gerou, AIA, ASID

Four-year degree; FIDER accreditation.
—Teresa Sowell, ASID, IFMA

Enthusiasm for design and people first, with skills in AutoCAD, creative design, color, and organization.
—Sandra Evans, ASID

Self-motivation.
—Pat Campbell McLaughlin, ASID

An educated designer with a four-year degree who can draw (both sketch free-hand and CAD), has a good attitude, and is willing to do whatever needs to be done.
—Melinda Sechrist, FASID

Ability to talk with me, a responsibility to the profession to always want to know more, ability to relate to my clients in a way that reflects well on my work and my firm.
—Michael Thomas, ASID

Retail Facilities

THIS DESIGN SPECIALTY addresses the interior design of any size or type of store that sells products to consumers. Department stores and specialty stores in shopping malls, freestanding stores, and specialty stores located in neighborhood open strip malls are included in this area of commercial interior design. Examples of projects are an independently owned apparel store in a shopping area, the interiors of a department store, and everything in between.

Merchandising is a familiar term to the retail facilities designer. It involves all the functions needed to effect the selling of merchandise, including advertising, the mix of merchandise, one-on-one selling, product displays, and the interior design and specification of the store itself. Because the total merchandising concept is so important to the success of a store, the interior designer working in this specialty must understand the business of retail.

In retail design, what is being sold has a critical impact on the plan and design of the store's interior. Customers must be induced to visit all parts of the store. The planning and interior design is meant to give customers the opportunity to see a large number of merchandise items. The type of merchandise obviously affects the way the merchandise is displayed. Many store fixtures—the equipment used to display merchandise, such as jewelry cabinets and clothing racks—are custom designed by the interior designer. Security measures intended to inhibit shoplifting are also important.

The independent interior design firm has more opportunity to work with the owners of small independent retail stores than with chain stores. Many department stores and franchise or chain specialty stores have in-house interior design teams that design new facilities. Corporate planners and interior designers as well as merchandising staff most often have the responsibility for the interior design of these stores.

The Electronics Boutique, Woodbridge Center, Woodbridge, New Jersey. John Mclean, RA, AIA, John Mclean Architect, White Plains, New York.

Corporate Headquarters, Restaurant, Retail, and Hospitality

JEFFREY RAUSCH, IIDA
Principal, Exclaim Design, Scottsdale, Arizona

What has been your greatest challenge as an interior designer?
Managing client expectations. What we do is more art than science, but unfortunately clients consider it the other way around.

What led you to enter your design specialty?
Trial and error. I first attempted residential while at university and decided it wasn't right for me. Then I did tenant improvement space planning, which, while easy for me, wasn't satisfying. This advanced into higher-end corporate work. My current mantra is that "I do design for those where design helps sell their product or service." This marries my design and marketing backgrounds.

Retail: store interior, Awesome Atoms. Jeffrey Rausch, IIDA, Exclaim Design, Scottsdale, Arizona. Photographer: Delstar.

What are your primary responsibilities and duties?
As managing partner, I do the business development, business strategizing, and lead design work.

What is the most satisfying part of your job?
Working with clients to create design solutions that are profitable for them.

What is the least satisfying part of your job?
Working with clients who don't understand the value of design to their business. They simply get in the way of satisfaction.

Can you describe the optimum portfolio for a job applicant?
One that exhibits thoroughness, accuracy, good communication skills, and basic design skills presented in an organized and attractive manner. Many portfolios now are emailed—this is great for a first-pass review of the candidate's skills. Ultimately, however, the original materials are necessary for a more thorough review.

What is the most important quality or skill of a designer in your specialty?
Flexibility and an ability to perceive the client's expectations. Flexibility to adjust to the naturally fluid design process. Perception to see reality as your clients do—to put yourself into their mindset.

Who or what experience has been a major influence on your career?
My first internship and my mentor there established the path of my career. Her tireless work ethic and detailed designs created a benchmark for my career.

Retail: store interior, Awesome Atoms. Jeffrey Rausch, IIDA, Exclaim Design, Scottsdale, Arizona. Photographer: Delstar.

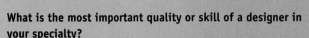

Healthcare

ANOTHER COMMON commercial interior design specialty category is healthcare facilities, including medical office suites, hospitals, dental offices, and senior care facilities. Other types are free-standing medical facilities such as physical therapy centers, diagnostic imaging (radiology) practices, laboratories, residential facilities for Alzheimer's patients, and other nursing care facilities. Another subspecialty in the healthcare category is veterinary clinics. Designers who love animals may enjoy this specialty.

Many interior designers who design other kinds of office suites are knowledgeable about the design of medical office suites. However, to be successful, the interior designer must understand the medical specialty that will be housed in the suite. A medical office suite is not just another project. Each medical specialty has specific functional needs and requirements. Interior design planning and specification of a suite for a cardiac specialist is different than that for a pediatrician or a surgeon. The interior designer must know enough about the medical specialty to be sure the spaces and specifications will support the functions of the medical suite. Aesthetic decisions must be made after careful planning for the medical and functional needs of the facility.

Hospitals of various kinds are more complex and difficult to design satisfactorily than a medical office suite. Functional requirements, codes, and health department regulations are strict with respect to the interior design of hospital departments. The interior designer must work closely with hospital administration and staff as well as with the architect and other consultants. Knowledge of the workings of the medical departments is important to the successful design of hospital spaces. The interior designer might be hired to design public spaces such as the lobby, cafeteria, and patient floor lounges, or medical spaces such as patient rooms, nursing stations, and specialized medical areas. Designers with this highly specialized knowledge can assist the hospital staff and architect in the planning and specification of areas such as the laboratory, emergency department, diagnostic imaging, pediatrics department, and other departments as well as patient rooms.

Designing general practice dental offices and dental specialties such as orthodontics requires knowledge about how the doctor provides service to patients. Although specialty manufacturers supply the necessary medical equipment, interior designers often lay out the interiors of the oportories and provide aesthetic treatments for architectural finishes and furnishings. The aesthetics and acoustical planning for interiors of this type of medical space must be made with care, as few patients enjoy dental visits. Thus, the interiors must function effectively for the dental practitioner as well as create a psychologically comfortable environment for the patient.

Healthcare Interior Architecture

JAIN MALKIN, CID
President, Jain Malkin, Inc., San Diego, California

What has been your greatest challenge as an interior designer?
My greatest challenge as an interior designer has been to acquire the education I needed because these courses were simply not available when I went to school. I had to do a great deal of on-the-job learning and also embarked on a lengthy process of self-education.

What led you to enter your design specialty?
When I moved to California from Chicago, I started fresh, with no clients, and I decided to specialize in an area that was underserved. In 1970, this was certainly the field of healthcare. I decided I would take a year off and read everything I could get my hands on in order to learn the field but, after two weeks at the library (way before the Internet), I had read both books written on healthcare architecture or design and just about every relevant article in the *Reader's Guide to Periodical Literature*. In short, there wasn't much there. I spent the rest of the year on site in hospitals doing research. Actually, my degree in psychology prepared me better than anything else could have in order to do this research, and it gave me a unique focus for the rest of my professional life, which was to be able to see the environment through the patient's eyes.

I came to the field with a research focus that few interior designers have, and this has led me to the books I have written, which have become principal references in the industry. After spending that year doing on-site research, I started writing articles for magazines on the psychological aspects of being a patient, and I proposed environment design changes. Because little was being written on this subject, every article I wrote was published, and I became an expert in the field before I had any practical healthcare design experience under my belt. A few years later, after I had gained experience, I decided to write a book to help other designers acquire this information without such a laborious course of study. This was the first edition of my medical and dental space planning book, the third edition of which was published in April 2002. The book has been continuously in print for over twenty years and is still the only book on the topic. It makes me feel good to know I've been able to contribute to others, and to the profession, in this manner. In 1992, I wrote *Hospital Interior Architecture*, which is a research-based approach to hospital design.

What are your primary responsibilities and duties?
As the head of an interior architecture firm employing twenty individuals, I am responsible for running the firm, for marketing, for financial liability, and for inspiring and encouraging the talented people who work in my organization, and I oversee the creative direction of most projects. In addition, I bring research to the projects.

Healthcare: Ethel Rosenthal Resource Library, Scripps Breast Care Center, La Jolla, California. Interior architecture and design, Jain Malkin, Inc., San Diego, California. Photographer: Glenn Cormier.

What is the most satisfying part of your job?

The most satisfying part of my job is the incredible thrill I experience when a project has been constructed and it meets— even exceeds—my expectations. Better yet, seeing the impact it has on patients and staff is very satisfying. Nothing can compare to this exhilaration, and each time it happens I think I must be the luckiest person in the world to be able to do this kind of work.

What is the least satisfying part of your job?

The least satisfying part of my job is managing employees. If one could clone the handful of employees who are creative, competent, have a good personality, positive attitude, and emotional maturity, this would be nirvana. The reality is that it is a challenge for me or any employer. Many other parts of running a business are simply not fun, such as billing. It's very important to have a tight rein on finances and constantly stay close to it in order to be financially viable. Preparing proposals and reviewing lengthy contracts is also drudgery—but, of course, necessary for any professional consulting firm.

What is the most important quality or skill of a designer in your specialty?

The field of healthcare design requires many skills, most of which center around technical competence—understanding codes, knowledge of materials appropriate for healthcare, understanding life safety issues. In this setting, as compared with corporate interior design, the wrong selection or a design that fails can actually be harmful to a patient. It's a big responsibility, and clients will hold your feet to the fire if something you've specified or designed fails.

Healthcare: waiting room, Smotrich Center for Reproductive Enhancement, La Jolla, California. Interior architecture and design: Jain Malkin, Inc., San Diego, California. Photographer: Glenn Cormier.

Who or what experience has been a major influence on your career?

There have probably been many influences on my career, but I would have to say that the individual who gave me my first job, while I was a student in college, got me interested in the field. I lied about my age and experience and was able to convince him (there it is again, that quality of persuasiveness) to hire me. By the time he found out I didn't know much, I had already learned a great deal in his architectural firm, and it set me on a new career path. Incidentally, after a speaking engagement some years ago, someone in the audience came up to ask me a question. He said that for years there had been a rumor in his office that I used to work there many years ago, and he wanted to know if this was true. He took delight in knowing that the kid they had hired who didn't even have basic drafting skills became a successful healthcare designer.

Healthcare: waiting room, neurosurgery suite. Interior architecture and design: Jain Malkin, Inc., San Diego, California. Photographer: Steve McClelland.

Healthcare

ROSALYN CAMA, FASID
President, CAMA, Inc., New Haven, Connecticut

What led you to enter your design specialty?
It was a quirk that in the recession I graduated in, there were no design jobs to be had, so I thought I'd go to graduate school. As I prepared for my GREs, I took a job at a local hospital as a draftsperson and, well, the rest is history. I was asked to stay on for a six-year, $173 million building project, and I learned hospital operations and the art of decision by committee. I also worked with two outstanding healthcare architectural firms. When the project was complete, I started my own practice and called on the alumni of that project, who helped build my healthcare design practice.

Healthcare: multispecialty waiting area. Rosalyn Cama, FASID, CAMA, Inc., New Haven, Connecticut. Architect: KMD, San Francisco, California. Photographer: Michael O'Callahan.

What has been your greatest challenge as an interior designer?
Realizing I was not practicing an art but rather operating within a social science. We impact the lives of so many and are proving in our professional research that all we do does impact human behavior.

What are your primary responsibilities and duties?
Some twenty years later, I am responsible for my firm's project marketing and development. I remain active in the design of our projects. I find it crucial to vision with our clients at the inception of a project. Their active leadership and clear view of what their facility will accomplish allows us to apply our best knowledge. We are then able to present the best solution for their project. This early groundwork allows me to manage my very talented team with a realistic end goal.

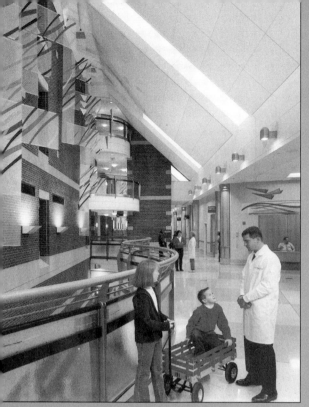

Healthcare: lobby. Rosalyn Cama, FASID, CAMA, Inc., New Haven, Connecticut. Architect: KMD, San Francisco, California. Photographer: Michael O'Callahan.

What is the most satisfying part of your job?
I believe that in healthcare design we impact lives at critical times. When we create an interior that reduces the stress one goes through during a medical procedure, I have great satisfaction.

What is the least satisfying part of your job?
I am most frustrated by the lack of appreciation this profession has. To too many, we are still the icing on the cake and are not called to the table when we can make the most difference.

How important is interior design education in today's industry?
Three states in the United States are actually recognizing the impact design has on life as a whole. They are instituting pilot programs that will incorporate the topics of this profession throughout their K-12 curriculum. I applaud those efforts and say it is about time!!!

What is the most important quality or skill of a designer in your specialty?
The ability to stay ahead of your client on the trends in the healthcare industry. Building flexibility into our projects is what makes them viable and lasts the length of time between renovations.

Healthcare: ambulatory surgery waiting. Rosalyn Cama, FASID, CAMA, Inc., New Haven, Connecticut. Architect: KMD, San Francisco, California. Photographer: Michael O'Callahan.

Senior living facilities are also often placed in this specialty because many such places provide, in addition to ordinary living spaces, specialized nursing care for residents who need short-term or long-term skilled nursing care. However, most of a senior living facility combines apartments and common spaces for active and healthy seniors. This specialty will continue to be an important part of interior design as the baby boomers (people born between 1946 and 1964) continue to make decisions about moving from their single-family dwellings to group living facilities.

Common areas and areas for nursing care are designed by the commercial interior designer who specializes in this area while the resident apartments are often designed by residential designers or the residents themselves. The interior design of this type of facility involves specification of materials and products to facilitate residents who use wheelchairs or walkers or have other special physical needs. Materials and color specification must consider reduced visual acuity to enhance safety as residents move through common spaces. Space planning must also adhere to accessibility standards such as the Americans with Disabilities Act (ADA) throughout the facility.

Artist rendering, private patient room, Tahoe Forest Hospital, Truckee, California. M. Joy Meeuwig, IIDA, Interior Design Consultation, Reno, Nevada. Artist: Larry Henry for HMC Architects.

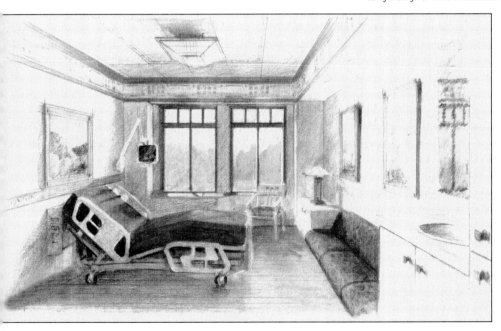

Institutional

MANY TYPES OF commercial facilities owned by government agencies or other public-sector organizations are under the institutional specialty umbrella. Among these are educational facilities, museums, libraries, government offices at the local, state, provincial, and federal levels, and churches, synagogues, mosques, and other religious facilities. The category of institutional design also includes prisons. Financial institutions such as banks and credits unions are often placed in the institutional category though they are not public-sector organizations. As you can see, this category covers a wide range of facility types.

To help you understand why these types of facilities are considered institutional, let's look at a definition of the term. According to the dictionary, an institution is "an established organization, or corporation, especially of a public character."[3] With this definition in mind as well as the kinds of facilities commonly placed in this category, it is easy to see that an institutional facility is one that is publicly funded rather than privately owned. Obviously, not all institutional facilities are publicly funded, but this is generally the case.

This wide range of facility types is extraordinarily diverse in client needs. Interior designers who specialize in any of these areas must design for at least four groups of stakeholders. Taking a county office building as an example, the first stakeholder to consider is its owner or the government entity responsible for it. Another stakeholder group that must be acknowledged and satisfied is the employees who will work in the building. These might include elected county officials, a wide variety of office workers, and even judges. A third group is the people who have business in the county building. A fourth stakeholder group that, to some degree, must be satisfied is the taxpayers who actually fund the construction and finishing of the facility. This last group may not have decision-making power in the development of drawings and documents, but its members certainly air their opinions when the facility is completed!

Because varied activities take place in an institutional facility, the interior designer must be sensitive to the part emotions play in the design. For example, although learning takes place in all kinds of schools, the age of the students using a particular school must affect the selection of furniture, colors, signage, even the mechanical systems. Each religious denomination has different requirements for the design of the place of worship. Even churches within the same denomination and located in the same city can have different design treatments based on the wishes of the congregation. These examples are merely to show how important it is for the interior designer to be sensitive to the stakeholders' wishes and needs in the design of institutional interiors.

Commercial: Healthcare, Corporate, Government, Institutional

BARBARA NUGENT, FASID

Owner, bnDesigns, Dallas, Texas

What led you to enter your design specialty?

My experience over the years has been in both the public and private sectors. Individual projects include hospitals, clinics, call centers, corporate headquarters, city halls, performing art centers, libraries, universities, art galleries, courts, bowling alleys, food service, lecture halls, auditoriums, renovations, banks, and others I can't recall. Sizes have varied from one room to multi-buildings on multi-campuses. Clients have varied from a single individual to a committee to multiple committees. Each has presented its own challenges, but the basic methodology is consistent.

Institutional, library: entrance, J. Erik Johnson Children's Center, Dallas, Texas. Barbara Nugent, FASID, F&S Partners, Inc., Dallas, Texas. Photographer: Craig Blackman.

What is the most satisfying part of your job?

I love designing libraries, all kinds: public, private, central, branch, and specialty (genealogy, law, children's, etc.). It is one of the few specialties that clearly requires the involvement of an interior designer early on. A well-designed library begins with consideration of the furniture (e.g., book stacks arrangement and dimensions). Their placement influences the development of the lighting, electrical, mechanical, and structural systems!

Institutional, library: stack and reading area, W. T. Cozby Public Library, Coppell, Texas. Barbara Nugent, FASID, F&S Partners, Inc., Dallas, Texas. Photographer: J. F. Wilson.

Can you provide any insights to help interior designers decide on a career direction?

Answering these questions may help one formulate a career direction within the wide variety of arenas composing our interior design profession.

- What is in your future as an interior designer?
- How can you prepare yourself to meet the qualifications of our profession, both today and tomorrow, when the world is changing daily?
- How will you maintain your skills to create built environments that promote appropriate human behavior and leave the world a better place because of your involvement?
- What are the dynamics within our profession that will feed your enthusiasm and thirst for knowledge so you continually create better environments?

Institutional, library: storytelling forest, J. Erik Johnson Children's Center, Dallas, Texas. Barbara Nugent, FASID, F&S Partners, Inc., Dallas, Texas. Photographer: Craig Blackman.

Government Design: State, County, Municipal, and Military

KIMBERLY M. STUDZINSKI, ASID

Project Designer, Buchart Horn/Basco Associates, York, Pennsylvania

What has been your greatest challenge as an interior designer?

Awareness of all disciplines involved in a project team is essential. Understanding of all of a building's systems—structural, architectural, electrical, plumbing, and HVAC (heating, ventilation and air conditioning), data and telecommunications, site and security—is necessary in order to create a successful space.

Designers need to be cognizant of budgets, scheduling, site and construction constraints, historical aspects, phasing logistics, and in the realm of government design, sensitive to public funding issues, politics, and community needs. Although it can be challenging to weave all of these elements together, it is the designer's job to make it appear seamless.

Institutional: first-floor lobby, County Administration Building. Kim Studzinski, ASID. Buchart Horn, Inc./Basco Associates, York, Pennsylvania. Photographer: Bryson Leidich.

Institutional: commissioner's office, County Administration Building. Kim Studzinski, ASID. Buchart Horn, Inc./Basco Associates, York, Pennsylvania. Photographer: Bryson Leidich.

What lead you to enter your design specialty?

Geography and chance. Some people decide upon doing a particular thing and go wherever it takes them. Others decide where they want to be and then make it work. I belong to the latter group. I have made a personal choice not to live in a major urban area. Since many commercial interior design firms are located in higher density urban areas situated near a larger client base, my employment options are more limited. I also enjoy working for a firm where I can focus on design more than marketing. Although I have tried to remain flexible about particular design specialization, I have had to search more intensely for the right fit within these parameters.

Fortunately, I have discovered wonderful opportunities in my backyard. Although my company is a large architectural and engineer firm with a diverse mix of clients, I have been able to focus on where the need has been—mostly with our government clients. Although it was not my purposeful intention, it happens to be an excellent fit.

What are your primary responsibilities and duties in your position?

No two jobs are identical, so the actual tasks vary each time. Some of the more common tasks—

- *Programming*—Develop a summary of personnel, space, and FF&E needs through client interviews, walk-through of existing spaces, and inventories of existing furnishings.

- *Space planning*—Design and create floor plans diagramming the organization of space. Preliminary designs are often sketches.

- *Client Proposals and Presentations*—I create and present proposals for professional services or design presentations of work created for client. Presentations that are more formal sometimes occur during public meetings. Often times, I sketch and render three-dimensional views to illustrate designs.

- *Furniture layouts and specification*—I make selections of furniture for projects including modular workstations, case goods, seating, and conference room furnishings. Depending on the job requirements, I may be assisting the client to procure utilizing purchasing contracts with manufacturers or through competitive bidding. I also have been involved with negotiating leasing on behalf of clients. Most clients utilize some furniture they already own, so I coordinate this as well.

Institutional: commissioner's hearing room, County Administration Building. Kim Studzinski, ASID. Buchart Horn, Inc./Basco Associates, York, Pennsylvania. Photographer: Bryson Leidich.

- *Finish Specification*—I select appropriate finishes and colors for interior materials. This is generally translated into a Finish schedule, a matrix for identifying materials by room. I also coordinate with a technical writer who prepares a specification of each project. Specifications are written legal documents that outline important requirements such as what materials should be, how they should be applied or finished, and performance guidelines. In most cases, finish boards are created to present selection samples to the client.

- *Quality Control*—I review drawings and specifications to check for accuracy and consistency with design intent.

- *Drafting*—Although I enjoy drafting, I do not typically do as much drafting as I used to. It is usually delegated to a junior member of the design team, utilizing computer-aided design (CAD) software.

- *Working on the computer*—Most of the tasks above are executed at least in part using a computer. I work with a whole host of software programs for word processing, spreadsheets, project scheduling, databases, and CAD, including both two and three-dimensional drawings.

What is the most satisfying part of your job?
I enjoy having the opportunity to improve people's environments. In many cases, I am designing a place where people work—a place where some people spend a third of their lives. In areas that are more public, I the have opportunity to create places that foster civic pride.

What is the least satisfying part of your job?

Occasionally a project is designed in its entirety only to have funding cancelled or direction drastically changed. It can be very frustrating to design something whole-heartedly and never see it come to fruition.

What is the most important quality or skill of a designer in your specialty?

I always try to remember that the project is not for me, but for the client. Therefore, I try to set my own ego aside and listen to what the client truly needs and desires. In addition, in most government design projects, the client is the public community. Decision makers are often elected officials whose terms may not span the duration of a project. I strive to create solutions with broad appeal to eliminate as may revisions as possible.

Being flexible and adaptive is also very important. My approach is to develop the most appropriate solution possible. Designs are not created within a vacuum, but within specific parameters defined by all the building systems, budget, ultimate use, and aesthetics. Moreover, sometimes late in the game, these parameters may change due to unforeseen circumstances. Therefore, what is the most suitable design in the end is not necessarily the *ideal* design.

Institutional: commissioner's conference area, County Administration Building. Kim Studzinski, ASID. Buchart Horn, Inc./Basco Associates, York, Pennsylvania. Photographer: Bryson Leidich.

Who or what experience has been a major influence in your career?

When I was younger, my family owned a small local hardware store. As I worked beside my father, he taught me, so I could in turn show our customers, how to do many things. I learned about plumbing, electrical, carpentry, hardware, building, and finish materials—how to use them, install them, fix them, and buy them. He also allowed me free rein with the merchandising and store layout. As our business grew, we added a kitchen and bath design center. A designer was born!

I remember the day I decided to pursue becoming an Interior Designer. I met a designer who, after finding out a little about me, told me about himself. Until that day, I knew what I liked to do, but did not fully realize it to be a bona-fide career choice—for which one could go to school, earn credentials, and get a "real job." On that day, I told myself, "that's what I'm going to do!"

Electronic Job Hunting

It has become increasingly common for large interior design firms to use electronic means to seek or prequalify potential employees. Firms also post job openings on company websites and Internet job sites. Job applicants can surf web-posting locations for information on potential positions. Students and professional members of ASID, IIDA, or another organizations can check the association's job bank or job service for potential openings or post their résumé there.

Electronic résumés need to be simple in style and format. Fancy typefaces, boxes, graphics, and other formatting methods that are appropriate to a printed résumé can be disastrous on an electronic résumé. Keep the file simple so the résumé will be read correctly by the receiving company. Use the key words of the industry as appropriate so the résumé will be picked out if the company uses a scanning program.

If you email your résumé, include it in the body of the email rather than as an attachment. Many firms are afraid of the viruses that may accompany attachments. Because of the profusion of spam mail, many receivers will not open email from people they do not know.

Whether you use email or fax, be sure to send a cover letter or note with your résumé. Blind mailing or spamming of your résumé will not get you in the door. You would not send a résumé by postal mail without a cover letter; the same goes for electronic means.

Library: children's area, Ocean County Library, Little Egg Harbor Branch, Little Egg Harbor, New Jersey. Suzan Globus, ASID, Globus Design Associates, Red Bank, New Jersey. Photographer: Diane Edington.

Entertainment

Entertainment facilities have become a challenging and growing category of commercial interior design. We go to places of entertainment to forget our troubles and have fun for a few hours. Perhaps we are vicariously transported to another land in movies and legitimate theater performances. Maybe we go to cheer our favorite sports team at a stadium. Other entertainment facility types are Las Vegas casinos, theme parks, golf clubs, and other small sports facilities. A more specialized area of entertainment interior design is the design of the sets and production spaces for television, radio, and movie studios.

The design of entertainment facilities requires strict adherence and attention to building and safety codes. The owners and designers must provide a safe environment for the large numbers of people who are welcomed into these facilities. There may be no compromises on safety issues in order to make the stadium or theater or studio somehow more attractive. The interior designer is challenged to design sports stadium skyboxes, casinos, and theaters safely as well as to attract consumers to the space.

As is true for most commercial projects, the interior designer is a member of a team in the design of entertainment spaces. Special considerations for lighting, acoustics, mechanical systems, and structural factors make entertainment spaces impossible for the interior designer to do alone. That is why most interior design firms who specialize in entertainment spaces work within architectural offices and hire experienced interior designers only.

Entertainment: PNC Park, Pittsburgh, Pennsylvania. Beth Harmon-Vaughn, FIIDA. HOK Sport + Venue + Event, Kansas City, Missouri. Photographer: Edward Massery.

Public Assembly/Hospitality

BETH HARMON-VAUGHN, FIIDA
Senior Associate, HOK Sport + Venue + Event,
Kansas City, Kansas

What has been your greatest challenge as an interior designer?
Weathering recessions and establishing respectful professional relationships with architects. I am most proud of the latter; most of my best friends and colleagues are architects.

What led you to enter your design specialty?
Interesting projects—I like large-scale work, and the specialties I am involved with are usually large-scale projects.

What are your primary responsibilities and duties?
Directing a group of eighteen designers, including design leadership, resource management of projects and the group, communication about projects, clients, and staff throughout the firm, the overall financial success of the group, personnel issues.

Entertainment: club suite, PNC Park, Pittsburgh, Pennsylvania. Beth Harmon-Vaughn, FIIDA. HOK Sport + Venue + Event, Kansas City, Missouri. Photographer: Edward Massery.

Entertainment: club lounge, PNC Park, Pittsburgh, Pennsylvania. Beth Harmon-Vaughn, FIIDA. HOK Sport + Venue + Event, Kansas City, Missouri. Photographer: Edward Massery.

What is the most satisfying part of your job?
Projects and clients; I still love this part and marketing new work!

What is the least satisfying part of your job?
Financial and numbers stuff—but it's absolutely essential to the success of my group and to me personally.

What is the most important quality or skill of a designer in your specialty?
Great interpersonal and communication skills and great creativity.

Who or what experience has been a major influence on your career?
Great mentors and teachers; the best teachers have been both patrons and peers. Great projects and great clients!

Entertainment: club balcony overlooking Star Bar, Reliant Stadium. Beth Harmon-Vaughn, FIIDA. HOK Sport + Venue + Event, Kansas City, Missouri. Photographer: Edward Massery.

Restoration and Adaptive Reuse

Residences and commercial buildings that have significant historical value are important to maintain in order for a community to understand its roots. Some interior designers specialize in the restoration of existing structures, working to preserve the past, if the structure has historical significance, or rehabilitating the structure rather than see it destroyed. Restoration means "to carefully return a structure to its original appearance and integrity."[4] Restoration project team members include an architect trained in historical construction, the interior design specialist, historians, archaeologists, and specialized craftspeople. Research by the interior designer and other team members determines a structure's original design, finishes, and furnishings. Original work and reproductions (or even authentic antiques) are returned to the interior to make the restoration as authentic as possible.

Restoration of interiors and, of course, exteriors is precise and highly specialized work. Design professionals in this specialty often obtain additional educational background in architecture, art and architectural history and even archaeology. In addition, the restoration of a historic building for contemporary use—not all become museums—involves special concerns for building code applications, safety, and the integration of modern materials with a structure built before the advent of modern codes and construction methods. The condition of the structure, what should and should not be restored, the availability of products and furnishings, and budget limitations are only a few of the issues that must be explored and resolved by the interior designer and design team engaged in restoration design work.

Adaptive reuse is a related specialty that involves modifying a structure and/or its interior from one use to a relatively different or even totally different use—for example, a residence that is redesigned as a bed-and-breakfast inn or a fast food franchise outlet as a real estate office. In many cases, the original exterior design remains the same or similar while the interior changes dramatically. Adaptive reuse projects by interior designers are often done in conjunction with an architect, as structural design work is often needed to complete the modification.

Adaptive reuse allows neighborhoods and historic districts to change with the modern needs of the community while maintaining their original appearance. The exteriors look the same while the interiors serve new purposes. For example, many communities change the zoning of older residential areas to allow businesses to use the former homes. Adaptive reuse helps maintain the appearance of the neighborhood while allowing professional offices, service companies, and perhaps hospitality businesses to operate in the area.

Schools, Churches, Public Libraries

W. DANIEL SHELLEY, AIA, ASID

Vice-President/Secretary
James, DuRant, Matthews & Shelley, Inc.
Sumter, South Carolina

What has been your greatest challenge as an interior designer?
One is personal—keeping abreast of the latest in products and materials and trying to remember product names and associated manufacturers. The second is professional—educating the client, other architects (I am also a registered architect), and bureaucrats on the work, merit, and legitimacy of a true interior designer versus an interior decorator.

What led you to enter your design specialty?
A personal friend who recognized my capabilities and potential.

What are your primary responsibilities and duties?
Everything—client contact, programming, visualizing and demonstrating concepts and actualities to clients, project coordination, execution, and follow-up.

School: elementary school (new construction/central core) cafeteria/commons. W. Daniel Shelley, James, DuRant, Matthews & Shelley, Inc.,

What is the most satisfying part of your job?
Having a satisfied client.

What is the least satisfying part of your job?
The long hours.

What is the most important quality or skill of a designer in your specialty?
Understanding the functions and operations of the facility (for example, public libraries).

Who or what experience has been a major influence on your career?
My first specialty client (a public library director) and my first specialty project (a public library).

Public library: Retrofit/adaptive reuse of nine-level 1970s department store (central browsing space created from former cashier/jewelry/cosmetic area). *Top:* after; *bottom:* before. W. Daniel Shelley, James, DuRant, Matthews & Shelley, Inc., Sumter, South Carolina.

"Can You Describe the Optimum Portfolio for a Job Applicant?"

The portfolio is not the number-one thing to me. The optimum portfolio is neat, organized, and shows diversity as well as most aspects of the design process.
—Donna Vining, FASID

No. I'm sorry, but it can be so many things. For entry level, I like to see original design work and an interesting presentation; CDs or websites are fine. For an experienced person, I want to see images of their finished work and any unbuilt projects they may have, preferably in an interesting format.
—Beth Harmon-Vaughn, FIIDA

We look for quantity, diversity of project type, technical experience, sketching, references, and organization.
—Fred Messner, IIDA

The portfolio should show a range of skills, not just pretty pictures.
—Rosalyn Cama, FASID

For an entry-level position, combine artistic school-work (freehand work) with technical documentation abilities (CADD and handwork drafting). For positions beyond these, present a broad spectrum of project work responsibilities: hand drafting, freehand sketches, trace work, materials boards/selections, programming documents, completed project photos, etc. These must be professionally organized in a manageable size. Not all examples need to be originals, but they need to be professionally photographed.
—David Stone, IIDA

A combination of work with an explanation of what was successful and what might have been improved.
—Sally Nordahl, IIDA

I look for creative thinking, for a broad knowledge of multiple areas of practice. I look for basic presentation skills, particularly in the applicant's ability to present ideas. I look for a passion for the profession!
—Linda Elliott Smith, FASID

A good balance of aesthetic and technical skills. AutoCAD and examples of documentation skills are essential, along with good examples of design presentation techniques and a polished résumé.
—Robert Wright, ASID

A portfolio that presents beautifully and creatively and that indicates pride in the work. Although a range of basic skills is the minimum requirement, I tend to put more emphasis on how a person explains her or his portfolio than its actual contents.
—Suzan Globus, ASID

Experience in a variety of types of projects. Experience in CAD. Attractive and/or exciting projects in the portfolio (you did say "optimum," right?). Good recommendations from previous employers. Good education from a reputable institution.

I think graduating students should do whatever they can to acquire experience—and perhaps intern at more than one type of firm.
—Linda Kress, ASID

Good CAD experience is a must! That being said, most young designers have never learned to draw—good drawing abilities are always a plus! I've also learned that many applicants exaggerate their involvement or responsibility on projects. I could never hire someone I felt was being dishonest about his or her role in the work being presented.
—Cheri Gerou, AIA, ASID

Related Career Options

AS YOU CAN see from this discussion and the lists of specialties in Exhibits 3-1 and 3-2, you can choose among many exciting types of interior design specialties for your career focus. A wonderful aspect of the interior design profession is that designing and planning interiors is only one of the career paths it offers. The following descriptions explain many other career options affiliated with interior design that a trained individual might find fulfilling. Some require specialized training or several years of experience in interior design but are open to anyone interested in pursuing these alternative career opportunities in the interior design profession.

TECHNICAL SPECIALTIES

- **Acoustics design:** Many kinds of commercial interiors require special attention to acoustic design. Theaters, large open office projects, hospitals, and restaurants are just a few of the interiors that often need the special services of an acoustician.
- **Kitchen design:** High-end residential kitchen projects are often very complex. Specialists working as consultants to residential interior designers or directly with homeowners often design residential kitchens. Commercial kitchens in hotels and restaurants, for example, are almost exclusively designed by kitchen design specialists.
- **Lighting design:** An important part of any interior is proper lighting. Many complex interiors require a specialist to consult with the interior designer to ensure that the lighting is appropriate for both function and aesthetics.
- **Wayfinding:** Finding one's way in large facilities such as schools and hospitals can be difficult. Specialists in wayfinding create graphics and signage to help visitors and employees stay "found" and to locate the exact part of the facility they are looking for.
- **Codes specialist:** Interior designers who become especially proficient in the application of building, fire safety, and accessibility codes may choose to become consultants to other design professionals in this area. Such specialists review drawings prepared by other practitioners and make recommendations to improve code compliance in the design.

TENANT IMPROVEMENT

Interior designers who specialize in tenant improvement generally work with building managers, real estate brokers, or directly with clients seeking to move into an existing building to determine if the space will accommodate the tenant's needs. Tenant improvement specialists also can help select architectural finishes but are less often involved in the actual specification of furniture products for the tenant.

PROJECT MANAGEMENT

Interior designers who are excellent project managers have created consulting businesses that offer project management services. Such consultants may be hired by clients to act as their agent. Others provide project management consulting to smaller interior design firms that need expertise beyond their in-house resources. Of course, project managers are employees in many interior design firms.

MODEL HOMES

Interior design firms may work with a custom home builder to help make the interiors of a spec home as exciting as possible to entice potential buyers. A spec house is built on speculation rather than for a particular client. Developers of large residential housing tracts hire interior designers to help the buyer with materials and color choices for the architectural finishes. These professionals are often called *colorizers* or *interior specifiers*.

CAD SPECIALIST

Interior designers who wish to work independently but not necessarily through all phases of projects may specialize in CAD. These specialists offer their services to designers who do not have the skill or time to prepare CAD drawings themselves.

PRODUCT DESIGNERS

Most product designers are actually trained in industrial design and work for major furniture and other product manufacturers. However, interior designers also find creating custom designs challenging after creating custom furniture products for their clients. Some make the transition to working for a manufacturer while others start their own custom furniture business.

MODEL BUILDING

Models are most associated with architectural firms, but occasionally interior design firms prepare them. Scale models are another way to help the client understand what the finished project will look like. Model builders might work independently or for a design firm.

RENDERER

Renderers prepare three-dimensional perspective drawings and other orthographic drawings to help explain design concepts. Many renderers use computer software that allows them to prepare these drawings from an almost unlimited number of viewpoints. Renderings are often completed in color using a variety of media such as markers and watercolor as well as pen and ink. Like model builders, renderers may work independently or for an interior design firm.

MARKETING SPECIALIST

Marketing specialists have strong sales skills or strong communications skills along with thorough knowledge of the interior design process. Most often they work for large design firms, prospecting and otherwise obtaining new work for the firm. Others form a consulting business to provide marketing services to a variety of sizes and kinds of interior design firms.

SALES REPRESENTATIVE

Sales representatives work for retail stores and office furnishings dealers. They sell directly to the end users of residential or commercial interior projects. Many sales representatives are former interior designers who have a greater comfort zone with selling rather than doing space planning and specification. Some individuals are attracted to work as a sales representative because of the potential for higher income.

FURNITURE AND INTERIOR PRODUCTS MANUFACTURERS

The manufacturers of furniture and other products used in interiors offer yet more employment opportunities for interior designers. Some manufacturers have an in-house interior design staff whose members work on projects for the company headquarters and showroom locations. Another position is manufacturer's representative, or *rep*. Reps are the people who sell the product for the manufacturer. They help interior designers, architects, and clients by providing information about the products; their goal is to get the products they represent specified and purchased by the end user.

TRANSPORTATION

Transportation interior design comprises two subspecialties: the interior design of terminals at airports, train depots, and the like, and the interior design of transportation vehicles themselves—airplanes, ships, yachts, train cars, and so on. Because terminals are generally multi-use areas, the interior designer must be familiar with many kinds of commercial space design. Most frequently, terminal spaces are designed in conjunction with an architectural office.

The design of transportation vehicles is highly specialized, as all design and specification decisions must be carefully considered in terms of the safe total engineering of the vehicle. If the wrong weight and size of furniture item is placed in the wrong location on a yacht, for example, the ship will not float and move through the water correctly, yielding an unsafe environment.

MUSEUM WORK

Historic sites, such as Colonial Williamsburg and the White House, and various kinds of museums, such as art, natural history, and presidential libraries, can be career venues for interior designers interested in museum cutorial work or this very specialized area of interior design. This career option requires advanced degree work in the field or even in archeology or museum science.

JOURNALISM

A career with a trade or consumer magazine that focuses on interior design or architecture is an interesting option for people who enjoy writing. Many interior designers have articles published in magazines via contributing author status as a way to further market their design practices.

TEACHING

Interior designers often teach part-time at community colleges and universities. Practitioners with advanced degrees may teach full-time in two-year or four-year programs. Teaching is a very fulfilling alternative career for interior designers who have gained several years of experience in one or more design specialties.

GOVERNMENT

In the United States, the General Services Administration (GSA) provides interior design services for a wide variety of federal facilities. These interior designers might design the new office for a senator or a large office project for an agency such as the Federal Aviation Administration. Many states, provinces, and local governments have facility planners and designers who do the actual design work or coordinate with outside design firms whenever government-owned public buildings are built or remodeled.

STILL OTHERS

Numerous other niches in interior design and the built-environment industry are related to interior design. Almost any aspect of the profession and any type of facility or portion of a facility can be a design specialty and career option—if there are enough clients to support the business!

Endnotes

1. Christine M. Piotrowski. 2002. *Professional Practice for Interior Designers,* 3rd ed. New York: John Wiley and Sons, p. 191.

2. Judith Davidson. *Interior Design.* "100 Giants," January 2003, p. 139.

3. *Merriam-Webster's Collegiate Dictionary*, 10th ed. 1994. Springfield, MA: Merriam-Webster, p. 606.

4. Rosemary Kilmer and W. Otie Kilmer. 1992. *Designing Interiors.* Fort Worth, TX: Harcourt Brace Jovanovich, p. 283.

Kitchen Design and Space Planning

MARY FISHER KNOTT, ASID, RSPI, CID
Owner, Mary Fisher Designs, Scottsdale, Arizona

What has been your greatest challenge as an interior designer?
My greatest challenge is managing my time correctly. I am known for wanting to take too much on. I am still learning how to say no.

What lead you to enter your design specialty?
I love to cook and have cooked since I was a child. I feel the family is the most important part of life and building a home that nurtures the family is very important. The kitchen has always been the center of family life. I like designing spaces that meet family needs.

Private residence: custom kitchen design. Mary Knott, Allied Member ASID, RSPI, CID, Mary Fisher Design, Scottsdale, Arizona. Photographer: Roger Turk, Northlight Photography.

What are your primary responsibilities and duties in your position?
My primary responsibility is working with the client and designing the space. I am also the primary draftsman on each project.

What is the most satisfying part of your job?
When my clients invite me to their homes after the project is finished and tell me how much they love their new space.

What is the least satisfying part of your job?
Collection of past due accounts from some clients.

What is the most important quality or skill of a designer in your specialty?
The ability to listen to the client and take good notes. It is the designer's responsibility to be a problem solver.

Who or what experience has been a major influence in your career?
My Mom and Dad. They encouraged me to follow my love for art and home. At the time I began my career as a kitchen designer and space planner [there] were very few designers specializing in this field.

Private residence: custom kitchen design. Mary Knott, Allied Member ASID, RSPI, CID, Mary Fisher Design, Scottsdale, Arizona. Photographer: Roger Turk, Northlight Photography.

Private residence: custom kitchen design. Mary Knott, Allied Member ASID, RSPI, CID, Mary Fisher Design, Scottsdale, Arizona. Photographer: Roger Turk, Northlight Photography.

Computer Modeling and Visualization, Project Management, and Graphic Design

DEREK B. SCHMIDT

Project Designer, Design Collective Incorporated, Nashville, Tennessee

What has been your greatest challenge as an interior designer?
Because I am a trained architect, it has taken time to become knowledgeable about and familiar with the specification of interior materials such as carpet, upholstery, and vinyl wallcovering. I also had to transition from the concepts of designing building enclosures to smaller details like millwork and drywall ceilings.

What led you to enter your design specialty?
The architecture program at Carnegie Mellon is fairly well focused on technology and makes powerful computer tools available to all their students. By the time I graduated, I was proficient in several software programs and had become skilled as a 3D modeler. When I began my job search, it didn't take long to realize my computer experience was my most valuable skill. Design Collective was very interested in selling and providing 3D modeling services as a way to distinguish itself from their competition; it was a good fit for me to join the firm with that as my specialty. Since that time my role has grown to include other specialties.

Why did you become an interior designer?
In 1997, I graduated from Carnegie Mellon University with a Bachelor of Architecture degree. I decided I wanted to work in a more detail-oriented field, so I took a position at a firm that practiced architecture but had interior design as its specialty.

CAD rendering: conference room, CAT, Inc., Nashville, Tennessee. Derek Schmidt, Design Collective Incorporated, Nashville, Tennessee.

What are your primary responsibilities and duties?

My position is called *project designer* rather than interior designer, graphic designer, or architect because I act generally as a designer on many types of jobs. Generally speaking, in my capacity as the computer guy, my role is to support the other designers in our firm in conveying design concepts to clients, specifically using computer technology. This takes many forms. Some examples: the preparation of a PowerPoint presentation to take to an interview with a potential client; the creation of graphic boards and stacking plans during schematic design; 3D modeling and rendering of a key room or area of an interiors project; CAD support of other designers preparing construction documents; the mockup of an exterior sign in Photoshop to show a client or building owner; design and mockups of custom interior signage for a client.

What is the most satisfying part of your job?

The most satisfying part is the variety of tasks I undertake—it's tough to get bored, because there are always new challenges. This month, I've learned a new software for constructing web pages because I am doing a website for a client.

What is the least satisfying part of your job?

On the flip side of that, because I have so many responsibilities, it can sometimes be hard to focus on a task because people are constantly requesting my help on other tasks, usually at the last minute.

Photo: conference room, CAT, Inc., Nashville, Tennessee. Derek Schmidt, Design Collective Incorporated, Nashville, Tennessee. Photographer: Michael Houghton.

What is the most important quality or skill of a designer in your specialty?

Proficiency with computers is key, but more important is the ability to learn new things quickly—software, hardware, etc. These things change rapidly, and it is not enough to be an expert at one technology because in time it will be outdated.

Who or what experience has been a major influence in your career?

That's difficult to answer. I try to look at all sources for inspiration in my work—colleagues, magazines, my travels, and movies. I think all good designers are inspired by the world around them and shouldn't be afraid to look at the work of others.

Design and Manufacture of Furniture for Hospitality, Contract, and Residential Interior Design

PAT CAMPBELL MCLAUGHLIN, ASID

President, Steel Magnolia, Dallas, Texas

What has been your greatest challenge as an interior designer?
Finding my niche.

What led you to enter your design specialty?
I always enjoyed opportunities to provide custom pieces on interior design jobs; then, all of a sudden, that was all I was doing—and I loved it!

What are your primary responsibilities and duties?
Design, overseeing the manufacturing process, developing new products, and marketing.

Product design: Steel Magnolia logo. Patricia McLaughlin, ASID. Steel Magnolia, Dallas, Texas. Photographer: Brad Kirby.

What is the most satisfying part of your job?
Every aspect.

What is the least satisfying part of your job?
Accounting!

What is the most important quality or skill of a designer in your specialty?
Attention to detail; producing the best product.

Who or what experience has been a major influence on your career?
Being laid off and coming to the realization that it is always a positive rather than a negative!! It is a time to reevaluate what your goals really are and how to get there!! Then just go with the flow!

Product design: deco chair. Patricia McLaughlin, ASID. Steel Magnolia, Dallas, Texas. Photographer: Brad Kirby.

Product design: tulip table. Patricia McLaughlin, ASID. Steel Magnolia, Dallas, Texas. Photographer: Brad Kirby.

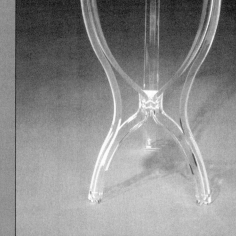

"What Do You Look for in Hiring a New Designer?"

Empathy (for client's needs), thoroughness (accuracy is *extremely* important), team player (with fellow employees and project team members), communication skills (oral and written), and, of course, the prerequisites: high level of basic design skills (space planning, material and finish selection, detailing, drawing, sketching, and CAD).
—Jeffrey Rausch, IIDA

Ability to define the problem, articulate a solution, and execute it. Problem solver. Someone who is willing to challenge the status quo and is open to new ideas and ways of doing things. Flexibility and humor.
—Sari Graven, ASID

The ability to communicate well and think logically. AutoCAD is a prerequisite.
—Suzan Globus, ASID

When hiring, first we look for design talent, but of almost equal importance is the ability to communicate—and not only graphically; the most important communication skill is verbal communication.
—M. Arthur Gensler Jr., FAIA, FIIDA, RIBA

Someone with good communication skills and a willingness to learn and work hard will always contribute, but specific skills are needed for specific positions. For instance, a CAD manager will need different skills than a project manager or project designer.
—Rita Carson Guest, FASID

Someone who is willing to listen and learn and take initiative.
—Sally Nordahl, IIDA

Intelligence, passion, design excellence, sketching skills, and CAD skills.
—Nila Leiserowitz, FASID

An overall well-rounded education coupled with natural ability.
—David Stone, IIDA

I look for designers with an open mind who are willing to learn, flexible, and willing to do whatever it takes to get the job done.
—Greta Guelich, ASID

Attitude and a willingness to go the extra mile.
—Donna Vining, FASID

Personality! How well the person interacts with me. A solid sense of good design—no gimmicks, just solid design. But personality is the real key.
—Charles Gandy, FASID, FIIDA

First, I look for a good attitude. I can teach people skills, but it's very hard to correct a bad attitude. Nirvana for me is finding someone who already has healthcare experience, but this is very rare.
—Jain Malkin, CID

Leadership skills first, then talent.
—Rosalyn Cama, FASID

We look for someone with technical skills and a strong work ethic—a team player.
—Linda Isley, IIDA

I look for commitment to professionalism, which consists of a degree in interior design. I look for someone who, if not currently certified by examination, is on the path to examination. And I look for good interpersonal skills.
—Linda Elliott Smith, FASID

College degree from a FIDER-accredited institution, preferably one where the interior program was in a college of architecture and five years, internship with a good firm or person, travel or work experience abroad, and something else. Something else can be a lot of things. I have worked with a world-class mountain climber, an artist, a chef, a pilot—the "something else" usually gives the person balance and dimension beyond their design education and experience.
—Beth Harmon-Vaughn, FIIDA

As a sole practitioner, I am kind of out of the hiring process. But if I were hiring new designers, I'd be looking for people who can do many things, not just design a project. The more they can do to help keep the business moving smoothly, like creating contracts and documents, ordering and expediting product, and that type of thing, the more valuable they would be to the firm. If you think about it, hiring a new designer who wanted only to design projects would do little for me as a small business owner beyond doubling the amount of paperwork and operational tasks I have to do. I'd be looking for someone to share the load and have the ability to cover all the bases in my absence.
—Terri Maurer, FASID

I look for three basic skills: the abilities to communicate, to work with others, and to be creative.
—Linda Sorrento, IIDA, ASID

Passion for design, creative thinking skills, communication ability.
—Marilyn Farrow, FIIDA

Talent, people skills, and a desire to improve—and to enjoy the journey.
—William Peace, ASID

Energy, enthusiasm, and a passion for design. But that doesn't go very far unless you add excellent written and oral skills, a sense of responsibility and thoroughness, and a strong design portfolio. How an individual performed in college can pretty much tell you how he or she will be in the professional world. Did the person attend class? Complete work on time? Participate in extracurricular activities? Travel? Work? I want to talk to someone who knew him or her in school—perhaps a professor or other students.
—Robert Wright, ASID

Education, experience, creativity, and ability to sell themselves and their ideas to others in the organization.
—Leonard Alvarado

I want someone who is creative, of course. I am also most interested in their training and life experiences. I look for someone with a degree from a FIDER-accredited program and someone who has traveled or had other experiences to expand that educational base. Work ethic is also important, as the person must contribute to the business revenue.
—Sally Thompson, ASID

"What Advice Would You Give Someone Who Wants to Be an Interior Designer?"

Have passion for growing your profession.
—Nila Leiserowitz, FASID

I would advise them to first understand themselves and then to understand as much as possible about others. Interior design, as do many careers, involves a great understanding of personal behaviors as well as the overall body of knowledge.
—Linda E. Smith, FASID

Each designer must have basic three-dimensional skills and a sense of color, proportion, and scale—which I don't believe can be taught if you don't innately have them. However, if you do have them, then taking the necessary courses and programs provided by an accredited college is a great way to start your career.
—M. Arthur Gensler Jr., FAIA, FIIDA, RIBA

Know what an interior designer is and does. Find out what is required of you to become an interior designer that goes well beyond coordinating carpet, draperies, and wall coverings, and prepare yourself for where our profession is going. This means a degree from a FIDER-accredited institution, work experience, and passage of the NCIDQ examination as your basic requirements. Then, if you live and practice in a jurisdiction that has regulations on the books regarding who can practice or use the name *interior designer*, be sure you are registered as an interior design professional.
—Terri Maurer, FASID

If you don't absolutely love this work, don't try to make a career of it; find something you're passionate about. We spend too much time at work to not love what we do.
—Beth Harmon-Vaughn, FIIDA

Get the best education possible.
—Charles Gandy, FASID, FIIDA

Get an education at a FIDER-accredited interior design program. Learn truly what an interior designer does. It isn't *Trading Spaces*. Research the profession—the technical and creative side of it. Practice your communication skills (graphic, written, oral). You'll never regret it. If you want to investigate the profession more, job shadow. Start analyzing the spaces you move through. Begin noticing the details. Pat yourself on the back. You couldn't have found a more rewarding or fulfilling profession.
—Stephanie Clemons, PhD, ASID, IDEC

Develop great people skills.
—Sally Nordahl, IIDA

Go for it! It can be tremendously demanding and tremendously rewarding. Get the best education you can and never stop learning. Be involved in the community; give back to the community.
—Jan Bast, ASID, IIDA

Don't do it because you think you have a flair for design. Millions of people have this. Do it because you understand that designers, by their work, are in the vanguard of the fight against the world's natural march toward chaos, decay, and entropy. Because of this, designers create beauty. What we do matters for this reason alone. All people can throw together one sort of design or another. Skilled designers alone have the ability to find order, structure, rhythm, and therefore beauty within the chaos of nature's entropy.
—Jeffrey Rausch, IIDA

Study, look, listen, and be passionate about design in all aspects of the built environment.
—Sandra Evans, ASID

Being an interior designer is an entire lifestyle—not just a job. Beginning designers must be willing to give interior design 100 percent for several years before they can put their arms around it. Be patient with your career path, and be flexible. Successful designers must be willing to adapt to outside forces like economic fluctuations, industry changes, new subspecialties, and new technology, and to their own personal growth.
—Robert Wright, ASID

My advice to an aspiring interior designer is to enter into the field with the proper education, continue with great experiences, and then test those experiences by completing the NCIDQ exam.
—Linda Sorrento, ASID, IIDA

It is not a glamorous job! Take an introductory class in interior design and drafting to get a feel for this field. Interior design is not about picking out colors and fabrics as seen on HGTV!
—Robin J. Wagner, ASID, IDEC

Make sure you are passionate about design because it will seem dull, redundant, and trying at times. But when the rewards arrive, they come in glimmering packages!
—Pat Campbell McLaughlin, ASID

Develop strong presentation and relationship building skills; each skill is critical to selling yourself and your ideas to potential clients and employers. Quickly accept the fact that a good design may never be realized unless it can be sold to the customer—then learn to sell conceptually.
—Leonard Alvarado

Look at everything around you; realize that someone had to imagine it first and then had to draw it so someone could build or make it.
—Melinda Sechrist, FASID

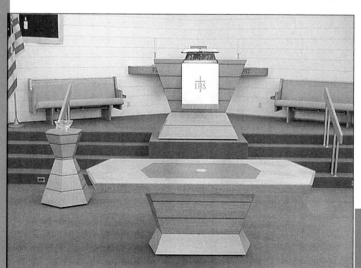

Desert Palms Presbyterian Church Sun City West, Arizona. Sandra Evans, ASID, Knoell & Quidort Architects, Phoenix, Arizona. Photographer: Jim Christy.

Work in the field for a summer to make sure you know what you are getting into.
—Fred Messner, IIDA

It is not all fluff and fabrics. A solid technical background will set you apart from the masses of decorators. Also, you need to pay dues to get to the point of job independence and leadership within a firm. Don't expect it all to be handed to you at the beginning of your career.
—David Stone, IIDA

Research, research, research! I think anyone considering the profession should do an ample amount of research to learn about the different aspects of interior design (hospitality, corporate, residential, facilities management, etc.). Students should also understand the commitment the profession requires.
—Christy Ryan, IIDA

A four-year FIDER-accredited education!!!
—Teresa Sowell, ASID, IFMA

Get an education, get experience, and be examined. You are entering what can be one of the most rewarding careers you could choose.
—Derrell Parker, IIDA

Get a great education (from a FIDER-accredited school) and find a good mentor. Active involvement in a professional organization has been my way of staying current with trends and getting the leadership training needed to be a great consultant.
—Rosalyn Cama, FASID

Try a variety of fields to find work that best suits your personal talents.
—Marilyn Farrow, FIIDA

It is a lot of hard work but can be very rewarding. Be open to new ideas, continue to embrace learning, and intern with a few companies before you step out on your own.
—Greta Guelich, ASID

Get the best design education you can and also take business courses. Expect to work many years before gaining enough on-the-job experience to feel competent and able to perform efficiently in any situation. This field has one of the longest learning curves of any profession.
—Jain Malkin, CID

Healthcare: multispecialty waiting area. Rosalyn Cama, FASID, CAMA, Inc., New Haven, Connecticut. Architect: KMD, San Francisco, California.

Literacy—both within the profession and external to the industry.
—Neil Frankel, FIIDA, FAIA

Quality education and training will set you apart from all the wannabes. In addition to the usual design curriculum, focus on technical training: lighting design, computer networking and technologies, basic construction techniques, and detailing. Learn computer programs such as AutoCAD, 3D illustration, Photoshop, and MS Project in addition to the standard office programs. Learn and understand marketing and business management.
—Suzanne Urban, ASID, IIDA

The best advice I can give someone who wants to be an interior designer is to listen to your client, develop your ideas based on the information you've received combined with your expertise, and communicate your ideas and your client's desires effectively.
—Linda Santellanes, ASID

Know that the days of interior design being a fun job are over. Interior design is a profession requiring knowledge and commitment and hard work.
—M. Joy Meeuwig, IIDA

Get to a four-year accredited design program and learn all you can. I also highly recommend taking business, accounting, and marketing courses along the way.
—Juliana Catlin, FASID

My best advice is to go to school to learn this profession. People do not realize how much knowledge is needed to qualify as a professional and to produce a good product for your client. After design school, working for a professional is the best possible leg up you can give yourself. There is even more to learn out of school.
—Debra May Himes, ASID, IIDA

Open your eyes to all the possibilities; interior designers are not just painters of texture and color.
—Linda Isley, IIDA

Find a FIDER-accredited school and study the widest variety of courses you can. Become proficient at computer skills and keep up with the latest trends.
—Ellen McDowell, ASID

Learn how to communicate orally and write very well. Be intensely curious; learn to love to solve problems.
—Lisa Whited, ASID, IIDA, IDEC

It is not an easy field to enter in. Be active in a professional organization starting with a student chapter, get your college degree, pass the NCIDQ, and be active in an organization that introduces you to potential clients.
—John Holmes, IIDA, ASID

Don't go into the profession thinking it's a get-rich scheme.
—W. Daniel Shelley, AIA, ASID

To focus and choose a specialty practice, become an expert in that practice and never forget the design principles that apply to all areas of good interior design.
—Beth Kuzbek, ASID, IIDA, CMG

Meet with interior designers and ask them about their careers, do an internship with a residential and/or commercial interior designer, and/or take an introductory interior design course.
—Michelle King, IIDA

Dismiss the public perception that interior design is all about glamour and spending other people's money frivolously. This image only represents a small percentage of practitioners.
—Jennifer van der Put, BID, IDC, ARIDO, IFMA

Get a four-year degree. Pay attention in all of your classes; if you are thinking of going far in your field at all, you will truly end up using all that knowledge they are making available to you! Get very good at all the computer programs related to your field. Without competent computer skills, you are limited in the sorts of jobs for which you are qualified. Jump at any chance you have to do those stand-up-in-front-of-a-group presentations. Become good at communicating your ideas orally as well as thorough your drawings; often, clients do not want to pay for elaborate drawings. That's when you need sketches and quick material displays and the ability to explain it all with energy and enthusiasm. Don't shirk business classes. Interior design is a 90 percent business and 10 percent creativity. (I'm not the one who first said that, of course.) Plan to take the NCIDQ. Support your profession (and it *is* a profession) by joining ASID/IIDA. (One hopes they will soon become a single organization!) And don't get into this field unless you love it. Your customers can tell the difference!
—**Linda Kress, ASID**

One must possess the passion to design. One must really love what one is doing and have fun on the projects to be creatively charged.
—**Alicia Loo, CID**

Be prepared for and open to many points of view.
—**Kristen Anderson, ASID, CID, RID**

Make your education an open book. Look for non-design-related sources of inspiration. Get a variety of work experiences within design. The perspective gained from a variety of experiences is priceless.
—**Sari Graven, ASID**

Study people, the way they live and work, and never overlook the building's architecture as a key element of your design. Use these elements to develop a unique and distinctive design that reflects your client's lifestyle or required work environment. Keep in mind—with every design project—function is always part of an empty building or space.
—**Sally Thompson, ASID**

I would advise two things:
(1) To be flexible in your pursuit of your initial professional jobs. There are so many, many types of jobs in the field of interior design, and they all yield great experience for the interior designer. Whether you work in an architectural or residential design firm or a furniture or carpet retail environment, you will learn essential skills for this field. In other words, I think I am saying, "Be willing to take baby steps" and don't expect your dream job right out of school. Each job will contribute significantly to your versatility as a designer.
(2) To always be up for the challenge, to be driven to excel at all times. The field of interior design offers many challenges. I believe meeting the challenge is what brings great satisfaction in this career.
—**Susan B. Higbee**

Take business management courses (accounting, finance). Although design and architecture are artistic pursuits, they are still a business. I have seen many talented individuals fail because they didn't have basic business sense or even the good sense to hire a business manager.
—**Trisha Wilson, ASID**

If interior design is your passion, allow yourself to enjoy the business and flourish without placing too much emphasis on monetary rewards. This industry seems to be in a constant state of transition, as it should be. Strive to be on top of and hopefully ahead of the game.
—**Janice Carleen Linster, ASID, IIDA, CID**

Residence. bedroom. William Peace, ASID, Peace Design, Atlanta, Georgia. Photographer: Chris A. Little.

suggest you start out in a generalized commercial firm where you will work in conjunction with a full range of professionals—architects, engineers, and contractors—and see many types of projects. Join a professional organization. Force yourself to learn building codes and general practices. Work on your business skills and watch your mentors carefully. Absorb everything you can while you come to realize your strengths.

—**Sally D'Angelo, ASID**

Investigate a variety of education opportunities and find the one that is the best fit for you.

—**William Peace, ASID**

Get as much formal education as you can and continue seeking education after you have graduated. Become NCIDQ certified and registered to practice in as many jurisdictions as are appropriate. Advocate for your profession and pave the way for those who follow.

Perhaps most important is to always act ethically and professionally.

—**Suzan Globus, ASID**

I would advise a person to get properly educated with either a two-year or four-year degree in interior design. I would recommend they read up on the profession of interior design and understand the many factors that propel a successful designer. It's much more than the ability to design. It's about marketing, sales, people skills, follow-up, relationship building, research, and continual education on product and technology.

—**Naomi Anderson**

It's an exciting field with endless possibilities for anyone with a creative flair. Plan to obtain the best FIDER-accredited education possible. Choose your first position with care, looking for a good mentor. Working in a small firm to start; perhaps working with six to twelve people is a good way to get exposure to various employee responsibilities. If you are not sure of the specialization you'd like to try, I

Enroll in a four-year program—at least. Concentrate on the practical side of the profession. It is foolish to think anyone can design without the knowledge to draw from the profession. Consider how much of the project you wish to influence. If you only want to choose colors and pick fabrics, interiors is not the best choice.

I would encourage anyone interested in interior design to seriously consider a higher level of education. If you don't understand structure and have adequate training in building systems, you will always be limited in your ability to design. I would invite interior designers to move forward in their education to become a licensed architect if you wish to explore the full avenue of design.

—**Cheri Gerou, AIA, ASID**

This is probably true for many career choices and holds true for interior design—do your homework. Seek guidance about possible career choices from those who know, such as professionals in the field. Ask a lot of questions about career opportunities, what they feel makes a successful designer, what they feel job prospects are in particular locations and specialties, and what they like and dislike about what they do. If possible, do an internship early on to get some first-hand exposure to the field.

A well-rounded education is an important foundation. Find a program that will allow you to focus on your particular interest but also develops broader skills. It's important to learn good business practices, including writing skills. Computer-aided design skills are also required for many design jobs.
—Kimberly M. Studzinski, ASID

Talk to working interior designers in various fields. (This book should be a great help!) Look at your own background, interests, and working style and try to get work experience or at least visit with designers who share your approach. For example, I tend to pay a lot of attention to people around me, so it is important for me to work in a quiet, isolated space. I also

love the independence of having my own firm. However, I have a friend who can't imagine wanting to work by herself out of her home; she is much happier surrounded by friendly coworkers.
—Corky Binggeli, ASID

Read. Go see projects. Select a FIDER-approved program.
—David F. Cooke, FIIDA, CMG

People interested in becoming a designer should spend time in the environment of designers. Try to spend a summer in a design firm, even if you are just picking up the department head's lunches. Work at a construction site—to

understand the most fundamental aspects of building and learn from those who actually have to put your design vision together with bricks and mortar. Visit museums and read books and magazines on design. Spend some time shadowing a designer for a day or more. Look at the built environment around you and try to figure out why certain places make you feel good and others do not.
—Kristi Barker, CID

Private residence: dining room. Charles Gandy, FASID, FIIDA, Charles Gandy, Inc., Atlanta, Georgia. Photographer: Ron Rizzo.

Go for it! If you love color, texture, space planning, and people, you'll love designing as a profession.
—**Mary Fisher Knott, CID, RSPI, Allied Member ASID**

Understand that it is a constant learning process and you will never know everything. Nevertheless, absorb as much as you can, whenever you can, and know that you will be a better designer because of that.
—**Jennifer Tiernan, IIDA**

From my experience, it seems that interior design programs don't place enough emphasis on technology. All the designers in our office, regardless of specialty, have some computer experience; at a minimum, they must have experience with some kind of CAD software and other computer skills like Microsoft Word and Excel. Candidates with excellent design skills and no computer experience will have a lot of difficulty finding jobs in our increasingly computer-based field.
—**Derek B. Schmidt**

Chapter Four

Where the Jobs Are

The environments in which interior designers work are almost as varied as the design specialties. You want to determine the kind of work environment that will satisfy your interests and suit your personality, but this choice is not easy. Many interior designers begin their careers in small firms, where they have the opportunity to learn about project management and business management. Others prefer working in larger firms, knowing that although they may be a small fish in a big sea, the experience will be valuable. Working for a small firm generally means lower compensation and a design reputation that remains close to home. Perhaps you hate to sell but love to design. In that case, small studios that depend on the sale of merchandise for the bulk of their revenues might not be a wise choice. If interior design is your second career, you may feel more comfortable working on your own. In fact, all of these choices represent one of the wonderful things about the interior design profession—it offers many choices to suit many interests and abilities.

Interior Design and the Economy

Interior design has a major impact on the economy. *Interior Design* magazine surveys the 100 largest design firms each year. In the January 2003 issue, those 100 firms reported total professional fees of nearly $1.4 billion dollars. The firms surveyed forecast a 2.27 percent increase for the next year. These firms also reported approximately 8,100 interior designers and installed work valued at $32.6 billion dollars for furniture, fixtures, and construction. [1]

In addition to those who work at the largest design firms, many interior designers own or work in small businesses with five or fewer employees or are sole practitioners working alone. Of course, there are also many who work in allied areas of the built-environment industry such as sales people in retail specialty stores such as a lighting fixtures store. That makes it hard to determine with precision how many people practice in the field. One gauge of the total is the number of interior designer practitioners affiliated with recognized associations. However, even that number is not accurate, as many professional interior designers choose to stay unaffiliated.

According to the U.S. Department of Labor Bureau of Labor Statistics (www.bls.gov), the occupation label *interior designer* [2] represented over 30,000 jobs in late 2001. The ASID reports that approximately 55,000 interior designers practice in the United States. [3] The median annual earnings for interior designers as reported by the Bureau of Labor Statistics were $36,540 in 2001. The lowest 10 percent earned less than $19,840 and the highest 10 percent earned over $66,470. [4] The statistics presented in the January 2002 "Interior Design 100 Giants" issue of *Interior Design* were higher. The median annual salary for principals/partners was $120,000, designers $58,000, and other billable design staff $40,000. [5]

The entrepreneurial practice by one individual is quite common, and many choose interior design as a career because of the opportunity to work as a sole practitioner. However, this goal should be approached somewhat cautiously. Because of the complexity of the interior design profession, it is unwise to begin a solo practice until you have gained experience and real-world knowledge of the profession. Working for some-

Law office: Alston & Bird LLP, hallway. Rita Carson Guest, FASID, Carson Guest, Inc., Atlanta, Georgia. Photographer: Gabriel Benzur.

one else for a while helps you learn about the business side of the profession while you gain experience in design and working with clients.

The options discussed in this chapter are by no means every conceivable work environment for the interior designer. These are both the most common types and the places that most entry-level interior designers find their first employment. By considering these options and the design specialties discussed in the previous chapter, you might find the combination that fits your goals as you begin your career as a professional interior designer.

Light Commercial and Residential

SALLY HOWARD D'ANGELO, ASID
Principal, S. H. Designs
Windham, New Hampshire

What has been your greatest challenge as an interior designer?
It's a wide-open field with many specialized possibilities, all of which take many years to learn. The greatest challenge for me is to decide on that specialty. The desire to explore new types of challenging projects in different specialties causes me to continually reach. This keeps my creative juices flowing, but the design process is not as systematized and therefore less profitable. The more practical course requires a designer to develop expertise and efficiency in a specialized area of work. Owning my own firm allows me to control the mix. I try to do a little of each.

What led you to enter your design specialty?
I like to be able to assess the problem, design the solution, and implement the design. I chose to run my own business

Teacher's lounge: Central Catholic High School, Lawrence, Massachusetts. Sally Howard D'Angelo, ASID, S. H. Designs, Windham, New Hampshire. Photographer: Bill Fish.

because I wanted to follow the project straight through, from contract to final payment. In order to control the whole process, I take on small to medium-size projects that can be easily managed from start to finish. I like the efficiency of commercial design process because the budget and time frame are exact and decisions are made quickly. Functionality and increased productivity are often the main objective, with a change in image as the exciting byproduct. I also like to work with residential clients who want to realize a better solution to an existing problem and are personally involved. Those are slower projects that require a large amount of client input but result in creative synergistic solutions.

What is the most satisfying part of your job?
Presenting a creative and functional solution to a client who could have never thought of that possibility before is worth all of the work. I am the momentary hero.

What is the least satisfying part of your job?
I get the least satisfaction from a cookie-cutter design. It takes time to develop a really creative solution, and sometimes I am not given that time. It's hard to discipline myself to stop designing.

Private residence: master bath remodel. Sally Howard D'Angelo, ASID, S. H. Designs, Windham, New Hampshire. Photographer: Bill Fish.

Nesmith Library, Children's Theater, Windham, New Hampshire. Sally Howard D'Angelo, ASID, S. H. Designs, Windham, New Hampshire. Photographer: Bill Fish.

What is the most important quality or skill of a designer in your specialty?

As a small business owner, assuming you are already a talented designer, you have to enjoy people and constantly be willing to get involved with them. Whether working in the commercial or residential market, you need to be cognizant of the client's ultimate goal for the project, how it will add value to the business or home and improve the lifestyle of the family or function of the business. You need to solicit and document that goal and design toward that end.

Who or what experience had been a major influence in your career?

My professional association, ASID, has played a major role in my professional development. It gave me extensive education and training in all areas of the business and design world. I've traveled throughout the country, served on many boards of directors, and discussed topics of every kind on behalf of the association. The more involved I became, the more I got out of it. It opened many doors to me throughout my career, and I've met talented associates of every kind who took the time to help and mentor me.

Career Decisions

DECIDING TO WORK in residential or commercial interior design is the first career decision you will face. The actual work of the interior designer as expressed by the design process described in chapter 2 is done in nearly all work environments under the interior design umbrella. Thus, the type of firm you wish to work at is another decision you must make. Some firms are unlikely to be open to entry-level designers. Others will welcome you to their staff. Before looking at specific work environments, let's discuss general factors you should consider.

One of these general considerations is the size of the company. First are sole practitioners working alone or with one assistant. Next are the small firms—those with ten or fewer total employees. Medium-sized firms have between ten and twenty-five employees. We will say that large interior design firms have between twenty-five and fifty employees. Multidisciplinary firms that offer a combination of interior design, architecture, engineering, and landscape architecture services can have well over one hundred employees.

Small or medium-sized firms generally can give you a broader range of experiences than any type of large firm can. Employees of small or medium-sized firms handle many parts of a project because fewer people are available in the company to take on the responsibilities. The owner or principal of the firm may involve you in projects quickly, giving you experiences you might not have expected at once.

Large firms can offer broad experience, but from a distance. In a very large firm, it is not just a cliché that all you may get to do for the first year is some small, repetitive task such as selecting materials palettes. In a large firm, it takes more time for the entry-level designer to be given major project responsibility. In some large firms, entry-level designers are not hired at all or work only as assistants to senior interior designers. The pressure to be productive and generate a large number of billable hours can be stressful for entry-level interior designers working in firms where this is critical to the performance evaluation of the design professional staff.

Compensation options are another general consideration. Compensation is not high in interior design in comparison to many other professions. The information on Interior Design and the Economy in this chapter clarifies this important issue. If the firm generates revenue by charging for services, the interior design staff is generally paid a set salary. An interior design firm that also sells furniture or a retail store with an interior design department often pays designers based on commission. This means you are paid based on the amount of furniture and other products you sell to the client rather than a salary. Being paid a commission provides the opportunity for higher total personal income than when paid a salary. However, small firms cannot pay as much or offer as much in company benefits as large firms can.

The smaller the firm, the less likely you will receive many noncompensation benefits such as company-paid health insurance, retirement, or investment programs. For example, a small firm may not be able to pay for your NCIDQ fees or

professional association dues. Larger firms encourage their employees to take the NCIDQ examination and often pay for continuing education seminars and workshops.

It is important to keep in mind that you must pay your dues and learn what it is like to work in whatever type of firm and specialty you enter. Regardless of size, most firms will not let an entry-level designer work alone with a client at first. You must be patient, learning and gaining experience so your boss will grow comfortable with turning you loose with a client.

As you plan your professional goals, keep in mind that you need to look for compatible colleagues and the opportunity to learn and grow to keep you motivated. If you want to gain a quick reputation or work for a prestigious firm, you need to plan your work experiences to carefully build skills that will be favored by the large multidisciplinary firms. If your goal is to have your own small practice one day, many types of firms and specialties will be appropriate work environments in which you can acquire skills and knowledge to help you when you open your own firm. As you learn what you want from the profession, you will be able to determine where to go for a position that will lead you toward your goals.

Lodging: atrium, The Palace of the Lost City, Sun City, South Africa. Trisha Wilson, ASID, Wilson & Associates, Dallas, Texas. Photographer: Peter Vitale.

Independent Design Firms

AN INDEPENDENT INTERIOR design firm—also called a studio—is probably the most common type of work environment open to the interior designer. In this situation, the owner or owners are free to focus on any specialty, providing design services while specifying and perhaps selling products to their chosen client target market. Independent firms can be of any size, from a sole practitioner working alone to a very large company with numerous employees. They can be highly specialized, working with only one type of client, or generalist, providing services to two or more design specialties. These firms often conduct business as a designer/specifier—that is, they plan and specify the merchandise for the project but do not sell the goods to the client. The designer/specifier provides the interior design services described in all phases of the design project process discussed in chapter 2 except for many of the tasks in the contract administration phase. Clients of such firms may buy the goods themselves from independent suppliers or use a competitive bid process to purchase the needed goods and installation services.

Other independent design firms choose to sell merchandise as well as provide interior design services. Commercial interior designers tend to be of the designer/specifier type; residential interior designers commonly sell merchandise to their clients as well as provide interior design services. The difference affects many aspects of the organization and management of the firm, regardless of its size, and it very well may affect your choice of work environment. For example, it is very important for designers in the designer/specifier work environment to bill as much as 90 percent of their work time to clients since the revenue for the firm comes primarily from fees. As mentioned above, designer compensation in this case is often less than compensation paid to designers who also sell merchandise.

Working for a small independent interior design studio with a limited number of employees has an important advantage: You are generally given more direct project responsibility faster than your entry-level colleagues who work in larger firms. Of course, entry-level interior designers always work under the direction of the owner in a small firm, as do entry-level designers working in a large firm. Depending on the reputation and experience of the owner, projects in a small independent firm might not be as large and exciting as those that come to large firms. However, small firms are great places to gain experience.

The owner (of a small firm) or the design director (in larger firms) is instrumental in determining what goes out the door. The project work done by other designers is often scrutinized and reflects the owner's personal style or style developed by the firm. Understanding this

Interior Design Portfolios

The portfolio is a visual record of the design skills you possess; the goal is to show you possess the skills necessary to do the job for which you are applying. A portfolio is a necessary job-hunting tool for any interior designer at any level of experience when seeking a job doing creative design work.

A portfolio must be organized to show the best work you have done or are capable of doing. For a student seeking a first job in the profession, everything in the portfolio should be the very best work he or she can do. These items are commonly included in a portfolio:

- sketches
- space plans
- furniture layout plans
- color boards
- working drawings and specifications
- perspectives
- photos, slides, or publication reprints of projects

For students, items should focus on the needs of the firm while showing a breadth of skills. For example, if you are applying to a residential firm, the majority of items should be related to residential projects. However, examples of other work can be included, especially if they show skills not evident in residential projects.

Designers who have been working for some time should present completed projects in their portfolio. Employers want to see both photographs of completed projects and examples of design documents, which illustrate the designer's mastery of technical skills.

Portfolios must be well organized. An interviewer may spend only ten or twenty minutes looking at an applicant's portfolio. Organize the items to tell your story as effectively as possible. Start with items that specifically relate to the job opening. If you have done your homework and know something about the firm and what they are looking for, your portfolio will be better organized and you will look organized yourself.

A portfolio should never be considered finished. As your skills improve or you produce more exciting or interesting work, replace less important pieces with those items. Professionals constantly document projects by having photos taken of completed work for their own marketing purposes and to have portfolio items should an opportunity to seek a new place of employment occur. Thus, it is important to get the highest-quality photos you can afford. Although digital photos are common today, when possible, have project photos taken by a professional architectural photographer.

work environment issue is important because your design ideas can be vetoed by senior designers; this is difficult for designers who want to make their own decisions on the concepts and solutions of a project.

For a designer/specifier firm, the interior design staff is commonly paid a set salary. Some of the compensation for interior designers working in a firm that also sells merchandise results from commission on the goods sold to the client. If you are paid a salary, you are paid that set amount regardless of the hours you work. If a commission is paid as part of your compensation, then the amount paid will vary quite a bit from paycheck to paycheck. More income can be generated from a commission-based compensation package. However, more risk is entailed. It will take time to develop selling skills and a client base to reach an effective commission level that matches a straight salary.

Independent design firms of any size look for employees with experience and education in the overall design process. Background in the specialty of the design firm, hospitality projects, for example, is also valuable. Experience with CAD, the ability to handle multiple tasks, and an understanding of project management are also skills expected in any size independent design firm. Depending on the size of the firm, it may take up to two years or more in order for you to be given full project responsibility.

Private residence: living room. Greta Guelich, ASID, Perceptions Interior Design Group LLC, Scottsdale, Arizona. Photographer: Mark Boisclair.

High-End Residential and Commercial

ROBERT WRIGHT, ASID
Owner, Bast/Wright Interiors, Inc.
San Diego, California

Commercial headquarters: typical workstation. Robert Wright, ASID, with Kellie McCormick, ASID, Bast/Wright Interiors, San Diego, California. Photographer: Brady Architectural Photography.

What is the most important quality or skill of a designer in your specialty?
Listening with a sixth sense and correctly interpreting the client's needs. It is difficult for some clients to communicate when it comes to an area so subjective and personal as aesthetics and design.

What has been your greatest challenge as an interior designer?
I challenge myself and my design staff to always place the client's needs front and center. Have we listened? Have we responded with the right solution? Have we exceeded the initial project goals? I want a satisfied client.

What led you to enter your design specialty?
An evolution in my career brought me to the residential specialty. Residential interior design allows me to tap into my client in the most personal way. I know that a well-functioning and aesthetically pleasing home can change one's outlook on all aspects of life.

What are your primary responsibilities and duties?

I own the design firm. I am responsible for overseeing the administrative operations as well as knowing what is happening with all of the client work. The majority of my days are spent dealing with the client. I spend a lot of time on the telephone and on the freeways!

Who or what experience has been a major influence on your career?

Several people have had a major influence on me. My first boss, Hester Jones, taught me 80 percent of what I still do today. This includes all aspects of business as well as how to work with people and how to put together a proper design presentation. She exposed me to ASID, which has been the common thread throughout my career. My second job, with Nevelle Lewis and Associates, exposed me to design refinement and project management. I also had the highest respect for my boss, Larry Herr, at Parron Hall Interiors. He held all his employees in the highest regard with the utmost in respect.

I started my career in Houston, Texas, during the late 1970s oil boom. Internationally known architects and designer were all doing projects in Texas. I was exposed to the best of design at a very good time in my career.

Travel is imperative, too. I make it a point to travel for both business and pleasure. Everywhere I go contributes to design details that can be incorporated into projects. A good designer needs to make it a point to go to markets and seminars to stay aware of what is happening in our industry.

What is the most satisfying part of your job?

It is twofold—seeing a project finish with both an incredibly pleased client and a healthy profit margin.

What is the least satisfying part of your job?

When I do not have a good balance between client work and administrative duties as an owner of the firm.

Commercial headquarters: office park. Robert Wright, ASID, with Kellie McCormick, ASID, Bast/Wright Interiors, San Diego, California. Photographer: Brady Architectural Photography.

Private residence: entry. Robert Wright, ASID, Bast/Wright Interiors, San Diego, California. Photographer: Brady Architectural Photography.

Architectural Offices

MANY ARCHITECTURAL FIRMS offer interior design services to their clients. The larger the firm, the more likely it has an interior design department. In most cases, the interior designers work on projects related to the work of the architectural firm. However, because interior design services are often a separate service offering, projects may be obtained without a connection to the architectural department.

Interior design positions in architectural offices vary with the size of the firm. Interior designers seeking direct project responsibility are far more likely to find an entry-level position with a small- to medium-sized architectural firm than a large one. The large multidisciplinary firms more often hire experienced designers to be in charge of projects and use entry-level designers as assistants to the senior designers. Assistants commonly are involved in materials specification, drafting details, or other portions of a project, preparing necessary paperwork and otherwise supporting while learning the actual work of the designers. Of course, the entry-level designer is expected to know CAD, be able to handle multiple tasks, and work as a member of a team.

Senior designers—also called *project designers*—create the ideas and direction of the whole project. A senior interior designer also supervises other designers, leading a team to complete all the documents necessary for a project. The senior designer is also the primary contact with the client—attending meetings, taking phone calls, negotiating concepts, and generally keeping the client informed of the progress of the project. If you begin working in an architectural firm, you will be given project design responsibility and the opportunity to work directly with clients only after you have proven your design and project management skills. Once again, depending on the size of the firm, this may take two or more years.

The architectural firm most commonly generates revenue from services only. Thus, the productivity of an interior designer is very important. It is common for designers in an architectural firm to be responsible for billing 90 or even 100 percent of their time. Being slow and methodical—as an entry-level designer might be—is not considered productive. Because revenues come from billable services, designers are commonly paid a salary. Depending on the firm, additional benefits might include health insurance, payment of professional dues, and reimbursement for continuing education seminars.

Commercial—Banking, Education, Healthcare, and High-End Residential

SANDRA EVANS, ASID
Principal, Knoell & Quidort Architects
Phoenix, Arizona

What has been your greatest challenge as an interior designer?
My greatest challenge as an interior designer is to write a program that interprets my clients' needs and dreams. After the program is written, the challenge is to educate them with sensitivity to the budget and their own knowledge or lack thereof concerning appropriate interior design for the project.

Private residence: living room. Sandra Evans, ASID, Knoell & Quidort Architects, Phoenix, Arizona. Photographer: Jim Christy.

What led you to enter your design specialty?
The roots of architecture at our firm are in residential design. While a great many of our projects are in commercial, banking, educational, healthcare, and industrial facilities, we still are extremely involved in private residences.

What are your primary responsibilities and duties?
They involve space planning, establishing a concept (style, period, color), designing furniture, specifying furnishings and finishes, and coordinating efforts between the owners, contractors, and vendors.

Private residence: great room and kitchen. Sandra Evans, ASID, Knoell & Quidort Architects, Phoenix, Arizona.

What is the most satisfying part of your job?
The most satisfying part of my job is when clients tell me my work has had a profound effect on their lifestyle.

What is the least satisfying part of your job?
The least satisfying part of my work is selecting accessories and designing window coverings.

What is the most important quality or skill of a designer in your specialty?
The most important quality of a designer is to listen to the clients and keep an open mind regarding their opinions about what they want when it does not relate to the architecture. Diplomacy requires knowledge and patience. I try to educate my clients without insulting their aesthetic sensibility. In designing liturgical furniture, it is critical to create elements that are dynamic to celebrate the worship service.

Who or what experience has been a major influence on your career?
My experience with Knoell & Quidort Architects, and especially the work and integrity of Hugh Knoell and Phil Quidort, has been the inspiring and major influence on my career.

Retail Design

JOHN McLEAN, RA

Principal and Design Director, John Mclean
Architect/architecture & industrial design,
White Plains, New York

What has been your greatest challenge as an interior designer?
Retail design is a challenge because it involves skill and talent in
three primary areas of human endeavor: quality, cost, and
schedule. Retail design is programmatically comprehensive. It
involves the integration of architecture, spatial composition,
lighting, display and store fixture design, point-of-sale graphics,
and graphic and store signage design.

Because I am also an industrial designer, I am educated to
design and think in terms of mass production/prototypical design
solutions. These design solutions often are then related to a
variety of sites, such as shopping malls, strip malls, small
town/urban storefronts, and boutiques. Keeping this variety in
mind, a dynamic frame is created through which I enter to meet
these challenges.

Commercial retail: The Electronics
Boutique, Woodbridge Center,
Woodbridge, New Jersey. John
Mclean, RA, AIA, White Plains, New
York.

**Why did you become an
interior designer?**
It is a natural outgrowth of
my architecture and
industrial design practice. I
view projects holistically.
This type of design is best
called *comprehensive design*.
The comprehensive design
approach gives all aspects of
the space program the look
of a natural flow and fit—
that is, from architecture to
the interior design to the
landscaping.

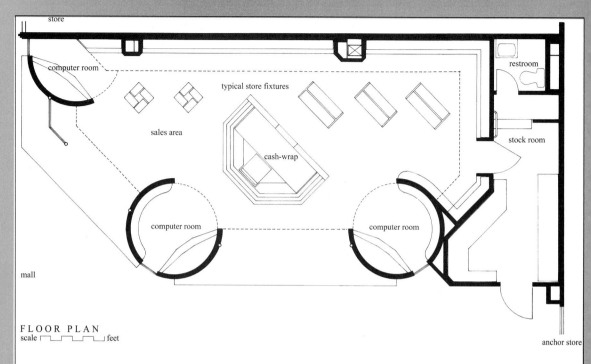

store

computer room

typical store fixtures

sales area

cash-wrap

restroom

stock room

computer room

computer room

mall

FLOOR PLAN
scale ⌐⌐⌐⌐⌐ feet

anchor store

THE ELECTRONICS BOUTIQUE WOODBRIDGE CENTER NEW JERSEY
John McLean Architect architecture & industrial design White Plains N Y

What led you to enter your design specialty?

Store design has been part of my psyche since childhood. The purpose of retail design is to entice or seduce a person to enter the store and then to create an atmosphere conducive to "yes" in making a purchase.

I remember the Bohack supermarket storefront design of my childhood. The façade was constructed of cream-colored porcelain enamel metal panels with the name *Bohack* in red, raised in relief, on the panels. Of historic note is the fact that Gordon Bunschaft of SOM designed this store.

Supermarkets did not have a general reputation for design quality prior to the 1980s. Therefore, when the opportunity arose for the office I was formerly associated with to design a supermarket, I was already primed to meet the challenge. I am proud to be credited with heading this team.

What are your primary responsibilities and duties?

I am the principal in charge and director of design.

Commercial retail: The Electronics Boutique, Woodbridge Center, Woodbridge, New Jersey. John Mclean, RA, AIA, White Plains, New York.

What is the most satisfying part of your job?

The most satisfying part of my professional life is having the opportunity to use the creative talents for which I have been trained. Being able to successfully meet the challenge presented by a project is a great reward.

What is the least satisfying part of your job?

The least? The best way to answer this part of the question is to acknowledge that good design has to be supported by economic viability. It is very important, therefore, for a professional to treat his/her practice as if it is an ongoing project where the parameters of quality, schedule, and cost are balanced.

What is the most important quality or skill of a designer in your specialty?

The most important quality and skill expressed by a designer should be to constantly strive to bring a fresh point of view to each project. Prototypical design can translate into variations on a theme rather than static repetition. This was the practice I followed in creating the Electronics Boutique stores. The result was distinct but recognizable store designs.

Who or what experience has been a major influence in your career?

Frank Lloyd Wright, who taught that design matters in the life of a person and a community.

Mies van der Rohe, who practiced as a comprehensive designer of commercial environments and brought the aesthetics of architecture and design to the corporate world.

Eero Saarinen, who kept the principles of the modern movement alive and showed that there is more than styling in linking architecture and design.

Louis Kahn, for his poetic approach to design.

Furniture Retailers

ANOTHER COMMON WORK environment for the interior designer is the furniture retailer. High-end furniture retailers sell the high-priced, high-quality products directly to the residential consumer, sometimes through a furniture store or the interior design department of a department store. This is an attractive work environment for many professional interior designers interested in the residential specialties. Job opportunities in the interior design departments of department stores and other furniture and specialty stores are excellent places for the entry-level designer to get started in the profession.

In many ways, the interior designers in stores function like small studios or even sole practitioners. The goal of the interior designer working in the retail store, however, is to sell the products offered by the store rather than items otherwise available in the market. In some companies, the designer cannot sell anything other than what is normally handled by the store. This is an important difference between working in an independent interior design studio and working in a retail furniture store.

Experienced interior designers working in a retail furniture store or in some department store environments often have assistants who are entry-level interior designers. Because few retailers are willing to let young, inexperienced interior designers work with clients, these design assistants help the senior designers produce sketches, draft floor plans, and develop color schemes. In this way, they learn valuable lessons about the work expected of designers in furniture stores and working with clients. Interior designers in large retail and department stores also have access to office assistance for help with some of the paperwork.

Compensation is commonly by means of a small salary, with the bulk of compensation being paid based on commission related to the sale of merchandise. Many retailers do not charge a design fee for interior design services, so the entire revenue generated by the design staff is based on the sale of merchandise. Thus, it is important for an interior designer in this work environment to be comfortable with selling. Because interior design assistants are generally not responsible for selling merchandise, they are compensated by some salary and perhaps a small commission.

Office Furnishings Dealers

OFFICE FURNISHINGS DEALERS are retailers who specialize in selling products for offices—sounds obvious, doesn't it? The name for this type of company came about as stores dealing with office products began to focus on selling furniture made by one or two specific furniture manufacturers. They became "dealers" by making special arrangements with one or more manufacturers based on the large volume of furniture they sold. Office furnishings dealers focus on specifying and selling those products with which they have the dealership arrangement, but they sell many other kinds of furniture and products appropriate for offices and similar commercial interiors.

Law office: Alston & Bird LLP, secretary's corner. Rita Carson Guest, FASID, Carson Guest, Inc., Atlanta, Georgia. Photographer: Gabriel Benzur.

Many of these companies have interior design departments. Projects primarily involve corporate offices and professional offices for financial institutions, law firms, medical office suites, and the like. These designers rarely design restaurants, hotels, retail stores, or private residences. Interior designers primarily work on projects brought to the company by the furniture sales staff. Sometimes the interior design departments of the large dealers also seek projects that are not initially obtained by the in-house sales staff.

Office furnishings dealerships provide excellent work environments for entry-level interior designers. You can learn a lot about how to space-plan and design, work with clients, and be part of a team. This work environment is often used as a stepping-stone to many of the interior design and architectural firms that specialize in other areas of the commercial interior design. Important employment criteria include excellent space-planning skills, knowledge of CAD, and an understanding of the bid process. Interior designers working at an office furnishings dealership also must be comfortable working as part of a team, as design solution presentations are often done in tandem with the sales staff.

For the most part, interior designers in office furnishings dealerships are compensated by salary. Some companies also allow a small commission related to the sale of a certain type of product. For example, the office furnishings dealer may pay the designers a commission based on the value of accessories purchased by the client.

Office/Corporate Design

LINDA SORRENTO, ASID, IIDA

Manager, Strategic Workplace Solutions/A&D
Arbee Associates
Gaithersburg, Maryland

Office furnishings dealership: Collaborative Idea Neighborhood, Arbee Associates Headquarters, Gaithersburg, Maryland. Interior design by Gensler, Washington, DC, in collaboration with Arbee Associates. Photographer: Kevin Beswick.

What is the most important quality or skill of a designer in your specialty?

The quality most needed by a designer in the office environment is problem-solving ability within critical project parameters.

What has been your greatest challenge as an interior designer?

My greatest challenge as an interior designer is to reasonably manage my interests in the variety of opportunities offered by this field.

What led you to enter your design specialty?

I was led into my specialty by my passion about how people work and solving their issues through the office environment. I first explored this interest during the design of my undergraduate senior project. Soon after graduating with a BFA in interior design, I began my career designing office spaces.

What are your primary responsibilities and duties?

As a representative for my company to the architectural and design community, I'm responsible for providing solutions to the designers' office projects. This effort begins in the early strategic stages of a project and continues well beyond job completion.

What is the most satisfying part of your job?
I am most satisfied in collaborating with designers in doing the best possible work for their clients.

What is the least satisfying part of your job?
The least is often the length of time necessary to complete the project.

How important is certification by examination and licensing of interior designers today?
The only way to continue to expand the interior design profession and to protect the right to practice is through examination and then jurisdictional certification or licensing.

Office furnishings dealership: executive management office. Arbee Associates Headquarters, Gaithersburg, Maryland. Interior design by Gensler, Washington, DC, in collaboration with Arbee Associates. Photographer: Kevin Beswick.

Who or what experience has been a major influence on your career?
A major influence on my career has been the continuation of my education through a graduate program in interior design. I took the time through this education to learn about research in interior design. This second degree and emphasis on research have become valuable assets in advancing my career.

Office furnishings dealership: Collaborative Idea Neighborhood, Arbee Associates Headquarters, Gaithersburg, Maryland. Interior design by Gensler, Washington, DC, in collaboration with Arbee Associates. Photographer: Kevin Beswick.

"Can You Describe the Optimum Portfolio for a Job Applicant?"

A good portfolio contains samples of a number of types of projects that relate to my target market (offices, small medical offices and facilities, and nursing homes), samples of one or two color and finish boards, some CAD drawings, some hand drawing and lettering, rough sketches, and perhaps something to show the applicant's creativity and problem-solving skills. The format should be easy to view and handle, and be self-explanatory in case I have to ask the applicant to leave it until I have time to look through it.
—Terri Maurer, FASID

If just out of school? Then enough to show their communication, technical, and design skill.
—Bruce Goff, ASID

Design creativity— drawing skills.
—Nila Leiserowitz, FASID

An optimum portfolio includes examples of all aspects of their talents, including drawings, plans, sketches, perspectives, color boards, and photos of completed projects in a 9" x 12" portfolio. The job applicant could bring in their best color board along with this portfolio or include a color photo of the color board in their portfolio. The 9" by 12" size is less cumbersome for the interview.
—Greta Guelich, ASID

The best portfolio shows me a wide range of the applicant's skills. I enjoy seeing early projects that have not been touched up and then later projects to see the development. Fabrics, finishes, and furniture selections are also important. Organization in the portfolio tells me a lot about the applicant. Basically, just a simple but solid presentation of the skills of the young designer.
—Charles Gandy, FASID, FIIDA

A portfolio should represent the best work that a person has done, with examples of construction documents, drawings, renderings, client programs, and photos of completed projects. KISS.
—Sandra Evans, ASID

Variety; good, clean work; accurate drawings; logical layouts, not cutesy; sketching ability; architectural printing a must!!
—Pat McLaughlin, ASID

A portfolio should include examples of work that detail the designer's role on the project, a brief description of the project scope, and digital photos or actual examples of color boards. Also, letters of referral are an added benefit when they document the designer's credibility and ability to work with people.
—Leonard Alvarado

CAD examples, hand-drafting examples, letters of recommendation, photos of work.
—**Debra May Himes, IIDA, ASID**

A progression of projects from first experience to the present and related things like art, photography, and writing. A well-rounded presentation of a person's interest and skills.
—**William Peace, ASID**

Several quick sketch items, several space-planning and concept design items, and several sets of drawings. Color and material boards that are either actual boards or photos.
—**Melinda Sechrist, FASID**

Projects on which the designer has been a participant, honesty in describing his or her personal role on the project, understanding of and responsiveness to the client's objectives in developing the design solutions evidenced by the projects.
—**Marilyn Farrow, FIIDA**

Portfolios should demonstrate your individual strengths. I do not care to see every project you completed during your education, nor every part of any project. Projects should be used as tools to explain what processes or skills you learned. Bottom line, I want to know your individual strengths. Use your portfolio as a differentiator; show your strengths.
—**Barbara Nugent, FASID**

Most applicants arrive with a poor portfolio that has few senior projects and a lot of flotsam and jetsam—an eclectic group of assignments that provide little insight into the designer's or architect's abilities in a real-world situation. I like to see a substantial senior project that isn't bullshit—one that really demonstrates the person has done some research, intellectually thought about the solution, and portrayed it in an aesthetically beautiful manner. Excellent presentation skills are important.
—**Jain Malkin, CID**

The optimum portfolio has hand-drawn sketches, a rendering, photos of school projects and/or actual work, AutoCAD drawings, a set of construction drawings and specifications, and a brief explanation of what part the designer had in putting together each of the projects submitted.
—**Linda Santellanes, ASID**

A portfolio should demonstrate your problem-solving process and logic. We are more interested in understanding your approach to problems then we are in pretty pictures. Focus on the results you created in completing a project. If you have a particular specialty that you excel in—for example, drawing or presentation development—we would like to see that as well. Show a small range of projects that demonstrate your approach to both small and large projects.
—**Sari Graven, ASID**

The portfolio should be a concise expression of the job applicant's skills with a focus on the type of work needed by the design firm.
—**Linda Sorrento, ASID, IIDA**

Facility Planning and Design

ANOTHER TYPE OF work environment is within the planning and interior design departments of large corporations. Best Western, Microsoft, Bank of America, and many other corporations employ facility planning and management personnel as in-house interior designers. In this work environment, interior designers are responsible for the space planning and interior design of corporate facilities. In some situations, they might work with an outside independent designer. These jobs might even have an international flavor, as so many large corporations have offices and facilities outside the United States.

Entry-level designers are rarely hired into this work environment. Most often, these companies need experienced interior designers. A broad range of design skills is required for facility planning, and interior designers are skilled in all phases of the design process. However, interior designers working for corporations are not often responsible for the actual ordering of merchandise because the company's purchasing department does it.

Working for a corporation can mean a higher salary and better health insurance, retirement, and vacation benefits than can be obtained working for independent interior design and architectural firms. Corporate interior design jobs often require considerable travel. Depending on your point of view, this is a positive or a negative aspect of working for a corporation. Frequent-flyer miles can add up for interior designers who are responsible for corporate projects throughout the United States—or around the world.

Sole Practitioner

AFTER WORKING FOR someone else, many interior designers decide to start their own design practice. These interior designers are commonly called *sole practitioners*, indicating that they work alone. Interior designers start their own practice for the same reasons as many entrepreneurs: They are looking for the opportunity to be their own boss and reap the rewards (and suffer the consequences) of business ownership.

The sole practitioner commonly specializes in one of the areas discussed in the previous chapter. Working alone, the interior designer cannot handle a large variety of work, so specializing in residential interior design or an area of commercial design is quite common. Depending on the design specialty and skills of the sole practitioner, he or she may find it necessary to outsource certain tasks to other interior designers or professionals. For example, a sole practitioner might outsource CAD services when construction drawings are required. Of course, sole practitioners also contract with vendors and tradespeople for the purchase of goods and to install items such as wall coverings and flooring.

Sole practitioners must be prepared to engage in all the activities of an interior design practice—that is, they must market their services to obtain clients, develop contracts or agreements for services, prepare necessary drawings and specifications of required goods, and recommend or arrange for the goods to be delivered to the client. In addition, sole practitioners are responsible for all the bookkeeping and paperwork that sustains a business. They must prepare all the paperwork involved in purchasing merchandise or services for the project, billing, and paying vendors.

The salary sole practitioners earn is drawn from the revenues of the firm—that is, they can pay themselves if revenue exceeds all the other expenses of operating the interior design practice. Of course, a solo practice operated out of a home office incurs minimal business expenses. However, making enough profit on a project requires excellent business control and management. Many sole practitioners find that the number of hours that must be worked to secure new clients, provide interior design services, and manage the business leaves them with less salary per hour than they made working for someone else. It can take several years for the sole practitioner to start to show profits and a satisfying income level.

The location of the solo practice varies with the owner's business goals. Solo practices are most commonly located in a home office. Some sole practitioners lease space in an executive office complex. In this case, the interior designer shares a receptionist and conference room with other firms while renting an appropriate amount of private office space. This is less expensive than renting an office suite and means that the hiring of additional staff can also be delayed. Other practitioners locate in a commercial office or retail location. Any type of commercial location for the interior design practice gives it a more substantial appearance than a home office does. It is, however, readily acceptable in this profession in today's marketplace for practitioners to work out of a home office or studio.

One day, sole practitioners find they have enough business to require assistance. The first person hired by a sole practitioner is usually a part-time bookkeeper or some other part-time office administration assistant. Sometimes a business can grow to need additional design staff. At this point, it is generally necessary to move the firm to a commercial office location, as most cities do not allow home-based businesses to function in a residential area when they add on-site employees.

Interior designers who decide it is time to start their own firm must realize that the endeavor is a *business*. To be successful and grow—even though that growth is only in terms of total annual revenue—the solo practice must be planned and operated like a business with employees. The practice owner must use the same good business techniques of planning and structure that every firm uses. Not to do so can mean financial disaster as well as harm to the interior designer's reputation.

Interior designers can find career opportunities in numerous other places of business. Several of these are discussed in the preceding chapter and in Exhibit 3-2 on page 73.

Corporate Offices, Small Healthcare Facilities, and Nursing Homes

TERRI MAURER, FASID
Principal, Maurer Design Group, Akron, Ohio

What has been your greatest challenge as an interior designer?
My greatest challenge continues to be making the public—that is, potential clients—understand exactly what interior designers do that makes them different from decorators.

What led you to enter your design specialty?
I realized early on, while I was still in college, that I did not have the personality type to do residential work and deal with residential clients. So, when I graduated, I focused on getting work in the commercial field. I am much more attuned to creative problem solving and love the challenges placed on designers in that field.

Office: media presentation room. Terri Maurer, FASID, Maurer Design Group, Akron, Ohio.

Office: reception area. Terri Maurer, FASID, Maurer Design Group, Akron, Ohio.

What are your responsibilities and duties?

As a sole practitioner and business owner, I assume not only the duties of designer but also all the facets of running a business. While I do the normal interviewing and programming, design concept development, and all that goes into the documentation and implementation of the design project from inception through postoccupancy evaluations, I am also responsible for marketing to bring in the jobs, creating the contracts and other necessary paperwork for the office and project to run smoothly, bookkeeping, purchasing, expediting, and invoicing for any product procured for the client. And I get to sweep the floor, empty the wastebaskets, and make the coffee too! Yes, I definitely outsource a few of those tasks, but I am ultimately responsible for seeing that it all gets done.

What is the most satisfying part of your job?

The most satisfying part of my job is to see the end result of my efforts not only change the aesthetic of an environment but also to know that I helped improve the client's productivity, improved their financial bottom line, and improved their employees' and customers' morale.

What is the most important quality or skill of a designer in your specialty?

I think all designers working with business owners need to have two skills. One is the ability to be a team player with your client and the other professionals and tradespeople on the job. The other is knowing about business so you can communicate with your clients as a partner, not an underling, and to understand what you have to do to effect important changes beyond the color scheme.

What is the least satisfying part of your job?
The least satisfying part is all of the business tasks that need to be taken care of when I want to be creative.

Who or what experience has been a major influence on your career?
Without a doubt, I have to credit the head of the interior design program at my college, Mary Kapenekas, ASID, and another local designer, Nancy Keiser, ASID, for their major influence on my career and the direction it has taken. Both of them impressed on me the need to join a professional design organization following school. Mary, as a faculty member, pointed out that this was one of the important steps to becoming a professional interior designer. Nancy, with whom I did an internship while in college, took me to a local ASID meeting. Through their encouragement, I became involved in the local chapter, then was asked to take (and accepted) leadership roles that eventually led me to becoming ASID's national president. The lessons I learned along the way and the skills and tools I achieved through my ASID involvement have placed me well above the level I would have achieved without that professional focus.

Medical office suite: waiting area. Terri Maurer, FASID, Maurer Design Group, Akron, Ohio.

"What Motivated You to Start Your Own Design Firm?"

At the time I began my own firm, I had been in a partnership, following a number of experiences working for several types of design entities. I became pregnant, the partnership ended, and I was faced with the opportunity to begin working on my own. The timing was right for me to work on my own so I could spend time with our son during his early years. Given my experience in building and managing the partnership, I had the tools and skills to begin building my own business.
— **Terri Maurer, FASID**

When I first began design classes, I knew I would start my own design firm and felt it was only a matter of time and experience before I actually set the wheels in motion. It was just an innate desire to build something that would be successful.
— **Greta Guelich, ASID**

I became my own boss because I had to move from state to state because of my husband's career opportunities. It is difficult to develop seniority at a firm while moving around but easy to gain varied experience that facilitates development of comprehensive knowledge beneficial to a consulting practice.
— **Marilyn Farrow, FIIDA**

One of the wonderful aspects of interior design is our ability to evolve professionally. For many years I was an employee in firms from small to international. I have now decided to be a sole practitioner and have opened my own design firm. Although I still team with others when needed, I am enjoying the freedom of being self-employed at this point in my career. Isn't it wonderful that we have so many opportunities in so many specialties (healthcare, hospitality, retail, corporate, residential, government) as well as in the formatting of our business?
— **Barbara Nugent, FASID**

I like being the decision maker and choosing who I want to work with and how I want to work.
— **Debra May Himes, ASID, IIDA**

I started my own firm for two reasons: (1) In 1968, there wasn't a design firm in my market that allowed a designer to provide professional services rather than purvey a product, and (2) I wanted to be able to integrate my professional life with my family life.
— **M. Joy Meeuwig, IIDA**

What motivated me to start my own design firm was the opportunity to design what I wanted to design, to have some control over my environment, to have some flexibility, and to receive some tax relief and company benefits.
— **Linda Santellanes, FASID**

High-End Residential

GRETA GUELICH, ASID
Principal, Perceptions Interior Design Group LLC,
Scottsdale, Arizona

What led you to enter your design specialty?
Although my education was geared toward the commercial market
and I always felt I would be a commercial designer, I just fell into
a job at a residential design firm and really enjoyed the more
creative aspects of the position.

Private residence: living room.
Greta Guelich, ASID, Perceptions
Interior Design Group LLC,
Scottsdale, Arizona. Photographer:
Mark Boisclair.

**What has been your greatest
challenge as an interior designer?**
The greatest challenge has been
relying on others to bring their part
of the project in on time. Suppliers
always promise on-time delivery but
deliver late.

**What are your primary
responsibilities and duties?**
As a business owner, I wear many
hats. I meet with clients, design the
space, find the products, present the
project, order the products, and
supervise the installation. I find I
spend too much time running the
business versus doing the business.

**What is the most satisfying part of
your job?**
The most satisfying part of the job
comes at the end when I've done
all the work, it looks beautiful
and functions well, and the client
loves it.

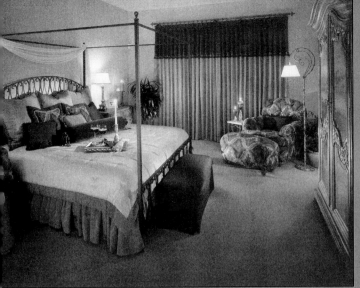

Private residence: master suite. Greta Guelich, ASID, Perceptions Interior Design Group LLC, Scottsdale, Arizona. Photographer: Mark Boisclair.

What is the least satisfying part of your job?

The least satisfying is what I call running my business—all the office paperwork that is necessary to keep the business going, such as sales tax, payroll tax, quarterly tax, and income tax reports.

What is the most important quality or skill of a designer in your specialty?

In residential design, the most important quality is listening. It is extremely important that the designer listen to the clients and interpret what they want in the design. Being able to sketch a thought or design idea is very important to make sure the designer is thinking the same thing as the client.

Who or what experience has been a major influence on your career?

My internship with an architectural firm during my senior year at the University of Nebraska was a major influence on my career. The partners of this firm introduced me to real-world experiences in the field of design. They allowed me to attend meetings with their clients as well as work on drawings and perspectives for their presentations and projects.

How important is interior design education in today's industry?

It is very important to be prepared and trained for a specific job, no matter what the position. With licensing just around the corner, education is even more critical for the interior designer.

Private residence: sitting area. Greta Guelich, ASID, Perceptions Interior Design Group LLC, Scottsdale, Arizona. Photographer: Mark Boisclair.

"What Do You Enjoy Most About Working in the Firm You Are in Right Now?"

The clients! Working in high-end residential jobs means that, for the most part, I work with interesting and creative individuals who are usually decisive yet respectful of the designer's role.
—Charles Gandy, FASID, FIIDA

I own it! Because I am a small business owner, my schedule can be somewhat flexible, which allows me to be involved in outside organizations.
—Greta Guelich, ASID

I like the independence of setting my own pace and schedule and not having to ask for clearance to proceed with a concept or to explore other avenues.
—Terri Maurer, FASID

Really high-profile projects, extremely high level of expertise, great resources.
—Beth Harmon-Vaughn, FIIDA

End results of projects—the happiness of the clients.
—Donna Vining, FASID

I work in a large architectural firm. The eight partners, all architects, view interior design as a completely separate discipline. They respect the full process of interior design and recognize its value and importance in complementing architectural work.
—Jennifer van der Put, BID, IDC, ARIDO, IFMA

We are a firm with many disciplines and types of expertise in retail, shopping centers, healthcare, environmental graphic design, marketing, public relations, and hospitality, and we have a formal alliance with three other firms. We have a relatively young staff—professional people who care about the service they deliver to their clients. Our culture encourages challenges to the status quo.
—Sari Graven, ASID

The opportunity to meet great clients and to work with great people. I find the collaborative team process the most enjoyable part of any project.
—M. Arthur Gensler Jr., FAIA, FIIDA, RIBA

I own it! I am involved with an interesting variety of projects and enjoy working with most of my clients.
—Melinda Sechrist, FASID

As a senior design professional, I enjoy the high-level decision makers with whom I generally work. It is likely you will see projects realized when you have the ability to talk to the true leaders of the firm or corporation.
—Marilyn Farrow, FIIDA

The challenge of our clients and the great team we have assembled to meet those challenges.
—Rosalyn Cama, FASID

I own part of it.
—Derrell Parker, IIDA

Coming to work most days is really a high. We have an extraordinary work environment and many clients who provide numerous opportunities for creative, cutting-edge design.

—Jain Malkin, CID

I enjoy the laughter the most. It appears in the creative energy and camaraderie of the staff and members of the design teams we partner with and the trust, loyalty, and delight of the clients.

—Suzan Globus, ASID

The scale of the projects.

—Teresa Sowell, ASID, IFMA

I have a good group of people who support me and my work for clients.

—Michael Thomas, ASID

Respect for the profession.

—Nila Leiserowitz, FASID

What I like the most about working in the firm I am in today is the professional environment created by the partners and employees. I contract at a small firm that is extremely organized. The environment is respectful of employees and clients alike. Not only have they managed to achieve a large workload from repeat business but also they enjoy their work. The partners convey a sense of great pride in what they have achieved and an understanding of where they came from.

—Linda Santellanes, ASID

The ability to totally vary my day and interact with many individuals keeps me fresh for new opportunities.

—Fred Messner, IIDA

I enjoy the inspiration given by the people I work with and the environment where I work.

—Linda Sorrento, ASID, IIDA

The opportunity to work with outstanding clients.

—Rita Carson Guest, FASID

It is my own firm; this gives me independence and the freedom to specify exactly what my client needs, not what someone might require me to specify in order to meet a quota or sales requirement.

—Sally Thompson, ASID

My firm is basically me at this point because I have leveraged my business experiences into another avenue: writing and presenting educational programs. I still maintain long-standing clients and work with them as their needs arise.

—Linda E. Smith, FASID

Teamwork!

—Pat McLaughlin, ASID

The freedom and flexibility I have to make decisions about my future.

—Sally Nordahl, IIDA

The nature of my firm now is that it has projects in a number of specialty areas, making it a true multidisciplinary firm. This exposes me to a broad spectrum of project types, responsibilities, and professionals.

—David Stone, IIDA

I do it my way.

—M. Joy Meeuwig, IIDA

The opportunity to lead and not be satisfied with the given.

—Neil Frankel, FAIA, FIIDA

I closed my firm after working there for fifteen years. I currently am the director of an interior design college within a large architectural school. What I love about this is that I now can share my nineteen-plus years of experience with students who are eager to enter the field. I also have the opportunity to solve problems of a different nature—but solve problems nonetheless!

—Lisa Whited, ASID, IIDA, IDEC

I teach at Colorado State University. I have incredibly wonderful, hardworking students to teach. I love being in the classroom and learning from them. That is what I enjoy most.
—**Stephanie Clemons, PhD, ASID, IDEC**

I am proud of the work we produce and the success we are experiencing. I enjoy watching our new designers finding themselves and building their confidence. There is so much for them to learn.
—**Robert Wright, ASID**

The type of projects and the clients.
—**Bruce Goff, ASID**

Being creative every day.
—**Michelle King, IIDA**

One of the best things about the profession of interior design is that you can branch out to other industries, and the principles you have gained in both your education and experience can help you flourish and excel in any area of endeavor. I currently am employed with a manufacturer working with interior designers and architects throughout the country seeking specifications of our products on their projects. The work keeps me in the A&D community and allows me to be involved with hundreds of projects and dozens of interesting and exciting architects and interior designers.
—**Beth Kuzbek, ASID, IIDA, CMG**

Control. I own it.
—**W. Daniel Shelley, AIA, ASID**

With Corporate Express, the ongoing expansion of technology used in design and the quantity of projects. With designquiz.com, helping other designers prepare for the national exam. Experiencing others fulfilling their professional goals.
—**John Holmes, ASID, IIDA**

I love owning my own firm, where I can work on projects I enjoy and set my own schedule.
—**Ellen McDowell, ASID**

I absolutely love the team of designers assembled here. I also like the upscale niche we have moved the firm into in the last few years. It is a natural fit for this team.
—**Jeffrey Rausch, IIDA**

Oh, I am having so much fun! I work for intelligent, funny, hardworking architects who have great integrity. They also all have a great sense of humor, which makes a pleasant working environment. Although they tease me by calling me the decorator, they have learned to value and appreciate what I can do to enhance and complete their projects. But what I like most is the variety of work I do. Sometimes I am doing the expected thing—furniture, finishes, equipment, furniture schedules, finish schedules, and so on. Other times I am meeting with clients—meeting the challenge of making sure the clients are happy to be working with Lotti, Krishan & Short. Other times I am on marketing trips or making presentations with our marketing principal. That's the excitement of competition. Often I am drawing interior elevations—I learned AutoCAD when I was fifty years old! I love it! Sometimes I use AutoCAD's 3-D features combined with Photoshop to make little computer studies of a space so we can help the client understand something better. I also meet with subcontractors and manufacturers' representatives. And attend seminars—there's always something interesting to learn! I guess I enjoy almost all of the aspects of my work.
—**Linda Kress, ASID**

The types of projects we work on are more varied and allow for a higher creativity challenge than those of other firms or what I could bring in on my own.

—Linda Isley, IIDA

Designers are well rounded if they are given the chance to participate in different phases of a project in order to enhance their skills. I enjoy my job because every day is different and I am consistently challenged to enhance my skills in different areas. It is good not to become pigeonholed or stuck doing the same type of task routinely.

—Leonard Alvarado

I enjoy the freedom that comes from owning my own practice; however, along with the freedom comes the responsibility to my clients, my employees, and my vendors.

—Juliana Catlin, FASID

I am involved in high-end hotel projects that are diverse in terms of geography, locality, and type of project, which can vary from a historic landmark hotel to a highly urban business hotel or a resort hotel.

—Alicia Loo, CID

The scope of the projects.

—Kristen Anderson, ASID, CID, RID

The relationships with coworkers and clients.

—William Peace, ASID

I have to say that it is the thrill of challenge. Every day is a challenge in our firm. We have a multidisciplinary staff of approximately eighty-five people, including architects, interior designers, civil and structural engineers, and traffic and land use planners. It is a fast-paced, multitask environment where client demands require an extreme sense of urgency and responsiveness. Our clients' needs present daily challenges daily related to design, budget, or schedule goals. I enjoy meeting the challenge!

—Susan B. Higbee

Operating as a subgroup with a unique culture and the brand identity of an interior design practice while taking advantage of the deeper resources of a full-service multidisciplinary firm.

—Janice Carleen Linster, ASID, IIDA, CID

It is a firm I helped build. I care about our clients and the people I work with. I'm doing what I love; I followed my bliss.

—Cheri Gerou, AIA, ASID

Endnotes

1. Judith Davidson. *Interior Design*, "100 Giants," January 2003, pp. 139–158.

2. U.S. Department of Labor, Bureau of Labor Statistics. Occupational Employment Statistics. Occupation Identification number 27-1025. From website: www.bls.gov.

3. American Society of Interior Designers. 1998. ASID Fact Sheet, "Economic Impact of the Interior Design Profession." ASID. Washington, D.C.

4. U.S. Bureau of Labor Statistics, November 2001. From website: www.bls.gov.

5. Judith Davidson. *Interior Design*, "100 Giants," January 2003, p. 158.

Chapter Five

Interior Design as a Business

The interior design practice owner must deal with the same business issues that challenge every business. The owner—or someone on the staff—must keep a steady stream of new business and clients flowing to the firm. Decisions must be made about how to charge for services. If products are to be sold to the client, their markup or discount must be determined. The process of performing the work—and assigning responsibility for each required task—must be clarified. Employees must be hired, motivated, and rewarded. These are just a few of the issues that must be addressed, controlled, and managed by business owners and employees.

Planning and organizing the business of interior design are just as critical to the ongoing success of a firm as are the technical skills and creative competence of the owner and staff. If the practice does not conduct itself in a

Business Practice Terms

Billable hours: The time the interior designer works on tasks directly related to the completion of the design documents, specifications, and supervision on the job site.

Income statement: An accounting report showing revenues and expenses for a specific period. Also called a *profit and loss statement*.

Letter of agreement: A simplified form of a contract for services.

Proposal: A response the interior designer makes to a request for a proposal (RFP) offered by a client. It is not necessarily a contract for goods and/or services.

Purchase agreement: The document used to clarify the furniture and furnishings that are going to be purchased for the client.

Referral: A positive recommendation from a client of an interior designer.

Request for proposal (RFP): Clients use this document to obtain specific information from a number of interior designers interested in designing the client's project.

Retail price: The price by value charged to the consumer. It is generally 100 percent higher than the wholesale price of the goods.

Retainer: Payments made by the client to the interior designer to cover future work by the professional in the interest of the project.

Scope of services: A description of what must be done by the interior designer to complete the project. It is listed within the body of the design contract or letter of agreement.

Wholesale price: A special price given to the interior designer by a manufacturer or other vendor that is lower than the price to the consumer.

purposeful business manner, it cannot survive no matter how creative the staff is. Neglect the business, and the firm can suffer financial hardships and even legal complications.

This chapter briefly discusses a number of key business challenges for the interior design practice owner. Its purpose is to give you a quick look at the business side of the interior design profession. Attention is focused on marketing, the importance of contracts, revenue generation, and legal issues.

Healthcare: West of the Moon Lounge, Scripps Breast Care Center, La Jolla, California. Interior architecture and design, Jain Malkin, Inc., San Diego, California. Photographer: Glenn Cormier.

"What Motivated You to Start Your Own Design Firm?"

These responses are from designers who own firms larger than a sole proprietorship.

I've always been an entrepreneur, from the time I was six years old. I never even thought of working for someone else; it just seemed natural for me to start my own firm, and I did so at a very early age.

　　—Jain Malkin, CID

I had a baby and didn't want to go back to work full time at the firm I was with and was not allowed to work part time. I was also bored with doing exclusively space planning for the company I worked for.

　　—Melinda Sechrist, FASID

Never thought of any other way.

　　—Donna Vining, FASID

For me, it would have to be my lack of understanding of how hard it is to sustain a successful practice. There is an implied goal in our profession of being an entrepreneur, controlling your own destiny. Ego drives many of us to try our own business. There are many hard lessons to learn along the way.

　　—Fred Messner, IIDA

I used to have my own residential design firm. I operated out of a home office. The greatest part, besides low overhead, was that I could control my schedule and take time off to go play with the grandchildren. I enjoyed it very much, and I have good friends in ASID who are operating in this manner today. They are very successful and probably make more money than I do! When you own your own design firm complete with employees, overhead, etc., that's another thing entirely. At this stage in my life and the state of today's economy, it's not what I want to do.

　　—Linda Kress, ASID

I didn't start it—I was hired as a draftsman and through hard work, diligence, and talent I now own it.

　　—W. Daniel Shelley, AIA, ASID

The thought that I had a better idea of how to operate a design firm and the desire to lead a team of people. Increased income potential also played a factor.

　　—Jeffrey Rausch, IIDA

Fell on my head one too many times. In reality, thought that I should do this my way if I were going to do it at all. Never worked for anyone, not even an internship. STUPID! But, oh well.

　　—Bruce Goff, ASID

Being laid off!

　　—Pat McLaughlin, ASID

We have exciting projects and great clients. The firm is an open studio that encourages the interaction of talented and professional persons who inspire each other.
—Sandra Evans, ASID

My husband encouraged me to open my own business. I was afraid I would never have clients, but one successful project led to another and another.
—Rita Carson Guest, FASID

Authority and responsibility.
—Neil Frankel, FIIDA, FAIA

Private residence: living room. Charles Gandy, FASID, FIIDA, Charles Gandy, Inc., Atlanta, Georgia. Photographer: Roger Wade.

I started my own business so I would be solely responsible for my vision and to have a chance to express that vision in my own way. Having one's own business is not necessarily the thing to do for everyone, but for me it was.
—Charles Gandy, FASID, FIIDA

I started a firm years ago to meet the market demand for a commercial interior design practice.
—Linda Sorrento, ASID, IIDA

Self-expression is very important. It was the only way for me to reap the biggest professional and economic rewards.
—Robert Wright, ASID

Insanity. I thought I knew it all. No, really, probably wanting to run things my way.
—Jan Bast, ASID, IIDA

Having just taken a weeklong leadership training course, I've found that my risk-taking component is such that it was a natural outcome. I graduated from school and initially formed a partnership with an individual. Within three years, the partnership dissolved, and I formed

my own design firm, which is now seventeen years old.
—Linda E. Smith, FASID

The opportunity to practice as the owner of an architectural firm was always my vision. However, the size and complexity of our firm was never planned or dreamed of. But the opportunities that this profession has provided me are certainly beyond my expectations. I love the opportunity to create spaces, to work with clients, and to be part of the design and construction profession.
—M. Arthur Gensler Jr., FAIA, FIIDA, RIBA

Sounds horrible, but I was working under a designer who didn't give a lot of guidance. I thought if I kept making mistakes, I could do them just as well on my own and probably make better money and be happier doing it.
—Ellen McDowell, ASID

I hit the glass ceiling at a firm and because I did not want to purchase it, I started another one in such a way that it made sense for my existing clients to do business with me and stay with me over the long haul.
—Michael Thomas, ASID

When I had graduated, no one was hiring. I wanted to design, so while I had a job outside of design, I went out and found my own projects. The business was formed from there.
—**John Holmes, ASID, IIDA**

I loved what I was doing. And I thought—hey, why kill myself, working all of these hours for $12,000? Why not start my own company and make it on my own? Yes, the first year I didn't make much money. But after that I sailed onward and made a very decent living, the best year grossing $250,000. Not bad for a twenty-three-year-old with a lot of gumption and a positive attitude!
—**Lisa M. Whited, ASID, IIDA, IDEC**

After starting a family, I needed more freedom than the large company I was employed with could offer me. As a mother of two children, I wanted more freedom in arranging my schedule to meet my family's and my client's needs. I had many clients of my own. At that point they were very willing to work around my family schedule; however, the corporate environment I was in was famous for 7:30 breakfast meetings,

and that was very difficult with children. However, you must remember that a steady paycheck has advantages during tough economic times. So each person has to weigh his or her need for freedom with the lack of security you have when you work for yourself.
—**Juliana Catlin, FASID**

I do not have my own practice. However, three years ago I had an opportunity to start up an interior design division within an established architectural office.
—**Jennifer van der Put, BID, IDC, ARIDO, IFMA**

Economics, control, freedom to succeed or fail by my own actions.
—**Derrell Parker, IIDA**

There was no one out there doing what we do.
—**Rosalyn Cama, FASID**

It seemed like a natural progression to grow in my field without the limitations of a structured corporate environment.
—**Sally Nordahl, IIDA**

To use my skills effectively and enjoy the experience of providing a positive design experience for my clients.
—**William Peace, ASID**

My entrepreneurial nature and a desire to be completely comfortable with management's decisions motivated me to start my firm.
—**Suzan Globus, ASID**

When I moved to the small town of Gainesville, Florida, thirty-three years ago, my only option was to start my own practice. I had worked for an independent design practice in Miami and wanted to continue to have the freedom to specify and design for my client's needs. I did not want to meet the quotas or specific manufacturer sales required by a furniture store or office furniture dealership.
—**Sally Thompson, ASID**

While I have ownership in my firm, I am one of several partners and unfortunately cannot take credit for starting the firm.
—**Janice Carleen Linster, ASID, IIDA, CID**

Control and freedom. Control over the type of practice I chose and freedom to work as I wish.
—**Cheri Gerou, AIA, ASID**

Marketing Methods

REGARDLESS OF WHETHER or not a particular interior design firm sells furniture and other products to the client, the essence of interior design is the provision of interior design services to clients. Marketing professional interior design services, however, is different from marketing products. Services are intangible; they do not exist until they are performed. The positive satisfaction the client is looking for cannot be realized until the project is done. Therefore, the client has to choose an interior designer on faith, hoping that the selected interior designer will provide the quality and professionalism required to complete the project. The interior designer must sell the client on his or her ability to solve the client's problem and execute the requirements within budget. This is why experience in a particular area of interior design, technical skills, and the designer's reputation are so important in the marketing of professional interior design services.

Because marketing can be done in many ways, it is important to know where the firm is trying to go. This is identified by developing a marketing plan. A big part of what goes into a marketing plan is the firm's goals. The goals of the design firm affect how the firm will market itself. For example, if the company wishes to grow, it must find a constant stream of new clients. When this is the case, a greater number of marketing methods are needed. On the other hand, if the firm wishes to remain small, marketing for new clients will likely focus on low-cost marketing methods such as referrals. Should the firm want to seek work in other geographic locations, marketing decisions must first be made to create awareness and obtain clients in those new areas. Firms whose goal is to enter a highly specialized area of design will need to employ different marketing activities than a generalist firm. These are just a few examples.

Most small firms obtain the majority of their new clients from referrals by existing clients. A referral occurs when a client provides positive comments about a firm to a potential customer. Providing excellent service and building a relationship with the client are the best ways to get referrals. Missed appointments and unfulfilled promises do not constitute excellent service. Caring about what the client needs rather than dictating to him or her is critical in establishing a positive relationship. You must develop a positive connection with the client in order for that relationship to build. Developing a good relationship with a client brings you back to the point of providing excellent service.

Generating referrals is just one way to market an interior design firm. Exhibit 5-1 lists a few marketing tools used by the professional interior designer. Most marketing activities are used to attract attention to the firm or to provide information about the firm. Whether the design firm places an advertisement in a local magazine, develops a website, or convinces a

Exhibit 5-1

Marketing Tools and Strategies

- business stationery, including logo
- company website
- project photos portfolio
- brochures
- advertising
- ongoing press release strategies
- entering projects in design competitions
- newsletters
- direct mail letters and flyers
- speaking at seminars
- distributing premiums
- preparing slides or CDs for presentations
- participating at industry conventions open to the public
- writing articles in local newspapers or other appropriate print media
- networking at events to meet potential clients
- multimedia marketing presentations

magazine to publish information about a project, the objective is to gain exposure that translates into an interview with a client so that a contract for a new project is developed.

Contracts

WRITTEN CONTRACTS ARE the best way to conduct business. One type of contract explains the services that will be provided by the interior designer. The other—often called a *purchasing agreement*—details the furniture and other interior goods the client has agreed to purchase from the designer. A contract signed by the client is the only legal recourse the designer has should the client not pay or otherwise try to get out of the project. If an interior designer begins design services without a contract or orders any goods before the client has signed a purchasing agreement, there is no way to ensure that the client will pay the invoices.

To be legally binding on the client, the document must contain these five elements:

1. the date
2. a description of the project location
3. the scope of services (for a contract for services) or a description of the goods to be sold by the designer to the client
4. the fee or price
5. the signature of both the client— the party being charged—and the interior designer

Exhibit 5-2

Elements of a Design Contract

- **Date:** Obvious, but necessary for the contract to be valid.
- **Description of project area:** It is important to identify the project area. For example, "provide design services for your residence at 1237 New York Avenue N.W., Washington, DC" is appropriate when you are responsible for designing the entire residence. When the project involves a smaller area, a phrase such as "for the remodeling of the family room and kitchen" is appropriate. This is done so you are responsible—and compensated—only for the areas of the project described in the contract.
- **Scope of services:** This section defines the services you will provide in order to complete the required work. Services are always listed in the order in which they will be executed relative to the design process (see chapter 2); this helps the client understand how the project will progress. The scope of services varies considerably depending on the size, type, and complexity of the project.
- **Method of compensation:** This critical element is a clear explanation of how the client will be charged and billed for the interior design services constituting the contract. A few common fee methods are explained in Exhibit 5-3. Designers can bill at the end of each month or with respect to the phases of the project. A retainer is usually required upon signing the agreement and is used to partially cover services to be performed.
- **Purchasing of goods:** If the designer intends to sell merchandise to the client, a clause is included that tells the client how this will be done. Relevant information includes terms of payment, pricing, and other details that clarify how the client will be charged for the merchandise sold by the interior designer.
- **Signatures:** A contract is not valid until the client signs it. Beginning work before you receive a signed contract is not good business practice, as you have no legal recourse to exact payment.
- **Other clauses:** Numerous other clauses can be included in a design contract. The more complex the project, the more complex the agreement. The items mentioned above, however, are the basic elements of every valid contract. See the references for books that detail other elements of strong, binding contracts for interior design services and the sale of merchandise.

Contracts for services can be fairly simple letters when the project is not complex. When they take this form, they are often called *letters of agreement*. As long as the letter of agreement contains the information on the above list, it is a binding legal document. However, when a project is complex, requiring several months or even years to complete, more formal contracts are prepared. A detailed, formal contract generally has additional clauses that deal with other responsibilities—a clause concerning arbitration in case of disputes; charges for extra services; disclaimers of responsibility for specific situations; ownership of docu-

ments; and other appropriate clauses are a few examples.

Very important in all contracts for design services are the clauses used to describe the scope of services. This element describes what will be done, how it will be done, and how much the client will be charged. The scope of services must be detailed to clarify the required work. If the scope of services is vague, then the designer can be responsible for providing services for no compensation. The design process described in Exhibit 2-1 mentioned many tasks that are included in a scope of services clause. Exhibit 5-2 explains several key clauses and sections of a contract for interior design services.

Designers who also sell goods must clarify in the design services agreement how this will be achieved. However, the contract for the sale of goods is different from the contract for services. This is because the law regarding the sale of goods departs somewhat from basic contract law. The interior designer prepares a separate document—most often called a *purchase agreement*—that explains what is being sold and the terms and conditions of the sale. Just as with the contract for design services, the purchase agreement for the sale of goods must be signed by the client, include a description of what is being sold along with prices and include the date the contract was offered to the client.

Lodging: lobby, Las Ventanas al Paraiso, Los Cabos, Mexico. Trisha Wilson, ASID, Wilson & Associates, Dallas, Texas. Photographer: Peter Vitale.

Restaurant (Hospitality) and Residential

LINDA ELLIOT SMITH, FASID

President, smith & associates, inc., and education-works, inc., Dallas, Texas

What has been your greatest challenge as an interior designer?
I think one of the greatest challenges of an interior design practitioner is the multitasking that is constantly part of the interior design process. This multitasking can sometimes become a great source of stress to the practitioner.

Restaurant: franchise prototype, dining area. Linda Elliott Smith, FASID, smith & associates, inc., Dallas, Texas. Photographer: Bill Lefevor.

What led you to enter your design specialty?
I got into restaurant design as a result of an opportunity that was presented, and it turned into a ten-year commitment to restaurant design. The residential aspect of my specialty actually was an outcome of an early opportunity for what I call contract/residential design, which involved the interiors of condominium/apartment developments throughout the Southeast.

What are your primary responsibilities and duties?
I am the principal in charge of all design processes.

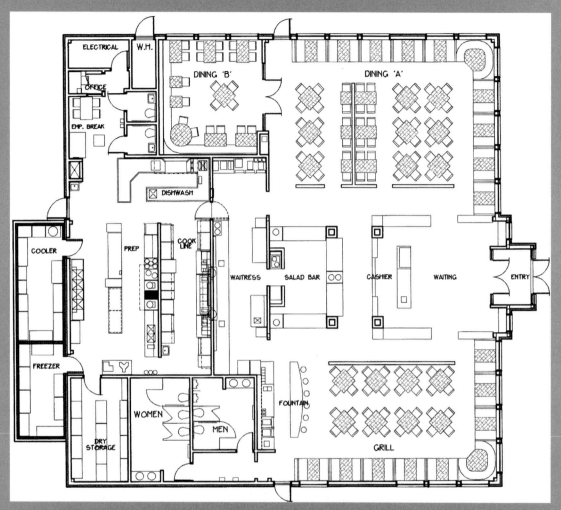

Restaurant: franchise prototype, floor plan. Linda Elliott Smith, FASID, smith & associates, inc., Dallas, Texas.

What is the most satisfying part of your job?
Knowing that I have met the clients' needs and fulfilled their expectations.

What is the least satisfying part of your job?
Dealing with people who have little respect for customer service and performance of project responsibilities.

What is the most important quality or skill of a designer in your specialty?
I think that in any specialty the most important skill is the ability to listen and then translate.

How important is interior design education in today's industry?

The knowledge gained through structured interior design education is invaluable as the basis for any practitioner. However, because the interior design profession continues to evolve and expand, the interior design practitioner's education must not stop at graduation. With sources, processes, and code requirements in a constant state of evolution, the interior designer must make a commitment to lifelong education.

Who or what experience has been a major influence on your career?

My involvement with the American Society of Interior Designers has provided me with skills and knowledge I could never have obtained out in the field. My association with other professionals nationwide has been one of the most enriching experiences of my life.

Restaurant: franchise prototype, counter. Linda Elliott Smith, FASID, smith & associates, inc., Dallas, Texas. Photographer: Bill Lefevor.

Hospitality, Municipal Government Facilities, Education Centers

Retail: store interior, Zie Spot, Norfolk, Virginia. Kristine S. Barker, CID, Hayes, Seay, Mattern & Mattern, Inc., Virginia Beach, Virginia. Photographer: Kristi Barker.

KRISTI BARKER, CID

Interior Designer
Hayes, Seay, Mattern & Mattern, Inc.
Virginia Beach, VA

What has been your greatest challenge as an interior designer?
One of the greatest challenges of interior design is finding your niche. I was fortunate to work in several types of design firms. I was exposed to residential design and commercial design and was able to determine what area would best suit my skills, interests, and personality. It can become discouraging when you are working in an environment where you do not feel successful. Continuing to explore your options and trying different project types until you determine where you can best apply your talent is the ultimate challenge.

What lead you to enter your design specialty?
After working in different environments with different personalities—you grow as both a designer and an individual. I found that my personality type was not suited for residential design—so I was able to avoid positions where that would be a focus. I learned in school that I was quite pragmatic—so commercial work was more suited to my interests and abilities. Projects where I could mix my pragmatic side with my desire for things to be creative, colorful, and fun has been my goal. Working on educational facilities like college student centers and hospitality oriented projects like restaurants have enabled me to work on projects that meet my professional goals and enhanced my strengths.

What are your primary responsibilities and duties in your position?

In my current position I am responsible for the interior design on all our projects in the Virginia Beach branch office. I am tasked with developing an interior design department for our office—which means I am working to develop and enhance our drawing standards and operational procedures. I also participate in the marketing of our company at industry and community events and mentoring of younger employees.

What is the most satisfying part of your job?

The most satisfying part of my job is the feeling of accomplishment I get when I have created a unique and viable solution for a project and the client is thrilled with the result.

What is the least satisfying part of your job?

The least satisfying thing is the frustration one can feel when a client just doesn't understand your design intent or is unwilling to release control over a situation and trust you to do your job to the utmost of your ability.

What is the most important quality or skill of a designer in your specialty?

One of my favorite quotes is from architect I.M. Pei:

"There are endless mysteries within discipline; infinite possibilities exist within a set of rules. It is not an individual act, architecture. You have to consider your client. Only out of that can you produce great architecture. You can't work in the abstract."

The client should come first and foremost in what you do. You must listen, even when you don't want to. You must bend a little, even when you don't think it's right. You must observe, even the most ridiculous things have a measure of value.

Food and beverage: Regattas Café & Market, Kingsmill Resort, Williamsburg, Virginia. Kristine S. Barker, CID, Hayes, Seay, Mattern & Mattern, Inc., Virginia Beach, Virginia. Photographer: Kristi Barker.

Entertainment: lower level, University Center, College of William & Mary, Williamsburg, Virginia. Kristine S. Barker, CID, Hayes, Seay, Mattern & Mattern, Inc., Virginia Beach, Virginia. Photographer: Jeff Hoerger.

Who or what experience has been a major influence in your career?

In my career I have been most influenced by my coworkers. I learned that it doesn't become you to be bitter and dour, overly self-involved, or chaotically disorganized. Approach each new project as a new opportunity for learning, be friendly, educate yourself on current events, listen. As a young designer, finding a mentor you can emulate is very important. I was fortunate to work with a designer who was a confident and independent career woman. I learned from her to develop a sense of style to compliment my strong technical skills. Her advice? Read all types of magazines, trade in your college wardrobe for one that conveys you have a sense of style, eat at fine restaurants, explore the world around you and be open to new adventures. My first mentor had admirable people skills and was able to deal with clients with ease. She taught me when to talk and when to close my mouth and listen. It can be difficult to learn that when you are an eager young designer right out of college!

Interior Design Revenue

As can be discerned from the section on contracts, interior design firms can obtain revenue by two methods. Residential interior designers most commonly generate revenue from the sale of the goods the client needs or by combining a design fee with the sale of merchandise. The most common method used by firms that specialize in commercial interior design is to charge the client a design fee for the required interior design services. Few professional interior design firms obtain their revenue solely from selling goods. This is more common in retail furniture stores and specialty stores that offer "free" interior decorating services.

Fees for professional interior design services can be calculated using several methods (see Exhibit 5-3). Because all designers have a limited amount of time to sell, an hourly fee is one of the most common ways for a designer to charge for services. In its simplest form, an hourly fee is charged for every hour or portion of an hour the interior designer works in the interests of the project as defined in the scope of services. The hourly fee approach is used by most service professionals, including attorneys, engineers, architects, and accountants.

How that hourly fee is determined is obviously an important question. It must be calculated to provide sufficient dollars to cover profit as well as the expenses of doing the work. Profit is the amount of money left over when expenses are deducted from what is charged to the client. Determining a fee amount for interior design services has three parts. The first is salary and benefits paid to employees. Next are operating expenses, which are overhead costs and other expenses not related to revenue production. The third factor is the desired profit. That profit can be realized only if the other two factors are accurately estimated.

The interior designer might also charge a fee for the project as a whole rather than by the hour. This is commonly called the *fixed fee* or *flat fee* method of determining fees for services. For example, after the scope of services is determined, the interior designer estimates how long it will take to complete the tasks, determines other costs of the project, such as printing scaled floor plans, adds a desired profit margin and then sets a fee for the project.

Some interior designers also gain revenue from the sale of merchandise or goods to the client. Interior designers, of course, can purchase merchandise for less than the consumer would. Interior designers (and others in the built-environment industry) then mark up the merchandise in order to produce revenue from the sale of those goods. There is no set markup because the seller—in this case, the interior designer—can sell merchandise to the consumer at essentially any price they like. (The buyer doesn't have to buy at that price, of course.) The markup amount represents additional

Exhibit 5-3

Fee Methods

- **Hourly fee:** This method is straightforward and similar to any professional service provider's primary fee method. The interior designer charges a set fee for every hour he or she works in the interest of the client's project. Interior design fees can range from $85 to over $200 an hour depending on the designer's reputation, experience level, and market competition. Due to competition, on average, it is common for the hourly rates of residential designers to be higher than those of commercial designers.

- **Fixed fee or flat fee:** The interior designer estimates a total fee for all the interior design services required for the project. The client agrees to pay one flat fee rather than an hourly rate. Contracts rarely allow the designer to charge the client additional fees if the fixed fee is insufficient to cover all actual project time.

- **Cost plus:** Using this fee method, the interior designer adds a percentage to the cost of the products needed for the project. Between 10 and 35 percent is usual, but the percentage can be higher. In most cases, the interior designer is also selling the required merchandise to the client or arranging for the purchase of goods in the client's name.

- **Retail:** The retail fee method, like the cost plus method, is related to the products specified for the project. In this case, the client pays the retail price for goods. Retail, often marked up a minimum of 100 percent from cost, is the price manufacturers recommend sellers (i.e., the interior designer and stores) bill consumers. For example, if the seller can buy a lamp from a manufacturer for $50, the retail price would be $100. In most cases, the interior designer also sells merchandise to the client.

dollars to the designer to help cover the expenses of operating the business and likely yields a certain amount of profit for the overall project.

Inherent problems exist, however, for the interior design firm that sells merchandise. When the firm takes on the ordering of goods, additional paperwork is needed to process the orders. In addition, the design firm must monitor the order and shipment of the goods to the job site. The interior design firm also has various responsibilities related to damages or loss in transit from the factory to the job site. When the goods are obtained from a source out of state, freight charges must be considered. Finally, the interior designer probably will have to spend more time at the job site to ensure that the merchandise is delivered and placed or installed properly. All these additional costs and expenses must be considered in the determination of the markup and added to the cost of the merchandise in order for the interior designer to realize any profit from the sale of the goods.

Legal Issues

As is true in every business and profession, the interior design professional can be affected by legal ramifications when work is incorrectly executed or otherwise outside normal professional performance. Clients can sue interior designers when work is done incorrectly. The first line of defense is to take on only those projects you know you are capable of doing with the utmost professionalism. The two areas of legal responsibility that most often affect working relationships relate to negligence and breach of contract.

Negligence, for the purpose of our limited discussion in this chapter, is when an interior designer does not use appropriate care in executing the project for the client, and the lack of care leads to some sort of harm. This can most often be summed up in the term *professional negligence*. When the interior designer is sued for professional negligence, he or she is accused of not doing the work in a manner that the courts define as normal for a professional interior designer.

Although negligence is very serious, many of these claims are negotiated to a resolution rather than going to court—unless, of course, serious injury has occurred.

Harm does not only mean physical injury. For example, if a business cannot open on time and the delay is due to a fault or error by the interior designer, then professional negligence has technically occurred. The interior designer can be accused of negligence if he or she specifies the project way over the budget or makes a mistake on the construction drawings such that construction work must be redone. For the most part, the interior designer is not literally sued by the client for these kinds of problems. Some compromise is usually worked out. However, this type of unprofessional work *can* lead to legal consequences that can harm the business and reputation of the interior designer.

Another legal issue that can involve the interior design professional is breach of contract. Once a contract between the interior designer and the client is signed, both parties have a responsibility to complete the tasks spelled out in the agreement. A breach of contract occurs when one of the parties to the contract does not do something agreed to in the contract. For example, if the interior designer is required to prepare the construction drawings and does not do so, he or she has breached the contract. If the contract calls for the client to pay design fees within thirty days of receiving the bill for those fees but the client does not do so, he or she has breached the contract.

Interviews

The interview is a critical hour in which you can make a good impression and convince the employer that *you* are the only person right for the job he or she is trying to fill. In that hour, it is up to you to build on the impression you made with the résumé that preceded your appearance at the office or studio. Remember that you only have one chance to make a first impression. That means everything about those first few minutes, from how you greet the receptionist to what you wear and how you shake hands can add or subtract from your interview opportunity.

You need to prepare for your interview to help you make it a positive experience and opportunity. First, reconfirm your appointment and make sure you know how to get to the office. Review your homework on the employer to be clear about what the firm needs, what they do, and how you can fit into the company. Then check your portfolio and rearrange it if necessary for the upcoming interview. Finally, prepare yourself mentally by going over the questions you anticipate the interviewer may ask you.

Even though the interior design profession is a creative one, the job interview is not a time to be too trendy or casual about your interview appearance. Even if you know the firm is casual in its business dress code, your apparel should be on the conservative side, meaning suits and ties for men, business suits or a dress with a jacket for women. Of course, residential firms are more accepting of trendier dress while commercial firms are generally more conservative.

When you arrive at the office or studio, try to relax as you wait for the interviewer. Some firms actually keep you waiting on purpose, and the receptionist reports later on how nervous or fidgety you were. So relax! Read a magazine and try to refrain from fidgeting with your portfolio or handbag. Everyone is nervous before an interview. Entry-level designers are even more nervous as they try to get that first great job. When the potential employer greets you, wait for him or her to shake your hand.

Some firms use team interviews or multiple interviews. In a team interview, one person leads the interview and then passes you to another member of the firm for additional questions. Team interviews are most common in large firms. You may experience multiple interviews instead. This means the firm may interview several potential employees on one day and then call back a few for more in-depth interviews. Multiple interviews can also be the pattern of large firms. If you apply to a small design firm, you will most likely be interviewed by the owner and not meet any other employee (other than the receptionist) unless the interview is going well and they are likely to offer you a position.

While you are being interviewed, don't bring up personal problems, argue, or sound like you are begging for the job. If you are asked if you have ever been fired, however, you need to be honest and say so if it's true. Briefly explain the circumstances without making it a focus of the interview. Some interviewers ask tough questions to see how you react under stress. The temptation might be to argue, but do not let that happen. Keep as cool as you can and focus on your strengths as they relate to the job.

Questions you are likely to be asked are:

- Why do you want to work for ABC Designs, Inc.?
- What do you know about our company?
- Tell me about the qualifications you have for this position.
- Tell me about yourself.
- How does your previous experience relate to this position?
- What are your strengths and weaknesses?

As the interview draws to a close, you will want to ask your questions about salary and benefits. If you understand the firm is interviewing several people for the position, be sure to ask when they will make a decision. If you are given an offer, be prepared to say yes. If the salary level of the offer or the type of job is quite different from what you were expecting, it is okay to ask for a day or so to decide. If you like the job but have another interview and want to wait until that interview, ask for overnight to decide. Don't make the employer wait—either one. If you like this offer, call and cancel the next appointment. Follow up all your interviews with a brief thank-you note. This is a courtesy that far too few people extend even though they should.

Many other strategies are involved in navigating interviews. Several of the books in the reference section can help you with specific questions.

Breach of contract between an interior designer and client seldom goes to court or requires the services of an attorney. In most instances, a compromise is worked out. Interior designers must be mindful of what they put into their design contracts and sales agreements. Whatever is stated must be done or provided—or, technically, the designer has breached the contract and the client may sue.

This discussion and the examples provided give you the very smallest explanation of legal responsibilities that affect the work of the interior designer. Several books listed in the references contain further information.

Libraries

SUZAN GLOBUS, ASID

President, Globus Design Associates
Red Bank, New Jersey

What has been your greatest challenge as an interior designer?
To keep focusing on how my work can enhance the lives of those using the space.

What led you to enter your design specialty?
I told a client I was considering starting my own firm, and he suggested I talk about offering interior design services to a library director who was building a new library. I started my own business with the contract for that library. Soon after, the referrals began and a specialty was born. It felt like a good fit for a former journalist.

Library: children's area, Ocean County Library, Little Egg Harbor Branch, Little Egg Harbor, New Jersey. Suzan Globus, ASID, Globus Design Associates, Red Bank, New Jersey. Photographer: Diane Edington.

What are your primary responsibilities and duties?
My primary responsibilities are obtaining new business, client communications, and managing staff.

What is the most satisfying part of your job?
Hearing clients describe how a finished project has changed their lives is most satisfying because it reminds me how profound the effects of a well-designed space can be on its occupants.

Library: reading area and staircase, Ocean Country Library, Brick Branch, Brick, New Jersey. Suzan Globus, ASID. Globus Design Associates, Red Bank, New Jersey. Photographer: Diane Edington.

What is the least satisfying part of your job?
The least satisfying part is managing poor staff performance, and I have been very fortunate in that regard.

What is the most important quality or skill of a designer in your specialty?
It is not specific to this specialty, but the ability to ask questions and listen to the answers has never failed to serve me well.

Who or what experience has been a major influence on your career?
Carlos Bulnes, a college professor who taught me that human beings are not an accessory in the space.

"How Important Is Certification by Examination and Licensing of Interior Designers Today?"

Living in a state where a practice act is in effect, I think it is very important to have laws that protect our right to practice. It is also important that the legislation include continuing education—so that the laws are similar to other professions like architecture and accounting.
　　—Ellen McDowell, ASID

Certification is necessary to become a full professional in the two major Interior Design Associations, as well as it is required to be "registered" in those states and provinces with Interior Design legislation.
　　—David Stone, IIDA

In my opinion, now is the time for interior design as a profession. Rules and exams and licensing are part of that evolution from job to profession. It is time we admit and celebrate the difference between design and decoration.
　　—M. Joy Meeuwig, IIDA

I believe it is an accepted method by which professionals seek to establish a recognized base line of skill and knowledge, and by which public entities seek to ensure the safety of the public.
　　—Sari Graven, ASID

We deal with too many areas of impact on HSW (health, safety and welfare) to not be licensed.
　　—Bruce Goff, ASID

It is the standard of today and the way of the future! Interior design affects the health and welfare of everyone in the design space. Provides a safe means of egress in emergency situations. Allows the disabled to live their lives on an equal level. These issues are too important to just hope the person knows how to design a space. It must be regulated.
　　—John Holmes, ASID, IIDA

If interior design is to survive as a profession then interior designers must become professionals, not hobbyists. With professionalism comes responsibility for the protection of the public (users, clients).
　　—Derrell Parker, IIDA

It is vital. It will define and protect our right to practice

our profession. Without it, our profession is vulnerable.
—**Suzan Globus, ASID**

To encourage our profession to reach to the level the professional designer needs it to be is the best argument for certification or licensing.
—**Debra May Himes, IIDA, ASID**

It certifies the commitment of the individual to their profession. Those that don't certify either have an ego issue about their abilities or are happy with the "lot" in life and are not interested in increasing their opportunities.
—**Linda Isley, IIDA**

VERY! It demonstrates a level of commitment the individual interior designer has to the profession. It legitimizes the profession for public consumption.
—**Jennifer van der Put, BID, IDC, ARIDO, IFMA**

Private residence: kitchen. Debra May Himes, ASID, IIDA, Debra May Himes Interior Design & Associates LLC, Mesa, Arizona. Photographer: Dino Tonn.

"What Is the Greatest Business Challenge for Interior Design Firms?"

Considering that many interior design firms are small, I believe the greatest challenge is maintaining the business side of the enterprise. Many firms seem to sacrifice business operations in favor of creative operations. This unbalance can be a death knell.
—Linda E. Smith, FASID

Finding a niche that matches the firm's skill set (this includes assembling a team whose members have the same skill sets) and then staying focused on that niche.
—Jeffrey Rausch, IIDA

I'd say that staying in a competitive mode during the ups and downs in the economy is the most difficult and challenging job facing any business owner today. The overall economy and the many directions it takes are a topic that all business owners need to keep a handle on if they want to remain in business. This takes planning and looking to the future so we are not blindsided by unexpected changes.
—Terri Maurer, FASID

Small firms? The need for the owner to be everything. Large firms? Keeping enough quality projects flowing in. Midsize? All of the above.
—Bruce Goff, ASID

To maintain design integrity and an ethical business practice on all projects.
—Beth Kuzbek, ASID, IIDA, CMG

Riding the ups and downs of the economy.
—Michelle King, IIDA

Flexing (firm and employees) with the economy.
—Stephanie Clemons, PhD, ASID, IDEC

To educate the public about what interior design firms do. The public needs to understand the value of good design—and the profession needs to understand the value of collaborating with other professionals (architects, engineers, landscape architects, and so on).
—Lisa Whited, ASID, IIDA, IDEC

Keeping a consistent run of projects coming in, in order to meet expenses. Using whatever marketing skills are needed to ensure referrals and interesting work. Taking on large and small designs to help even out the cash flow.
—Michael Thomas, ASID

Creating value for the client.
—Nila Leiserowitz, FASID

The greatest business challenge for most designers is simply being a good businessperson. Just because we are a creative bunch does not mean we should not also be good businesspeople. I think creative people often think they cannot be businesslike—but this is just not the case. The more businesslike one is, the more respect one commands, and thus the better a designer one is. To me, creativity and business go hand in hand.
—Charles Gandy, FASID, FIIDA

Finding the best partners—that is, the subcontractors who make your design a reality.
—Donna Vining, FASID

Staying current in a changing world.
—Fred Messner, IIDA

Getting paid for the real value of our expertise and services.
—Sari Graven, ASID

The greatest business challenges for interior design firms are to maintain accurate records of time, to write contracts/agreements, and to keep qualified employees. Time is money, and we have to earn a living while fulfilling our creativity.
—Sandra Evans, ASID

Continuing to bring in enough fee revenue to pay our designers what they are worth.
—Rita Carson Guest, FASID

The greatest business challenge today is to be diverse and flexible in services provided so as to prosper in any economic situation.
—Linda Sorrento, ASID, IIDA

First, there's a great deal of competition and people who are prepared to provide design services at unreasonably low fees. The greatest challenges are to recognize that interior design is a profession and a business and to be able to listen to clients and provide solutions for them—not just for the designer.
—M. Arthur Gensler Jr., FAIA, FIIDA, RIBA

Paperwork—keeping track of the minutiae inherent in design. Thank heaven for the Design Manager software program!
—Jan Bast, ASID, IIDA

Identifying the right road to profitability.
—Pat McLaughlin, ASID

Attracting and retaining experienced and talented designers in today's competitive workplace.
—Leonard Alvarado

Developing a good client base and remaining competitive.
—Sally Nordahl, IIDA

Making sure we stay within the scope of work for which we have contracted and that we are paid for all the work that is done. Keeping track of when the scope changes and communicating that to the client. Also, hiring competent staff and managing the staff you do have.
—Melinda Sechrist, FASID

Competitive fee structures in juxtaposition with real labor costs. Clients have been very successful in asking for the moon without expecting to pay for the level of professionalism we bring. We all need to respect our own abilities and agree that they are worthy of payment.
—David Stone, IIDA

Recessed economy.
—Beth Harmon-Vaughn, FIIDA

To reinvent ourselves, as the architectural community and furniture dealers have distilled our value into nothing more than furniture specifiers. We need to use research to show that our value is in how we change behavior.
—Rosalyn Cama, FASID

Balancing the art with the business of design. Managing personnel time so as to facilitate good design executed in a timely fashion.
—Marilyn Farrow, FIIDA

Today, the greatest business challenges for interior design firms are identifying our target market and building a marketing plan that grabs attention and showcases our skills and imagination.
—Greta Guelich, ASID

Professional viability is the greatest business challenge for small interior design firms. We keep meticulous records of time spent on individual projects, and we have historical data for many years on fees expended for various types and sizes of projects that enable us to accurately price new work. However, it's always difficult, if one is doing really creative design, to turn out a project at a profit. It takes tremendous effort to monitor productivity, keep billings current, and watch expenses. Work seems to come in clumps. On three occasions in the past twenty years, in a brief few months, every large project we had under contract was either abandoned or in abeyance. This type of loss is hard to recover from; one can't lay off employees who take years to train for healthcare design. At other times, so much work is coming in that it's like being on a treadmill that never stops. It never seems to be an even pace.
—**Jain Malkin, CID**

The greatest business challenge for interior design firms is to not lose sight of the company's goals and how to achieve them. It seems that in this busy world we can become immersed in what is happening today and not look out for the future. Having a business plan for your firm can make the dif-ference between calculated survival and luck.
—**Linda Santellanes, ASID**

Finding clients; getting projects completed on time and on budget.
—**Debra May Himes, ASID, IIDA**

Knowing when the business is too large and complex to be treated like the family checkbook. Finally admitting that we became interior designers for the creative aspect, not the day-to-day running of a business.
—**Derrell Parker, IIDA**

Understanding how to charge effectively for the services we provide. Many times, designers go beyond the scope of their fees for a project; because of our desire for the project to be fully complete, we get involved in many aspects not originally planned for. It is hard to stop the design process and say, "Hold on! This is not in our contract." We need to be more effective in charging and not giving away our design services.
—**Juliana Catlin, FASID**

Investment in new knowledge and research.
—**Neil Frankel, FAIA, FIIDA**

To educate the public about the talents and benefits of hiring an interior designer, and that we are worth the money.
—**Linda Isley, IIDA**

Keeping organized! We tend to be artistic and have trouble with the business side and planning ahead.
—**Ellen McDowell, ASID**

Reinventing the firm to meet the changing needs of the marketplace.
—**M. Joy Meeuwig, IIDA**

Marketing. Getting clients through networking, advertising, and referrals from clients to avoid rollercoaster income.
—**John Holmes, ASID, IIDA**

Marketing yourself and your profession.
—**W. Daniel Shelley, AIA, ASID**

Staying competitive without undermining the profession's value. I find some of my peers price their design services so low that they project a perception to the public that devalues interior design.
—**Jennifer van der Put, BID, IDC, ARIDO, IFMA**

In small firms, too many designer/owners try to do it all themselves. We need to hire the right people instead. We are not office managers, draftspeople, or assistants. Do what you do best: Design and work with the client.
—**Robert Wright, ASID**

Either keeping up your marketing efforts constantly, and I mean constantly, or convincing people that interior design is as important as the architecture and the construction job. It seems that there is always a nonprofessional around who feels he has a knack for design, and a project committee is tempted to try to save money by eliminating the interior designer. Often, of course, this costs them money—because they have to redo a bad paint selection, or replace inappropriate floor coverings, or live with very bad lighting—all problems that can be avoided if a proper professional does the job.

Or, perhaps the greatest challenge today is getting interior designers changed over from selling stuff to charging for their professional services.
—**Linda Kress, ASID**

To keep up with technology, to compete globally, to complete projects on a timely basis.
—**Alicia Loo, CID**

I would say developing core competencies that strengthen the firm for present and future needs. It is essential today to be versatile and flexible in the services offered in order to be able to meet all your clients' needs and to stay competitive with other designers. Over the years, Group Mackenzie Interiors has evolved with the needs of our clients. It is important to continue growing into new markets by developing and maintaining a diversified range of client types.
—**Susan B. Higbee**

Being professional in your business practices, which results in respect from clients, vendors, and others.
—**William Peace, ASID**

Education. If the field is not credible, it will not succeed in business. The profession will gain recognition by title only through education.
—**Cheri Gerou, AIA, ASID**

Educating the public about the value of using interior designers.
—**Suzan Globus, ASID**

To be successful economically while treating clients fairly, meeting their needs and expectations. A designer must

be able to work both *on* the business and *in* the business.
—**Sally Thompson, ASID**

I imagine the challenges of an interior-design-only firm may vary from those of a multi-disciplined architectural, interior design, and engineering firm. Speaking on behalf of all design disciplines within our industry, I believe our biggest challenge is the lack of recognition as a valued profession in comparison to other professions. Our profit margins pale in comparison.
—**Janice Carleen Linster, ASID, IIDA, CID**

I would say slow the economic climate is the greatest challenge facing design practices today. Because design is a want and not a need, clients can live without the expense until the climate changes.
—**Naomi Anderson**

Chapter Six

Educational Preparation

There was a time when individuals who had a good sense of color and enjoyed rearranging furniture could become decorators. In fact, many of the earliest decorators had very little formal training in the field. There was a reason for that: No real educational programs in interior design or decoration existed before the early part of the twentieth century. For anyone wishing to be a professional interior designer in *this* century, however, a formal education is required. In fact, in states that certify, register, or license interior designers, formal education is a requirement. In addition, the examination required for licensing and professional-level membership in the associations also requires formal education in interior design. The profession has become too complex to allow minimal educational preparation.

Interior design education in the early twentieth century evolved from the fine arts, home economics, and architecture. One of the most notable early schools where interior decoration courses were offered was the New York School of Fine and Applied Arts, now known as Parsons School of Design. Courses were added there after 1904 when a number of interested students helped encourage the formation of the educational program. Schools of fine art as well as colleges of home economics and architecture gradually added more classes and extensive programs of study. As the profession grew, curriculums became more comprehensive, acknowledging that interior decoration and interior design called for more than developing a sense for color and knowing furniture and architectural styles. Students and employers increasingly realized the importance of formal course work in the profession.

The profession changed dramatically after the Depression in the 1930s and World War II. Commercial interior designers in particular required more training in building systems and the development of construction drawings. Business and industry in the United States and throughout the world changed in the 1940s and 1950s, creating many specialties in interior design. Professionals working in these areas required even more specialized information to practice effectively.

If your goal is to be known as a professional interior designer capable of designing the interiors of high-end exclusive residences, a casino in Las Vegas, a children's hospital, or any kind of commercial interior, you must obtain formal education. The day of the self-taught decorator is long gone in this serious profession.

Educator

JAN BAST, ASID, IIDA
Design Institute of San Diego
San Diego, California

Why did you become an interior designer?
I had always loved reading floor plans, even as a child; I had worked for several developers—one in the architectural department—and had always been interested in space planning. And then the social worker in me also liked the idea of working with people to create living environments that functioned well.

What advice would you give someone who wants to be an interior designer?
Attend the best school possible, take a well-rounded group of general education classes (including psychology and sociology), and always maintain the highest standards in both schoolwork and your dealings with people.

What is the purpose of your program?
From our mission statement: "To teach, preserve, and expand the knowledge of design which is essential to the quality of life in the diverse society it serves, and to educate individuals capable of assuming significant roles in the interior design profession. Our objective is to educate interior designers who are prepared for the professional world they will enter upon graduation."

What are a few characteristics of a good student?
Attends class and participates in the class discussions; pushes herself to create the best work possible; asks questions; is involved in the design community, whether in a student chapter of ASID or IIDA or as a volunteer or participant in design community events.

How do you prepare students for the workforce?
Students must complete 135 hours of internship with an approved design or architectural firm.

What is the single most important skill a designer needs to be successful?
Empathy and intuition and honor.

How important is certification by examination and licensing of interior designers today?
Very important.

Educator

ROBERT J. KRIKAC, IIDA
Washington State University
Pullman, Washington

What advice would you give someone who wants to be an interior designer?
Make sure there is something about this profession that is your passion. Some days, it will be the only thing that can get you out of bed to face another day in the office.

What is the single most important skill a designer needs to be successful?
"Flexistence": a combination of flexibility, necessary to deal with the ever-changing nature of design projects, and persistence, required to bring a project to fruition.

What is the purpose of your design program?
The purpose of our program is to develop critically thinking graduates who have the necessary skills to identify and creatively solve design problems.

What are a few characteristics of a good student?
Passion about the work combined with the understanding that critical statements are about the work itself. An understanding that the professor is a guide, not an answer source, that the answers must come from the student's investigation and exploration of the issues. Flexistence.

How do you prepare students for the workforce?

In general, by instilling in them the need for passion and curiosity about the built environment. Specifically, through a range of interdisciplinary course work in project types; aspects of theory, history, and practice; experiential learning programs; travel; and interaction with practitioners. Our faculty members have a great deal of practice and academic experience and can relate classroom experiences to aspects of practice. They are able to show the students at all levels of the program how the material being covered is utilized by the profession.

How important is certification by examination and licensing of interior designers today?

These two steps are crucial if interior designers are to become respected as professionals.

Why did you become an interior designer?

I had wanted to be involved in the built environment since I was four or five. Of all the things going on, the workers and their tasks fascinated me the most. Being raised in a rural community, I did not encounter much emphasis on the design professions, but I took as many courses as I could that would prepare me for a career in architecture. I say *architecture,* as I had no idea that interior design was a profession unto itself. In college, I was exposed to the profession of interior design as a career option. When the possibility of a career path in interior design became clear, my academic life became much more exciting, engaging me in a much more passionate manner. After many years working in small architecture firms and then in the interiors group of a large AE firm, I obtained a master's degree and pursued a career in design education. Choosing the education path has allowed me to continue to be a part of the design profession and to give back something to this profession that has provided me such a satisfying career.

Four-Year Educational Preparation

THE MAJORITY OF degree programs in interior design are found in departments of interior design, fine arts, architecture, and human ecology. Depending on the college, university, or professional school and the department in which the program is located, the four-year degree can be a bachelor of science, bachelor of arts, or bachelor of fine arts. Several institutions offer a five-year bachelor's degree in interior design. These programs are most commonly associated with a college of architecture.

The number of semester or quarter credits required varies by institution. A four-year program commonly includes at least 120 semester credits, of which 60 or more are interior design–related. Institutions on the quarter system usually require 180 quarter credits, of which 90 quarter credits or more are interior design. This matches NCIDQ's qualification requirements in education at this time.

Let's look briefly at the type of course work you might experience in a typical four-year major in interior design. These programs all begin with a large dose of liberal studies classes in the first year. A few introductory classes in interior design and design theory, beginning drafting, whether manual or computer-aided drafting (CAD), and perhaps a basic art studio may be required during the first year.

The second year includes additional liberal studies classes as well as more intense interior design classes. This may be the point where you have the opportunity to expand on CAD skills and take classes in programming, furniture or architecture history, perhaps media classes to learn rendering, and other basic technical or art classes. Elective hours in business, fine art, or other areas of interest may also be taken.

Many schools require a portfolio of work to be presented for entry into the third and fourth year (sometimes referred to as professional-level classes). If this is the case, you submit examples of art and design work completed in the early classes as well as evidence of overall academic performance.

The third year is when the real interior design work begins! You are finally in major studio classes, where you produce floor plans, furniture layouts, and other basic design documents for small residential and/or commercial spaces. The third year is where the basic skills and theory classes are combined in studio classes that require design solutions commonly addressed by interior designers. Other design classes likely include technical classes related to materials, building structure, codes, and mechanical systems. Upper-level liberal studies classes and electives in other areas of interest to the student or required by the university are common in addition to the interior design and related major courses in the third year.

Classes in the fourth year are advanced studios that challenge you to plan and design larger complex spaces. Advanced classes in such areas as lighting design, business practices, and research are also required in the fourth year. Depending on the program, a senior thesis project or culminating project might be required. The fourth year also includes discussions about and development or refinement of your portfolio, résumé, and job-hunting skills. The last of the liberal studies and elective classes are also part of the fourth-year program.

If the school requires a fifth year of studies, this year is typically focused on an extensive special project—sometimes called a thesis project though it is not the same as a thesis produced in a masters degree program—investigated and developed over the year. The fifth year also allows students to take additional elective courses that prepare students achieve professional goals.

Many schools require an internship experience. This is an important opportunity for you to work for several weeks or up to a full semester in an interior design firm. Through the internship, you discover how to connect what you learned in classes and studios to the working world. The internship is usually taken either after the end of the third year or fourth year of classes. When is the best time? That varies with each student's overall performance in the first three years of course work as well as with the policies of the institution.

Postgraduate Education in Interior Design

Postgraduate education in interior design is important to many people in this profession. Most individuals who seek a postgraduate degree (masters or doctorate) do so because they are interested in teaching. Of the approximately fifty institutions offering postgraduate degrees in interior design, eight have a PhD (doctoral) program.

Education at the postgraduate level is generally oriented to research. The focus is on a thesis or a doctoral research effort in subject areas such as human factors, the history of decorative arts, and environmental design. Most programs allow for an individually designed program that may also include areas of practice such as facility planning and design, lighting

design, design for special populations, and professional practice.

Practitioners interested in moving up the ranks in the larger design firms sometimes obtain a master's degree in business administration or organizational management. These business-focused degrees provide the in-depth background the largest design firms often find valuable for their highest-level design and management staff.

A list of institutions offering postgraduate studies in interior design can be obtained from the Interior Design Educators Council (IDEC) website at: www.idec.org. The address and phone number of this organization are included in the appendix.

Educator

DENISE A. GUERIN, PHD, FIDEC, ASID, IIDA
University of Minnesota, St. Paul, Minnesota

What is the purpose of your design program?
To teach the relationship between design and human behavior and how to provide design solutions to support human behavior and needs.

What advice would you give someone who wants to be an interior designer?
Be prepared for labor-intensive projects that stimulate you to reach beyond your knowledge. Shadow interior designers from several areas of specialization (hospitality, healthcare, residential, corporate, etc.) and interview them so you have a good understanding what an interior designer does. Do this before you make up your mind to be an interior designer.

Work by Jamie Smith, student at Department of Design, Housing and Apparel, University of Minnesota, St. Paul, Minnesota.

What are a few characteristics of a good student?
Passion for design; good time management; curiosity about the world; critical thinking ability.

How do you prepare students for the workforce?
We prepare students to be the leaders of the profession. We do this with a heavy emphasis on research and theory. Students study the relationship of design and human behavior and how to identify and solve problems within this framework. In addition to course work and internships, we use a one-semester thesis project as a bridge between academic life and the work world.

What is the single most important skill a designer needs to be successful?
Communication skills (oral, written, drawing/sketching, drafting).

Why did you become an interior designer?
To work with people and improve their environments so they functioned better (remember, that was more than thirty years ago!).

How important is certification by examination and licensing of interior designers today?
I believe it is mandatory for all qualified interior design practitioners to be NCIDQ certificate holders and licensed/registered/certified if their jurisdiction has this regulation. With

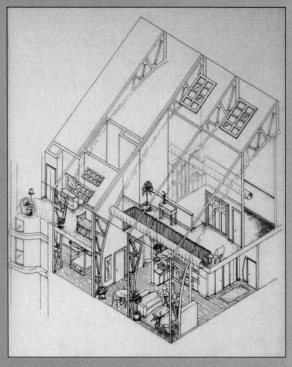

Work by Jamie Smith, student at Department of Design, Housing and Apparel, University of Minnesota, St. Paul, Minnesota.

the appropriate education and experience, interior designers can sit for the NCIDQ exam whether or not their jurisdictions are regulated. This is one way to improve the profession. Then, if it is possible to gain legal recognition in their jurisdiction of practice, interior designers must take the responsibility to do that so they can show they are able to protect the health, safety, and welfare of the public.

Work by Jamie Smith, student at Department of Design, Housing and Apparel, University of Minnesota, St. Paul, Minnesota.

Educator

TOM WITT, ASID
Arizona State University, Tempe, Arizona

What is the purpose of your design program?
The purpose of our program is to prepare verbally and analytically competent leaders for the profession.

What advice would you give someone who wants to be an interior designer?
Spread your education as broadly across the university curriculum as you possibly can—art, music, writing, chemistry, biology, and philosophy.

Perspective. Work by David Hobart, student at School of Design, Arizona State University, Tempe, Arizona.

What are a few characteristics of a good student?
Self-motivated and directed; a creative, critical, and analytical thinker interested in both art and science.

How do you prepare students for the workforce?
We have a faculty involved in both research and practice. Projects are grounded in the practice of the profession, and professional architects and interior designers are engaged regularly as consultants, as are practitioners of allied professions. The students are required to complete a summer internship under the direct supervision of a master designer.

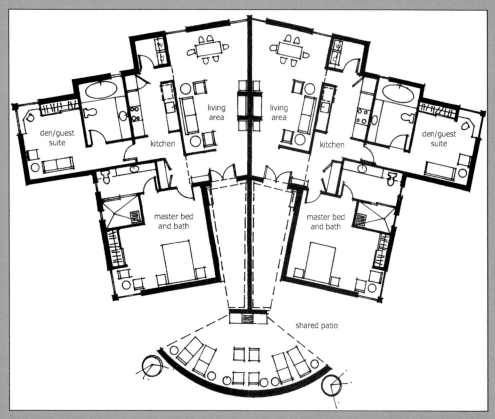

Floor plan of assisted living
facility. Work by Jill Gibney,
student at School of Design,
Arizona State University, Tempe,
Arizona.

What is the single most important skill a designer needs to be successful?

To be successful, the professional interior designer needs to be a critical, analytical thinker.

Why did you become an interior designer?

I love architecture and believe that interior design is the most intimate form of architecture, that is, has the greatest potential for improving the lives of people.

How important is certification by examination and licensing of interior designers today?

At the present time, registration does not seem very important. But registration is the next logical step in the evolution of the profession. The importance of registration is increasing, with more and more interior designers doing ever more complex projects and working in teams with architects and engineers. Increasing liability issues and the potential impact of this work on the health, safety, and welfare of the users will mandate registration.

Two-Year Associate Degree

NOT EVERYONE WISHES to spend four or five years in school pursuing a bachelor's degree in interior design. Perhaps you already have degree in another field and have decided to change careers and enter the interior design industry. The two-year degree offered by community colleges and some professional schools is referred to as an *associate degree*. Depending on the number of interior design classes, a two-year associate degree in interior design is acceptable to studios and retail stores that hire sales associates as well as interior designers. Generally, a two-year degree will not be sufficient to obtain employment with large interior design or multidisciplinary firms. Of course, some firms might hire an individual with a two-year associate degree in interior design and several years of full-time work experience in design or a related field.

At this time, two-year programs should require at least 40 semester credits or 60 quarter credits of interior design–related coursework in order to qualify for the NCIDQ exam. Not all two-year programs offer this amount of course work. Remember that states and provinces that legally register or certify interior designers unanimously require the NCIDQ examination for licensure. However, a jurisdiction may require a four-year degree for legal regis-

tration. Thus, it is important to check with your appropriate state or provincial registration agency, school or NCIDQ as the educational requirement to take the exam can change.

During the first year, introductory interior design classes such as basic design, color theory, history of furniture, textiles, and drafting are required. Most two-year programs require a number of liberal studies classes, especially English, math, science, and other liberal studies classes or electives. The emphasis is, however, on preparation in the major.

The second year emphasizes such classes as CAD, space planning, business practices, studio projects in residential and perhaps commercial interiors, and materials. Elective courses in interiors that allow the student to develop skills in space planning and furniture specification through project problem solving are encouraged or required. Of course, most programs also require students to study building and safety codes and mechanical systems. Most two-year programs also require students to complete an internship.

Students who have completed a two-year associate degree program can transfer to many four-year bachelor degree programs in interior design. Of course, the four-year program may require additional course work in liberal studies or other required preprofessional courses that were not a part of the two-year program. It is quite common to require transfer students to submit a portfolio of work to evidence skill mastery or overall performance.

Educator

MIMI MOORE, ASID, CID
San Diego Mesa College, San Diego, California

What advice would you give someone who wants to be an interior designer?

- Do a self-assessment and ask the following questions: How do you see yourself in the future? What lifestyle do you want? What kind of an income do you need? What makes you happy?

- Do research: Do informational interviews with practicing interior designers. Develop a list of questions to ask the practitioners. Ask to see examples of projects they do. Review a variety of interior design textbooks to gain an overview of the subject matter content required. Read the description of a professional interior designer.

After completing the self-assessment and research, answer the following questions: Do I want to be an interior designer? Why?

Work by Pamela Parvini, Kim M. Pilla, Doreen Owens, Sandra Jimenez, Kathie Missett, and Pat Richter, students San Diego Mesa College, San Diego, California.

What is the purpose of your design program?

Our program is designed specifically to put graduates into the workforce. Many of our students are changing careers and already have degrees in other fields. We also have a transfer track for those seeking a bachelor's degree.

What are a few characteristics of a good student?

Inquisitiveness, open-mindedness, and self-motivation.

Work by Sandra Jimenez, Kathie Missett, Doreen Owens, Pamela Parvini, Kim M. Pilla, and Patricia Richter, students San Diego Mesa College, San Diego, California.

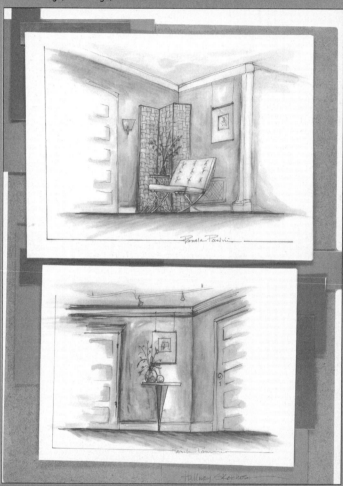

What is the single most important skill a designer needs to be successful?

Many skills are important, but the one that has been the most helpful to me is flexibility.

How do you prepare students for the workforce?

Students complete the required course work. They have many opportunities through their classes to hear guest speakers and to take field trips related to interior design. Part of the course work is an interior design work experience (internship) where students are placed in a design firm for 180 hours during the semester. This experience may be repeated. They also have the opportunity to participate in community service projects that compare to real work. Our student chapter of ASID provides exceptional extracurricular learning experiences also.

Work by Pamela Parvini, Kim M. Pilla, Doreen Owens, Sandra Jimenez, Kathie Missett, and Pat Richter, students San Diego Mesa College, San Diego, California.

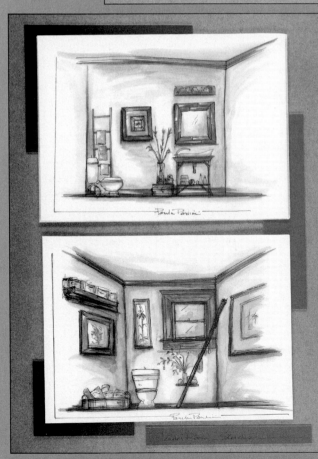

Why did you become an interior designer?
I wanted a way to express and use my fine arts background, so I pursued a degree in interior design.

How important is certification and licensing of interior designers today?
It is very important if we want to see our profession progress. We stand a chance of losing our right to practice.

Work by Sandra Jimenez, Kathie Missett, Doreen Owens, Pamela Parvini, Kim M. Pilla, and Patricia Richter, students San Diego Mesa College, San Diego, California.

Educator

SUSAN COLEMAN, FIIDA, FIDEC
Orange Coast College, Costa Mesa, California

What are a few characteristics of a good student?
Curiosity, motivation, readiness to learn, passion about design.

What is the single most important skill a designer needs to be successful?
Communication skills, a genuine interest in people, and a willingness to work to meet their needs.

What advice would you give someone who wants to be an interior designer?
Get experience/internships or work-based learning as part of your educational experience to give you the necessary skills; understand the relevance of what you are learning in the classroom to the practice of interior design and to help you confirm that you really do want to be an interior designer.

What is the purpose of your design program?
To educate entry-level designers for the profession of interior design. To help students make good career choices and understand all of the requirements of becoming a professional interior designer.

How do you prepare students for the workforce?
We provide them with the education and experience to function in the workplace as an interior design assistant. We provide them with learning experiences related to the real world so they can see and experience the relevance of what they are learning in the classroom to what they will be doing in the profession of interior design.

How important is certification by examination and licensing of interior designers today?
I think certification is vital to the practice of interior design. Until we have certification or legal recognition in all states, we will not have credibility as a professional practice.

Why did you become an interior designer?
It was an evolution from birth. I was always drawing, painting, coloring, and making things with my hands. I had a lot of exposure to all types of design, but it was the college program that helped me focus on interior design.

Educator

DENNIS McNABB, ASID, IDEC

Houston Community College System/
Central College, Houston, Texas

What is the single most important skill a designer needs to be successful?
Communication.

Model of barrier-free kitchen.
Work by Bev Newman, Allied Member, ASID, student at Houston Central Community College, Houston, Texas.

What advice would you give someone who wants to be an interior designer?
Do your homework concerning all aspects of the profession.

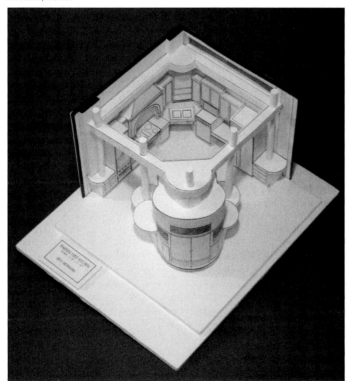

What is the purpose of your design program?
To train the individual in as short a period of time as possible to become employed.

What are a few characteristics of a good student?
Organization, focus, and determination.

How do you prepare students for the workforce?
Provide them the technical skills needed to become employed in the profession.

Sample Board. Work by Bev Newman, Allied Member, ASID, student at Houston Central Community College, Houston, Texas.

How important is certification by examination and licensing of interior designers today?

I have mixed feelings about this question but would have to say that for many aspects of interior design it is vital for the future of the profession.

Why did you become an interior designer?

I have always wanted to create. I found early on that my talents led me to interior design. I have always had a passion for creating environments where people felt nurtured and appreciated the space.

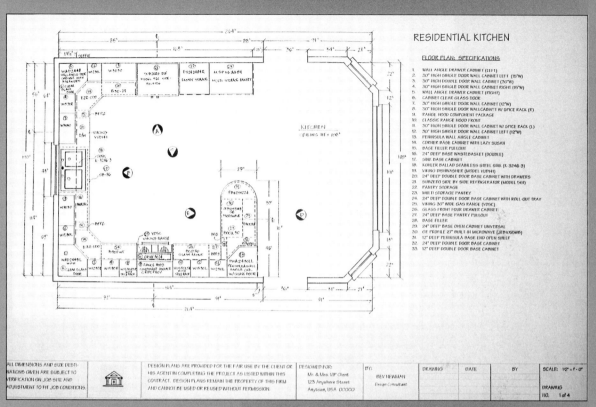

Floor plan. Work by Bev Newman, Allied Member, ASID, student at Houston Central Community College, Houston, Texas.

Choosing an Educational Program

CHOOSING THE EDUCATIONAL program that is right for you is a highly individual process. One of the key determinants in this decision is your goal in the profession. For example, if your goal is to work in a large commercial interior design or architecture firm, you must complete a four- or five-year baccalaureate program. If you would rather work in a smaller firm or already have a bachelor's degree in another area, a two-year community college or professional school program might yield many excellent job opportunities that satisfy your goals.

One factor in choosing an educational program is whether it meets the requirements you need to qualify for the NCIDQ examination. As noted above, states and provinces that license interior designers require the NCIDQ exam for licensure. If the program you are considering does not meet the minimal educational requirements established by your state or province and by NCIDQ, you will not be allowed to take the exam. This could limit your role in the interior design profession even if your jurisdiction does not have interior design legislation at this time. More states are regulating the prac-

By the Numbers

According to FIDER, approximately 115 baccalaureate programs are accredited in interior design and an additional 15 pre-professional programs that are non-baccalaureate programs—are FIDER-accredited. As of 2003, pre-professional level programs will no longer be accredited by FIDER. Those that are will have to seek accreditation at the professional level of curriculum when it is time for them to renew accreditation. An estimated 19,000 students are enrolled in these accredited programs. Courses are taught by an estimated 500 full-time, 350 part-time, and 800 adjunct faculty members. Interior design education has been a fast-growing program at many schools. There is no accurate estimate of how many students enroll annually beyond the figures estimated by FIDER; it is likely to be several thousands. Many other schools offer some kind of interior design program. These range from a few classes meant for students interested in working in a retail store as a sales associate to strong two-year associate and baccalaureate programs that might prepare students to work in interior design firms.

Foundation for Interior Design Education Research (FIDER)

FIDER is a private not-for-profit organization whose purpose is to lead the interior design profession to excellence by setting standards and accrediting academic programs. It was founded in 1970 and is the recognized body for accrediting interior design educational programs in the United States and Canada.

An interior design program that receives FIDER accreditation offers interior design–related course work that develops knowledge, skills, and abilities in design fundamentals, the design process, space planning and furniture planning, building systems and interior materials, regulations and standards that affect interior design, business and professional practice, communication, and professional values. In addition, accredited programs include a minimum of 30 semester credit-hours of liberal arts, sciences, and humanities courses. The exact mix of classes is left to the individual school as long as student learning demonstrates achievement of FIDER standards.

FIDER standards for accrediting academic programs are maintained through research into the field of interior design and building community consensus regarding requirements to enter the profession. FIDER maintains a close relationship with the major professional associations and the National Council for Interior Design Qualification (NCIDQ) through representation on the board of directors. Many state regulatory bodies governing use of the title or practice of interior design refer to FIDER in their educational requirements.

Over 100 FIDER-accredited programs are taught in the United States and Canada. For more information about FIDER accreditation, contact the organization through www.fider.org. The address and phone number of this organization are included in the appendix.

---

tice of interior design all the time, and the NCIDQ examination will most likely be the primary licensing tool in these states as well. (See chapter 1 for further discussion on this topic.)

Another factor to consider in choosing your educational preparation is the faculty. The background and experience of those teaching the classes is important. A strong faculty whose members have practice backgrounds is vital. In four- and five-year schools, one or more of the faculty may be oriented to research rather than practice. These teachers provide valuable instruction in lecture classes such as design theory and history of furniture. Both practitioners and research-oriented faculty are important to the program.

Some faculty members are full-time, providing classroom instruction, academic and career advising, and administration of the program. Other schools utilize part-time faculty members who work full-time as professional interior designers and teach one or two classes. One learns from both kinds of faculty members. Full-time faculty are more common in four- and five-year programs, and part-time teachers are commonly used in community colleges. Of course, four- or five-year programs also have some part-time teachers to fill certain teaching slots, just as community college interior design programs can have one or more full-time faculty members. The background, design interests, and teaching schedule of the faculty may be important considerations for you when choosing a program.

FIDER accreditation is another important factor to consider when selecting an interior design program. Accreditation from FIDER means that the curriculum, faculty, facilities, and support of the school's administration meet standards accepted by the profession. In fact, some states require that licensed interior designers who practice in that state have graduated from a FIDER-accredited program.

Investigate the curriculum and faculty, visit the facilities, and even ask for names of graduates who might talk to you about the preparation they received. Talk to potential employers as well to find out what kind of educational preparation they require of entry-level employees. All this research will help you determine the right academic program for your goals and needs.

Private residence: hall table and mirror. Greta Guelich, ASID, Perceptions Interior Design Group LLC, Scottsdale, Arizona. Photographer: Mark Boisclair.

Commercial Offices and Tenant Improvement

SUSAN HIGBEE

Director of Interior Design, Group Mackenzie,
Portland, Oregon

What has been your greatest challenge as an interior designer?
I think initially, it was establishing a role that was accepted and recognized in the industry as essential to the architectural design process. Our culture here, is that architecture and interior design is an integral process. Our best successes are produced when we have a collaborative team working on a project.

What lead you to enter your design specialty?
I have worked in all aspects of interior design, but I have seen the greatest challenges and rewards in Commercial Interiors. It is a very fast paced industry with many different project types. Clients are not involved so much on a personal level, and hire you for your expertise and direction to lead them through the process. It is exciting every single day.

Corporate: employee café, Regency Blue Cross Blue Shield of Oregon. Susan Higbee, Group MacKenzie, Portland, Oregon. Photographer: Sergio Ortiz.

Corporate: office lobby, Krause IV office building. Susan Higbee, Group MacKenzie, Portland, Oregon. Photographer: Randy Shelton.

What are your primary responsibilities and duties in your position?

I am currently the Director of Interiors at Group Mackenzie. I direct a staff of seven interior designers. I also manage larger teams that consist of a multi-disciplined group of architects and engineers depending on the nature of the project. My primary departmental responsibilities include management of the following:

- Workload distribution
- Team collaboration
- Team performance and efficiency
- Quality control of work output
- Quality of design
- Fiscal performance
- Staff development

As a senior leader in the firm, I am also responsible for Business Development for interior design and space planning/tenant improvement projects.

What is the most satisfying part of your job?
Satisfying the client is the most rewarding part of my job. It brings great pleasure to gain the confidence of a client, and to meet their needs no matter what the challenge brings.

What is the least satisfying part of your job?
I do not enjoy anything that compromises the ability to provide this service.

What is the most important quality or skill of a designer in your specialty?
I think it is most critical to be skilled at listening and understanding the functional requirements for a project. A commercial project will have many functional requirements that must be met to be successful operationally. It is our job to provide innovative, aesthetic environments while meeting the functional requirements. If this is done poorly, businesses loose efficiencies. If done well, businesses can see increased efficiencies as well as improvement in morale, worker productivity, etc.

Who or what experience has been a major influence in your career?
Growing up overseas in Japan played a significant role in influencing my career. It was the upbringing in different cultures that made me aware that everything in your environment shapes who you are.

Corporate: office lobby, Waggener Edstrom office. Susan Higbee, Group MacKenzie, Portland, Oregon. Photographer: Randy Shelton.

The Importance of Internships

MOST EDUCATIONAL PROGRAMS require students to complete an internship experience. The internship is the students' opportunity to work for a concentrated period in a practitioner's studio or office. Often, each student's adviser or another faculty member arranges the internship with input from the student. Most schools involve students in setting up their internship experience to give them valuable interviewing experience.

Each internship experience is different. Depending on the actual office needs and the student's requirements and interests, the intern might spend time assisting designers in researching products for specifications, preparing sketches, drafting floor plans or other drawings needed for construction documents, meeting with clients and the practitioner designer, and attending meetings or presentations by vendors and suppliers. Not every student gets the opportunity to actually work on portions of projects. Some may serve as a strong support person to a senior designer, helping make product specification decisions and developing specification documents. Other offices give students the opportunity to prepare drawings—always under the supervision of a professional designer.

In general, the larger the design firm, the more structured the internship. Students may spend a portion of the internship doing "grunt work": filing in the design library of catalogs and samples; visiting showrooms to search for appropriate samples; drafting small details needed in construction drawings. As mundane as these tasks may appear to the student, they are a part of the profession. Gradually, the student may be allowed to sit in on client interviews, draft more important parts of the construction documents, and have more direct interaction with the senior designers in the firm.

It is important for the student and the faculty members responsible for supervising the internship experience to carefully discuss and evaluate the student's abilities and career interests before determining an internship location. Although any internship experience teaches the student valuable lessons about actual professional work, one established to closely support the student's goals and current skills will be most valuable to his or her overall educational preparation.

Continuing Education

AS WITH ANY PROFESSION, interior designers must keep up with the latest advances in technology, business practice, regulations, and information on the design specialties in which they work, and they must continually improve their design skills. One way this is done is by taking continuing education unit (CEU) seminars and workshops. Some jurisdictions require a certain number of CEUs in order for practitioners to renew their license or certification.

CEU seminars and workshops are of varying lengths, depending on the topic and outline. Seminars can be as short as one clock hour, which will earn participants .10 CEU credits. For example, the interior designer can take a seminar on a specific aspect of marketing for one hour. Another workshop on a broader topic in marketing might last for three hours and be worth .30 CEU credits. An all-day workshop on working with markers as a method of doing renderings could be worth from .60 to .80 CEU credits.

Programs are available through the professional associations at national and chapter programs and meetings. Major trade markets for interiors products also offer continuing education seminars. Correspondence courses enable interior designers who cannot travel to study at their convenience.

Upon completion of the seminar, the designer participant completes forms that are forwarded to NCIDQ. Registering the completion of classes is especially necessary for designers who work in jurisdictions that require a certain number of CEUs per year to retain legal registration. Some employers require employees to register the course completion to obtain reimbursable funding.

Of course, designers can take college-level classes to upgrade skills or add new knowledge areas. For example, it is not unusual for practitioners to take college-level business classes, perhaps to obtain a masters degree or simply to increase their knowledge in specific areas of business. College-level classes are not eligible to receive CEU credits, however.

Continuing Education Units (CEU): Facts

Seminars are approved by the Interior Design Continuing Education Council (IDCEC).

Members of the Council are:
- American Society of Interior Designers
- Interior Designers of Canada
- Interior Design Educators Council
- International Interior Design Association
- Network of Executive Women in Hospitality

According to NCIDQ, approximately 8,000 CEU classes are approved by IDCEC. Seminars emphasize knowledge, skills, and competencies in a wide range of interior design practice knowledge.

Specific courses are approved in the areas of:
- theory and creativity
- interior design (such as design process, universal design, and space planning)
- interior design education
- design specialties
- technical knowledge (such as lighting, acoustics, and textiles)
- codes and standards
- communication systems
- business and professional practice
- ethics
- history and culture

Healthcare, Education, Offices

M. JOY MEEUWIG, IIDA
Owner/sole proprietor
Interior Design Consultation (IDC)
Reno, Nevada

Healthcare: seating alcove, General Surgical Unit, Washoe Medical Center, Reno, Nevada. M. Joy Meeuwig, IIDA, Interior Design Consultation, Reno, Nevada.

What has been your greatest challenge as an interior designer?
Proving, over and over, that I have a valuable service to offer. Also, re-creating my niche as the market changes. I kept the fortune from a fortune cookie that pretty much says it all: "You are capable, competent, creative, careful. Prove it."

What lead you to enter your design specialty?
When I began my career as an instructor of interior design at a small university, a new School of Nursing building was being constructed. The faculty needed decision-making help. My scope of work evolved from helping thirteen professionals agree on a color scheme to developing the finish schedule and writing furniture specifications of the total facility. When I made the move from professor to practitioner in the late 1960s, the thing called "systems furniture" was becoming known. There seemed to be a niche for a commercial designer/specifier in my small metropolitan market. And, my personality type and style are much better suited to commercial work than to residential work. The medical specialty happened because it was the piece of the market left over after the local furniture dealers took their piece of the design pie. Once I started working with medical, I found it fit. Solving functional and code problems are a challenge. And as one gets older, meeting healthcare needs has meaning! I guess my work is very personal to me.

What are your primary responsibilities and duties in your position?

As a sole practitioner, I am responsible for everything from creative to clerical. My style is to become an attachment to and extension of the client, whether an architect, a facilities department, or an end user. When a client retains my firm, they retain my commitment.

What is the most satisfying part of your job?

I remain a sole practitioner because I get my satisfaction from the totality—from the "idea" to moving day and beyond.

Hospitality: Hidden Valley Country Club, Reno, Nevada. M. Joy Meeuwig, IIDA, Interior Design Consultation, Reno, Nevada. Photography by Perspective Image, Seattle, Washington.

What is the least satisfying part of your job?

The least satisfying part of my job is "politics."

What is the most important quality or skill of a designer in your specialty?

Regardless of specialty, the most important skill is the ability to make decisions.

Who or what experience has been a major influence on your career?

Education and educators! A high school art teacher showed me new options. A college professor of interior design helped me focus on a path. Studying the pioneers of late nineteenth and early twentieth century American architecture showed me the power of the built environment.

Educator

SUE KIRKMAN, ASID, IIDA, IDEC
Harrington Institute of Interior Design
Chicago, Illinois

Steel table. Project: Experimental Design. Work by Pawel Witkowski, student at Harrington Institute of Interior Design, Chicago, Illinois.

What advice would you give someone who wants to be an interior designer?
Find a very good school that specializes in curriculum based on industry needs and whose faculty comprise by professionals in the field who have academic credentials.

What is the single most important skill a designer needs to be successful?
Attention to and understanding of human behavior and to people's needs and wants. The designer needs to be able to listen carefully, interpret the *real* needs and concerns, and then solve the issues.

What is the purpose of your design program?
To educate students with a body of knowledge and level of experience that prepares them for above-entry-level positions in the design industry.

What are a few characteristics of a good student?
Focus and good class preparation. Attention to detail in all things. Strong time management skills combined with team and individual skills.

Chair. Project: Experimental Design. Work by Kathleen Ferris student at Harrington Institute of Interior Design, Chicago, Illinois.

How do you prepare students for the workforce?

All students are required to take a minimum of 300 hours of approved internship along with a practicum course that works through job issues such as goal setting, preparing for the NCIDQ, professional organization, employment issues (sexual harassment, job interviewing, résumés, and working with clients). Students also take a portfolio class, which helps them define and refine their portfolio and customize it with technology.

Why did you become an interior designer?

To use my creative response to interior space in a unique way; to solve problems for the client so as to enhance their use of an interior space; to fulfill a natural curiosity about how space is used.

How important is certification by examination and licensing of interior designers today?

Because we deal with health and safety issues and issues that affect the human condition—how we move, feel, understand, function, and so on—it is important that interior designers have the education, experience, and training necessary to make those decisions.

Double lounge chair with table. Project: Experimental Design. Work by Natalie Schebil, student at Harrington Institute of Interior Design, Chicago, Illinois.

Educator

JOY DOHR, PHD, FIDEC, IIDA
University of Wisconsin—Madison
Madison, Wisconsin

What is the single most important skill a designer needs to be successful?
Be a creative and critical thinker; demonstrate that you see, know, and can make something.

What advice would you give someone who wants to be an interior designer?
Obtain a solid education, build knowledge of the complex relationships of humans and their environments; sustain and develop skills in working with people in their places and know how to listen and interpret needs; know architectural interiors, material and visual culture, history, business practice, and communication. Learn to see, to listen, to think creatively, and to make; be passionate about what you do and about past, present, and future opportunities; be a good communicator, both orally and in writing and in visual, technical, architectural, and quantitative symbols. Be culturally sensitive.

How do you prepare students for the workforce?
Besides attending to our teaching/learning and design research mission, we involve students in campus service projects; team projects with other majors; interaction with practitioners and industry representatives in class critiques; engage actual clients; complete case studies; have a required internship and professional practice course; and encourage students to participate in professional events.

What are a few characteristics of a good student?

Good students are reflective and contemplative; they are passionate about design; they are energetic, productive, responsible, disciplined, and timely. They seek to develop knowledge and skills; to obtain a wealth of interesting information, understanding, and application of design research; to grow through student/faculty interaction and sharing. We must bring these characteristics to the teaching/learning experience. For example, I put the following in my course syllabi:

- Be contemplative—read, study, think, and get to know the topic in a new way.

- Be passionate about design. Beauty is a manifested, physical reality of a sound idea, a caring, knowledgeable interpretation of client's needs, the content of an inner person that speaks to others. These will be heard if you care enough.

- Be energetic and productive—care for, state, and make things better.

- Be timely—be disciplined and on schedule—focus on the task at hand.

Why did you become an interior designer?

For multiple reasons:

- To be a steward to our environment, creating designs that work, are inspirational, and focus on the quality of life for humans.

- To be engaged in a field that is interdisciplinary in nature, is creative, and that involves people their places, paths, and products.

- To be in a field that requires me to use my whole brain and other talents, requires both analytical abilities and synthesis toward a sense of order, and that offers equality and efficiency.

How important is certification by examination and licensing of interior design?

Extremely important. Regulatory agencies and expected credentials are part of practice for any profession. Interior design is a practice, and to stay current you must meet expectations and continue to develop and inform your practice. These steps are part of that development.

NCIDQ Examination

ONE CRITERION OF a profession is the administration of an examination that tests professional competency. For interior design, the NCIDQ examination is the professional benchmark. This examination is required by state and provincial regulatory agencies where practice regulation and licensing exist. The examination is also required by the ASID, IIDA, IDEC, and IDC professional associations in order for members to advance to the highest level of membership.

The NCIDQ is a private, not-for-profit corporation founded in 1974. Its primary purpose is to develop and administer the examination used to provide credentials to professional interior design practitioners. Its other responsibilities include identifying public health, safety, and welfare issues; defining, researching, and updating bodies of knowledge; and analyzing the performance of exam candidates. In addition, the NCIDQ is responsible for records maintenance on certificate holders, continuing education credits taken by practitioners, working with authors to develop single-topic monographs, and administering the Interior Design Experience Program (IDEP), an internship program for entry-level practitioners.

The current examination is an intensive two-day, three-part test consisting of multiple-choice questions and practicum sections. The multiple-choice sections test the candidate's knowledge about practice issues in all sections of the design process. The practicum sections require the candidate to produce a design solution, and create a floor plan and other common design drawings or documents.

To take the examination, candidates must have six years of education and work experience, including at least two years of interior design study. Graduates of four- or five-year interior design programs must have two years of full-time interior design work experience as well. Candidates who have a two-year certificate in interior design need four years of full-time work experience in interior design to qualify for the examination. The NCIDQ has announced that by January 1, 2009, candidates will be required to have three years of interior design education and three years of work experience. Address your specific questions on your qualifications to the NCIDQ.

Programs and materials are available to help candidates prepare for the examination. A study guide including practice practicum sections is available from NCIDQ. The ASID offers a program called Self-Testing Exercises for Preprofessionals (STEP). This is an intensive weekend study program—open to any examination candidate regardless of association affiliation—covering both the practicum and multiple-choice sections of the examination. Some community colleges offer study workshops.

Completing the NCIDQ examination should be a goal for all professional interior designers whether or not they work in a state or province with licensing legislation or wish to affiliate with a professional association. The exam is a measure of competence that, in conjunction with your design education, indicates to potential clients that you are a professional.

Commercial, Hospitality: Food and Beverage

CORKY BINGGELI, ASID

Principal, Interior Designer
Corky Binggeli Interior Design
Arlington, Massachusetts

What has been your greatest challenge as an interior designer?
Because I have my own, one-person firm, and work from a home office, I miss out on the exchange of information, feedback on design, and peer support that a larger office provides. After the BAC (Boston Architectural Center), I formed a small group of designer friends, who got together to exchange job leads and talk about our work. I still keep in touch with these folks, and I also benefit from membership in ASID, which gives me a wide network of design relationships. I have also developed a close relationship with another designer, Christina Oliver, ASID; we share sources, sometimes do projects together, occasionally refer clients to each other, cover for each other on vacations, and generally enjoy our friendship and mutual support.

Retail: Linear Aveda Salon & Spa, Boston, Massachusetts. Corky Binggeli, ASID, Corky Binggeli Interior Design, Arlington, Massachusetts. Photographer: Gregg Shupe.

What lead you to enter your design specialty?
While I was at BAC, I became interested in restaurant design. Soon after leaving, I interviewed with someone who was opening a restaurant and wanted a student designer to do the design for free. I got the job, but also insisted on a modest fee. The project—the Iguana Cantina in Waltham, MA—was a success, and got quite a bit of publicity, mainly because of the 28-foot-long robotic iguana that I built with three of my friends. This led to other projects for the same and for other clients, and I was on my way.

What are your primary responsibilities and duties in your position?
I pretty much do everything from marketing to designing, construction drawings, bookkeeping, and filing. My husband, Keith Kirkpatrick, helps me with a sideline, scheduling local artists to show their work at several of my client's restaurants. I teach one course per term, either at Wentworth Institute of Technology or at Mount Ida College. I have also written a book, *Building Systems for Interior Designers*, published by John Wiley & sons.

What is the most satisfying part of your job?
I love the types of projects and the clients that I get to work with, mostly entrepreneurial owner/operators of restaurants, hair salons, and fitness centers, as well as hotel people. My relationships tend to be one-on-one with decision makers, and most of my clients are high-energy people who work hard and

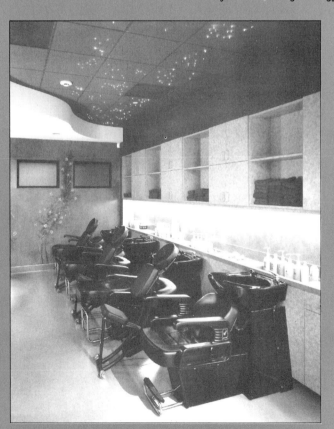

truly like other people. The projects tend to be creative, high visibility, and fast turnaround. Although I like working with people, I also need a lot of quiet time by myself, and the balance between client contact and the isolation of my design office is just right. And I get to pet my cat during breaks!

What is the least satisfying part of your job?
The least satisfying part is sometimes having too much work and sometimes having not enough, or having clients be slow about paying. It is not fun to nag people for money.

Retail: Linear Aveda Salon & Spa, Boston, Massachusetts. Corky Binggeli, ASID, Corky Binggeli Interior Design, Arlington, Massachusetts. Photographer: Gregg Shupe.

What is the most important quality or skill of a designer in your specialty?

Listening to what the clients says, both verbally and nonverbally, about their priorities and concerns. Although I am always happy to follow my own creative muse, I try to get my ego out of the way and really find out what the client is trying to achieve. I don't always go in exactly the direction a client might expect—they are paying me for my expertise and experience—but I do pay close attention to their conceptual and business concerns, and I explain my work in that light. Their business success is the basis of my future work, so I respect their perspective and budget.

Who or what experience has been a major influence in your career?

I have known quite a few architects and designers who have their own firms, and find that they spend most of their time getting new work, massaging clients, managing employees, and administering their offices, while the actual design work gets done by someone else. Knowing that I wanted my own business, I was determined to structure it so that I would be doing my own design work. I have had employees before in other types of work, and I know I don't like hiring, managing, and firing people. I

Hospitality: Appetito Restaurant, Boston, Massachusetts. Corky Binggeli, ASID, Corky Binggeli Interior Design, Arlington, Massachusetts. Photographer: Douglas Stefanov.

could possibly make more money working for a large firm, and could definitely take on larger projects as part of a larger team, but I prefer the flexibility and independence that comes with my do-everything approach.

"How Important Is Interior Design Education in Today's Industry?"

Interior design education is very important. You need to learn all of the basics in college.
—Rita Carson Guest, FASID

I would not be a partner in an architecture firm without my interior design education. Design is complex, and it involves critical and analytical thinking.
—Sandra Evans, ASID

Issues that designers deal with and the knowledge base required to understand them are growing. The complexity of the issues we work with is also increasing; therefore, a baseline of education is extremely important so you can hit the ground running. Education also gives you time to define a working style and methods of approaching the creative process.

I also cannot stress enough the importance of continuing education for all designers. Our knowledge base becomes obsolete at an ever-increasing rate. It must continue to evolve.
—Sari Graven, ASID

Education is very important! And continuing education is a must to ensure the professional is providing clients with the most up-to-date information. I cannot imagine the building industry without professional interior designers.
—Jennifer van der Put, BID, IDC, ARIDO, IFMA

Education is more important than ever because the profession, and especially my specialty of healthcare, demands great technical knowledge as well as excellent communication and CAD skills.
—Jain Malkin, CID

Important, but the professional societies need to build stronger bridges between them.
—Michael Thomas, ASID

The only way to become a professional interior designer is through education, experience, and testing.
—Linda Sorrento, ASID, IIDA

Very important! The biggest role of education is providing a foundation in the designer to understand what he/she *knows* and *doesn't know*. When you know what you don't know, you can research the information and/or find help from others in the field.
—Robin J. Wagner, ASID, IDEC

A must.
—W. Daniel Shelley, ASID, AIA

Interior design has extreme importance, and I think this is best demonstrated by the fact that almost half of the states now have some sort of legislation protecting the profession.
—Ellen McDowell, ASID

As an educator, my bias is toward a FIDER-accredited interior design program education. It sets up the entry-level interior designer for success.
—Stephanie Clemons, PhD, ASID, IDEC

If you don't have it, you are very limited. As times goes on, I believe you will not be able to practice as a designer without a degree. Would you hire a lawyer or a doctor without a degree?
—**John Holmes, ASID, IIDA**

Unfortunately, not important enough—it lost its role when we substituted space planning for design.
—**Neil Frankel, FAIA, FIIDA**

It is of the utmost importance. We are moving toward a master's degree as a minimum requirement.
—**Pat Campbell McLaughlin, ASID**

Education is becoming increasingly important as the industry becomes more specialized. The amount of knowledge required to successfully design projects today is tenfold that of when I graduated.
—**Jeffrey Rausch, IIDA**

Very important.
—**Teresa Sowell, ASID, IFMA**

Education is crucial to the interior designer. I think it is fundamental to have a four- or five-year degree in interior design from a FIDER-accredited school, the years of experience working and being mentored, and then the NCIDQ qualification exam. I believe all these steps are necessary to protect the health, safety, and welfare of the public.
—**Christy Ryan, IIDA**

Very.
—**Jan Bast, ASID, IIDA**

Education is the backbone of our industry.
—**Robert Wright, ASID**

Without an accredited degree in interior design, one cannot become certified by NCIDQ, nor obtain registration/licensure in more than half of the United States and most of Canada, nor become a professional member of ASID or IIDA. *It is imperative!*
—**David Stone, IIDA**

Education provides us with knowledge and, hopefully, helps us develop wisdom. Education gives us the tools to be flexible—adaptable—able to meet new challenges and take advantage of new opportunities. That is what survival in today's industry is about.
—**M. Joy Meeuwig, IIDA**

An interior design education in today's industry is crucial. I believe a structured education is essential to attaining a personal goal of advancement and to aiding in your credibility to others.
—**Linda Santellanes, ASID**

Getting a design education is one of the most important decisions a designer can make.
—**Debra May Himes, ASID, IIDA**

Very important.
—**Sally Nordahl, IIDA**

The process of learning and the interaction with others is as important as the information received.
—**Michelle King, IIDA**

Changing technology and today's fast-paced business climate have made it important to be educated in order to bring the very best products, techniques, and principles to clients.
—**Beth Kuzbek, ASID, IIDA, CMG**

Very important, with today's focus on licensing the professional, but as important is the quality of the education. *Professional* is a title. It's the knowledge or expertise the person has that differentiates between the professional and the decorator. A decorator's primary focus is on enhancing the aesthetics of an environment with colors, textures, and finishes. A professional interior designer does that and much more in the area of workplace productivity, safety, and efficiencies. The professional affects how people work.
—**Leonard Alvarado**

Education is paramount—and to be able to apply the skills learned. Those who learn through experience may learn one task well but will not become innovative problem solvers. They only learn to become solution appliers—repeating responses learned from experience.
—Linda Isley, IIDA

Essential—not many more years are left for the nonprofessionals who just one day hang out their shingle. The public is becoming more and more aware that real designers have a design education.
—Linda Kress, ASID

Extremely important. I tell all students that, at minimum, that they *must* graduate from a FIDER-accredited school with a bachelor's degree in interior design. An associate degree does not cut it anymore. (And I told this to students before I entered my current job in education!)
—Lisa Whited, IIDA, ASID, IDEC

It is imperative to be trained formally at school—for example, attending a professional-level program.
—Alicia Loo, CID

Extremely. Be sure to include structural knowledge of buildings and footprint relationships to the site plan.
—Kristen Anderson, ASID, CID, RID

Extremely important; it is the future of design. The collaboration of all design disciplines starting in the early stage of design education will elevate our status with the public.
—William Peace, ASID

I believe it is very important. Fewer jobs are available in this economy, so competition among individuals pursuing jobs is very high. A solid, strong education is essential, with emphasis on both design and technical skills.
—Susan B. Higbee

The body of knowledge is growing so rapidly that I can't imagine it will be long before design services offered by people without education will not be valued.
—Suzan Globus, ASID

Interior environments provide more than just shelter. Design is both life-enhancing and capable of being a healing art. As designers, we have the ability to design the stresses and irritations out of people's lives. The aesthetics are always important, and design education enhances our ability to create peaceful, functional spaces while attending to the philosophical and environmental safety issues facing us today.
—Sally Thompson, ASID

I believe a minimum of four years is essential, as is ongoing education throughout our careers.
—Janice Carleen Linster, ASID, IIDA, CID

It's very simple: As in most professions, education is the key. A properly educated job candidate stands a much better chance of landing a job than someone with a little experience and no education. Education also brings a degree of confidence. The public will be served better by a designer who is properly trained and educated. A definite must.
—Naomi Anderson

It is the sole hope for survival of the profession.
—Cheri R. Gerou, AIA, ASID

Chapter Seven

The Future

"What Do You See as the Future for the Interior Design Profession?"

Our profession is growing and maturing at a very rapid rate. The importance of what we do and how we affect the built environment is expanding and being recognized by the public. Every project we work on, no matter how small, affects the lives of those who live, work and play in the environment we design. What we do affects the health, safety, and welfare of the public. The level of responsibility for designers is rising as well, so we must prepare to shoulder this additional responsibility through our education, work experience, and qualifying examination. Regulation of our industry will be the norm, as will a first-rate education and a strong qualifying examination.
　　—Terri Maurer, FASID

A more technically oriented profession that continues to evolve in its understanding of the design of spaces for human experience and the impact of what we do in our society.
　　—Beth Harmon-Vaughn, FIIDA

The profession is going to continue to evolve, with opportunities arising in heretofore unidentified areas. Interior designers are problem solvers and as such bring much-needed skills to a wide variety of specialty areas and associated fields.
　　—Linda Elliott Smith, FASID

The future of the profession is very strong. The field is still in its infancy, and as it gains in recognition and respectability, consumer demand will grow.
　　—Dennis McNabb, ASID, IDEC

Positive. Respect for creating the built environment.
　　—Nila Leiserowitz, FASID

The future is bright if we take the initiative to regulate legally the practice of interior design. We must build consensus on the body of knowledge and advance it, supported by research and theory. Our profession is much more complex than it was twenty or even ten years ago. Research is the key to understanding how to improve the human condition through design.
　　—Denise A. Guerin, PhD, FIDEC, ASID, IIDA

Interior design will only get better and stronger. Technology will play an even greater role in the future of our world, and design is not an exception.
　　—Charles Gandy, ASID, IIDA

As professions go, we are a toddler, and as such all of us must be the best we can be, setting the stage for the future. We must not only preach the talk but walk the walk. Three *Es*: education, experience, examination.
　　—Donna Vining, FASID

It must become a united front that stands on the foundation of one professional organization. With all of us working together, interior design will gain stature and provide a rewarding profession for all who practice.
　　—Mimi Moore, ASID, CID

The field continues to expand in opportunities as public perception of our value expands. There will continue to be more and more specialties as the knowledge of specific codes, materials, methods, and design specialties becomes more intricate.

—Fred Messner, IIDA

I think the field will continue to become more technical. I think it will continue to gain recognition as a viable, respected, and necessary profession within the larger design community.

—Jan Bast, ASID, IIDA

I am certain that interior designers will always be in demand and that the consumer will realize the value in working with a designer. We will be expected to know more technically as well as be more aware of building systems and codes that govern them. The interior designer of the future will be expected to appropriately work with the limited resources our Earth has to offer and help curb our country's enormous consumption habits.

—Robert Wright, ASID

The future of the interior design profession is a collaborative effort involving all the players in the interior environment.

—Linda Sorrento, ASID, IIDA

I know what I would like it to be—right now some egos in both the interior design and architectural design field need to be checked for it to go anywhere.

—Robin J. Wagner, ASID, IDEC

We will be part of a greater whole made up of all professional design practices. Today as we practice, we work as an important piece of a team. It is obvious that in order to solve the problems in building design, it takes a group brain made up of many disciplines. The results of the research being done today about the effects of the built environment will inform a new approach to building structures for humans to inhabit for living, learning, working, playing, and healing. We will need to be ready to respond with a broadened scope of services.

—Rosalyn Cama, FASID

Through all areas of the interior design profession—residential, commercial, hospitality, retail—the list goes on and on, with both large and small projects—are unlimited opportunities. But success will come only to those prepared to make the commitments to time and education and dedicated to creating great environments and wonderful places.

—M. Arthur Gensler Jr., FAIA, FIIDA, RIBA

Our practice continues to become more complicated as the world changes.

—Rita Carson Guest, FASID

Increased specialization, broader recognition of the value of design, more complex technical knowledge requirements (for example, environmental concerns, clients' technology requirements).

—Marilyn Farrow, FIIDA

A strong future for designers who focus on specialty areas and who provide expertise in workplace productivity, sustainable interiors, energy conservation, and health and safety. All of these disciplines affect an organization's bottom line, and that is the driving force for hiring a consultant or professional today.

—Leonard Alvarado

I would like to see interior design become incorporated in the architecture curriculum at all architecture colleges so that design is integral.

—Sandra Evans, ASID

Defining interior design as a profession is more important than ever; the field is challenged from all sides. Our specific area of expertise, based on education, internships, and continuing education, must be defined in a title act or a practice act.

—Pat McLaughlin, ASID

More prominence in the field of workplace solutions, whether for a corporation, healthcare client, or hospitality project. Also, more respect from our fellow design professionals for bringing a critical area of knowledge to the table. We do not design buildings, but we are an integral and important part of the whole building experience as well as capable of taking the lead on renovation projects.
　　—David Stone, IIDA

The design process is applicable as a creative problem-solving approach to a wide variety of situations and problems. Our ability to gather and organize large amounts of information, channel it into a working, cohesive concept, and then implement it is what every business is looking for today. Our education has never been more relevant to the issues we face today in business as well as our personal lives.
　　—Sari Graven, ASID

Increased specialization and segmentation resulting in more professionalism, consumer value, and higher income potential. Along with this will come increased educational requirements and liability.
　　—Jeffrey Rausch, IIDA

I think that interior design as a profession is in its infancy and is fighting to become or be recognized as a profession. We need to market what we do and seek legal recognition so that it becomes a profession instead of a hobby.
　　—Susan Coleman, FIIDA, FIDEC

The profession of interior design is relatively new. More and more states are seeking and accomplishing licensure. I think the states that have already accomplished the Title Act will be seeking the Practice Act. I see interior designers having total independence and ownership of their work and responsibilities. In other words, an interior designer would not be required to go through an architect to stamp interior drawings.
　　—Christy Ryan, IIDA

Licensing.
　　—Teresa Sowell, ASID, IFMA

With some states gaining licensing, it is only a matter of time before all fifty states license designers. Through licensing, the public will recognize interior designers as true professionals.
　　—Greta Guelich, ASID

The future is as a service industry, providing plans and specifications for interior architecture. Interior designers need to get out of the business of selling furniture or, at a minimum, separate the two activities into separate businesses. Our ideas are our most valuable assets.
　　—Tom Witt, ASID,

The future is not clear. The media aspect of our profession implies that what we do is all about vision and touch. There is a clear threat from architecture to severely limit what an interior designer can do without being legally subservient to architects. Last, we have too many professional organizations, a fractured voice that inhibits our ability to effectively deal with these challenges.
　　—Robert Krikac, IIDA

Two avenues. First, the Home Depot/Expo/Crate and Barrel concept; good design for the masses. Second, high-end design, either commercial or residential; people who hire problem solvers and consultants.
　　—Bruce Goff, ASID

The intimate relationship between the human animal and his or her little piece of the built environment just keeps becoming more important. The interiors specialist needs to become an integral part of the A&D team. It isn't just knowledge about interior finish materials and use of space but also about how people perceive their surroundings. People are adaptable, but wouldn't it be wonderful if interior spaces supported people rather than people having to adapt to the spaces?
—M. Joy Meeuwig, IIDA

I envision the interior design profession in the future requiring an individual to be more creative, competitive, and educated in order to keep up with global markets, tighter budgets, and more educated clients.
—Linda Santellanes, ASID

CAD will be very important in this field. Hand drawing is also important in order to communicate your ideas to the client. Customer service will set one designer apart from another.
—Debra May Himes, ASID, IIDA

An expanded role in the strategic decisions our clients are facing. Interior designers are going to be called upon to have expansive knowledge of branding and an understanding of the full design experience and sustainability in a world with limited resources.
—Juliana Catlin, FASID

More people will understand and use the services of the design profession. Interior design services will be used for all sizes and budgets of projects, both expensive and inexpensive.
—John Holmes, IIDA, ASID

The future will only put more emphasis on the technical abilities of the interior designer. In addition, the more educated the public becomes, the more designers will be pushed toward better design solutions. Licensing, of course.
—Stephanie Clemons, PhD, ASID, IDEC

Competition with creative people in other professions. A cross-pollination of design disciplines as we look for fresh ideas.
—Michelle King, IIDA

I'm just glad I am not a commercial designer, because the growth is in residential, from all I have tracked.
—Michael Thomas, ASID

I see a brilliant future for the profession, with many opportunities for growth, especially on the periphery of the industry—for example, manufacturing. I see an enormous number of people seeking to bring interior designers and their expertise into their arenas.
—Beth Kuzbek, ASID, IIDA, CMG

The potential for deserved public and legal recognition.
—W. Daniel Shelley, AIA, ASID

I think it's good, as opposed to great. Probably more people are out there with design degrees than there is income to be made in the field. If you're not dedicated or educated, or good at it, you will soon end up on an alternate career path. I also think there may be a trend for many young people interested in interior design to go for a degree in interior architecture.
—Linda Kress, ASID

A lot more than fluffing pillows and selecting color swatches. I see the business lending itself more to structural building concerns and code issues and understanding and dealing with the various building departments and creating a whole end picture for our clients, including all working drawings and specifications. Technical knowledge of materials and elements.
　　—**Kristen Anderson, ASID, CID, RID**

The future of the profession, in my thinking, is strong. The field has matured and has many support vehicles in place. A central need of societies is interiors; thus the designer is in a central position as well. The stewardship needed in relation to architectural interior environments is similar to that of the natural environment. We'll continue to see new means of working with technology. We will see an increasing interest in and attention to custom design. The social consciousness and ecological concerns related to the built environment will become increasingly understood and acted upon. Designers with such knowledge will emerge with a stronger voice and will be able to see the gestalt of a project, providing translations for clients.
　　—**Joy Dohr, PhD, FIDEC, IIDA**

This is part of the reason I earned my MS in Organization—I think there are incredible opportunities for interior designers to provide organizational development consulting services. When I was working with companies, designing their spaces, I would always ask for an organizational chart and strategic plan. If they didn't have a strategic plan, I would lead them through that process (one of my services). I told them that, in my view, their greatest asset was their employees. If they wanted to reach goals as a company, then we needed to design a space that would help their greatest asset (their employees) to be productive. There is a great opportunity for interior designers to provide strategic planning, organizational development, and other consulting services to companies.
　　—**Lisa Whited, ASID, IIDA, IDEC**

I think the profession will continue to grow, become even more computer-oriented, and be a great profession to be part of.
　　—**Ellen McDowell, ASID**

As the world continues to generate uncertainty, people will continue to want designers to bring peace and certainty to their immediate environment (something more under their control). Interior designers help their clients grasp and understand what is important to them personally and help them surround themselves with those important items.
　　—**Linda Isley, IIDA**

I see interior design being universally recognized in North America as its own profession.
　　—**Jennifer van der Put, BID, IDC, ARIDO, IFMA**

If we commit to a new body of knowledge, our profession could be very important.
　　—**Neil Frankel, FAIA, FIIDA**

A standalone profession where education, experience, and examination are the fundamentals for the right to practice.
　　—**Derrell Parker, IIDA**

Since the time I graduated back in 1988, I have seen advancement in the direction the profession is going. Today there are more FIDER-accredited programs producing well-trained young designers.
　　—**Alicia Loo, CID**

Being a design consultant and problem solver and not being known for providing product only will elevate our profession.
　　—**William Peace, ASID**

I believe that the interior design profession will continue to gain acknowledgment and greater respect, as it has in the last decade. Our job becomes more and more essential every year to create healthful living environments. Rising issues in ergonomics, worker productivity, sustainability, and so on can no longer be ignored. Our role is critical in the creation and success of healthful interior environments.
—Susan B. Higbee

I see the profession expanding to encompass all the various specialties. Consumers are becoming increasingly conscious of the benefits of good design and aware of the long-term effect of everything that is manufactured and placed in our environment.
—Suzan Globus, ASID

I see my profession becoming more important as we serve as consultants with architects and engineers, working as a team, to create better living and working environments.
—Sally Thompson, ASID

Changes will continue to move in the direction of a more defined and encompassing field. Education, accreditation, and examination issues will have to be assessed and changed as issues are identified.
—Sue Kirkman, ASID, IIDA, IDEC

It's still a young profession, fighting for respect among the building professionals. We've made tremendous progress in the last twenty years in the areas of education and professional recognition. I can only see the profession becoming stronger and more widely ingrained in society and business. The U.S. Department of Labor projects the interior design field to grow by 17 percent by 2010.
—Sally D'Angelo, ASID

The future is very bright for the profession. With organizations such as ASID, which effectively promotes and, to some degree, protects the profession, it will only get better. The public is constantly being educated on the many benefits of hiring a designer, and designers in return have tailored their skills, billing procedures, and so on to cater to the needs of the public. By keeping up with the needs and wants of the public, interior designers will continue on a path of growth and success.
—Naomi Anderson

I believe our profession is rolling through a fluid metamorphosis. While the changes that have taken place in the last twenty years are exciting, I believe the growth and transition of our profession will continue. Because we most often design environments to be experienced by people, I think our business in the future will require us to be much more knowledgeable about our human instincts, our feelings, our health, our learning process, and so on. There is also much to be gained from understanding the developments in the world around us that directly affect our clients' business and therefore our design solutions. This does not imply that we ourselves have to know everything there is to know; however, we will need to know how to partner, how to collaborate, and how to engage outside resources.
—Janice Carleen Linster, ASID, IIDA, CID

Unless the profession is able to increase the level of knowledge and education, I believe it will disappear. Society has a knack for eliminating those things that are not deemed valuable. We've all heard the jokes about interior designers. This profession is facing a lack of credibility.

Education to a much higher degree is the only enduring path for interior design. A greater understanding of the building process and its components are mandatory for any success of this profession.
—Cheri Gerou

The profession will continue to change and be even more competitive. But there will always be a profession of humanizing built spaces. I see a move in the balance of art and science.

—David F. Cooke, FIIDA, CMG

The interior design industry seems to be working on developing a unified voice so the goal of passing certification and regulation laws in all fifty states can be achieved. With regulations in place, there can be more control over who can call himself an interior designer. Interior designers are responsible for implementing design solutions that affect the safety and welfare of the public in an interior environment. Certification would let the public know that the designer they hire understands current codes, regulations, and standards for interior environments. Those who call themselves interior designers should be educated at approved institutions of higher learning and pass rigorous exams. Those who do not meet these requirements should not be able to call themselves interior designers. I think we will see more action from lawmakers on regulation of our industry.

—Kristi Barker, CID

Marrying technology with the human need to be comfortable within a space, be it at work or home.

—Mary Fisher Knott, CID, RSPI, Allied Member ASID

I think the demand for interior designers will increase as state legislation becomes more defined. I have noticed that general awareness of what designers do increases where licensing or certification is required. I also anticipate that designers will be utilized more as the design/build approach becomes more popular. Also, the hierarchy of designers, depending on experience level, will become more universally defined.

I find more clients demanding flexibility in design. Meeting rooms are becoming multipurpose rooms with furniture that can be reconfigured. Workstations need to be adaptable to workplace personnel churn. This requires interior designers to be more creative.

I also believe that further development and increased availability of wireless technology and battery-operated equipment will change the landscape of spaces, enabling desired flexibility. Computers won't be tethered to a wall or cubicle by wires. The approach to furnishing and space planning will change, just as the development of the powered workstation panel changed layouts decades ago.

—Kimberly M. Studzinski, ASID

As I mentioned, I think the profession will continue to use technology both in the creation of the design and in the designs themselves. Raised flooring, computer-controlled HVAC, engineered materials— all these will become more prevalent. I also think that the field of so-called green design will grow as companies become more environmentally sensitive, as natural resources become more scarce, and consumers and even corporate shareholders demand that companies use resources efficiently.

—Derek B. Schmidt

Resources

INTERIOR DESIGN ORGANIZATIONS

American Society of Interior Designers (ASID)
608 Massachusetts Avenue NE
Washington, DC 20002-6006
202-546-3480
www.asid.org

Foundation for Interior Design Research (FIDER)
146 Monroe Center #1318
Grand Rapids, MI 49503-2822
616-458-0460
www.fider.org

Interior Design Educators Council (IDEC)
9202 N. Meridian Street #200
Indianapolis, IN 46260
317-816-6261
www.idec.org

Interior Designers of Canada (IDC)
Ontario Design Center
260 King Street East #414
Toronto, Ontario, Canada M5A 1K3
416-964-0906
www.interiordesignerscanada.org

International Facility Management Association (IFMA)
1 East Greenway Plaza #1100
Houston, TX 77046-0194
713-623-4362
www.ifma.org

International Furnishings and Design Association, Inc. (IFDA)
191 Clarksville Road
Princeton Junction, NJ 08550
609-799-3423
www.ifda.com

International Interior Design Association (IIDA)
13-122 Merchandise Mart
Chicago, IL 60654-1104
312-467-1950
www.iida.com

National Council for Interior Design Qualification (NCIDQ)
1200 18th Street NW #1001
Washington, DC 20036
202-721-0220
www.ncidq.org

National Kitchen & Bath Association (NKBA)
687 Willow Grove Street
Hackettstown, NJ 07840
908-852-0033
www.nkba.org

ALLIED ORGANIZATIONS

American Institute of Architects (AIA)
1735 New York Avenue NW
Washington, DC 20006
202-626-7300
www.aiaonline.org

Building Office & Management Association Int'l. (BOMA)
1201 New York Avenue NW,
Suite 300
Washington, DC 20005
202-408-2662
www.boma.org

Color Marketing Group (CMG)
5904 Richmond Highway,
Suite 408
Alexandria, VA 22303
703-329-8500
www.colormarketing.org

Construction Specifications Institute (CSI)
99 Canal Center Plaza,
Suite 300
Alexandria, VA 22314
703-684-0300
www.csinet.org

**Illuminating Engineering
Society of North American
(IES)**
120 Wall Street, 17th floor
New York, NY 10005
212-248-5000
www.iesna.org

**Institute of Store Planners
(ISP)**
25 North Broadway
Tarrytown, NY 10591
914-332-1806
www.ispl.org

**Leadership in Energy and
Environmental Design (LEED)**
U.S. Green Building Council
1015 18th Street NW, Suite 805
Washington, DC 20036
www.usgbc.org

**National Trust for Historic
Preservation**
1785 Massachusetts Avenue NW
Washington, DC 20036
202-588-6000
www.nationaltrust.org

**U.S. Green Building Council
(USGBC)**
1015 18th Street NW, Suite 805
Washington, DC 20036
202-828-7422
www.usgbc.org

Selected Interior Design References

Abercrombie, Stanley. "Design Revolution: 100 Years That Changed Our World." December 1999. *Interior Design*, pp. 140–198.

American Society of Interior Designers. 2002. Website information. www.asid.org

_____. 1993. ASID Fact Sheet, "Economic Impact of the Interior Design Profession." ASID, Washington, DC.

_____. 2001. "ASID: FAQs About Us." ASID, Washington, DC.

Baraban, Regina S., and Joseph F. Durocher. 2001. *Successful Restaurant Design*, 2nd ed. New York: John Wiley and Sons.

Barr, Vilma. 1995. *Promotion Strategies for Design and Construction Firms*. New York: John Wiley and Sons.

Barr, Vilma, and Charles E. Broudy. 1986. *Designing to Sell*. New York: McGraw-Hill.

Berger, C. Jaye. 1994. *Interior Design Law and Business Practices*. New York: John Wiley and Sons.

Birnberg, Howard G. 1999. *Project Management for Building Designers and Owners*. Boca Raton, FL: CRC Press.

Bureau of Labor Statistics. November 2001. Website information. www.bls.gov.

Campbell, Nina, and Caroline Seebohm. 1992. *Elsie de Wolfe: A Decorative Life*. New York: Clarkson Potter.

Cohen, Jonathan. 2000. *Communication and Design with the Internet*. New York: W.W. Norton.

Coleman, Susan. 2002. *Career Journey Road Map*. Costa Mesa, CA: Orange Coast College.

Davidson, Judith. "100 Interior Design Giants." January 2003. *Interior Design*, pp. 139–158.

Farren, Carol E. 1999. *Planning and Managing Interior Projects*, 2nd ed. Kingston, MA: R.S. Means.

Hampton, Mark. 1992. *Legendary Decorators of the 20th Century*. New York: Doubleday.

Harmon, Sharon Koomen. 2000. *The Codes Guidebook for Interiors*, 2nd ed. New York: John Wiley and Sons.

Haviland, David, ed. 1994. *The Architect's Handbook of Professional Practice*, student ed. Washington, DC: AIA Press.

Interior Designers of Canada (IDC). 2002. Website information. www.interiordesignerscanada.org.

International Interior Design Association (IIDA). 2002. Website information. www.iida.org

Israel, Lawrence J. 1994. *Store Planning/Design*. New York: John Wiley and Sons.

Jensen, Charlotte S. September 2001. "Design Versus Decoration." *Interiors and Sources*, pp. 90–93.

Kilmer, Rosemary, and W. Otie Kilmer. 1992. *Designing Interiors.* Fort Worth, TX: Harcourt Brace Jovanovich.

Kliment, Stephen A. 1998. *Writing for Design Professionals.* New York: W. W. Norton.

Linton, Harold. 2000. *Portfolio Design*, 2nd ed. New York: W. W. Norton.

Malkin, Jain. 1992. *Hospital Interior Architecture.* New York: John Wiley and Sons.

_____. 2002. *Medical and Dental Space Planning*, 3rd ed. New York: John Wiley and Sons.

Marberry, Sara, ed. 1997. *Healthcare Design.* New York: John Wiley and Sons.

Martin, Jane D., and Nancy Knoohuizen. 1995. *Marketing Basics for Designers.* New York: John Wiley and Sons.

McGowan, Maryrose. 1996. *Specifying Interiors.* New York: John Wiley and Sons.

Merriam-Webster's Collegiate Dictionary, 10th ed. 1994. Springfield, MA: Merriam-Webster.

Morgan, Jim. 1998. *Management of the Small Design Firm.* New York: Watson-Guptill.

National Council for Interior Design Qualification. 2000. *NCIDQ Examination Study Guide.* Washington, DC: National Council for Interior Design Qualification.

_____. 2003. *Practice Analysis Study.* Washington, DC: National Council for Interior Design Qualification.

Washington, DC: National Council for Interior Design Qualification.Pelegrin-Genel, Elisabeth. 1996. *The Office.* Paris and New York: Flammarion.

Pile, John. 1995. *Interior Design,* 2nd ed. Englewood Cliffs, NJ: Prentice Hall.

_____. 2000. *A History of Interior Design.* New York: John Wiley and Sons.

Piotrowski, Christine M. 1992. *Interior Design Management.* New York: John Wiley and Sons.

_____. 2002. *Professional Practice for Interior Designers*, 3rd ed. New York: John Wiley and Sons.

Piotrowski, Christine M., and Elizabeth Rodgers. 1999. *Designing Commercial Interiors.* New York: John Wiley and Sons.

Rutes, Walter A., and Richard H. Penner. 1985. *Hotel Planning and Design.* New York: Watson-Guptill.

Stipanuk, David M., and Harold Roffmann. 1992. *Hospitality Facilities Management and Design.* East Lansing, MI: Educational Institute of the American Hotel and Motel Association.

Tate, Allen, and C. Ray Smith. 1986. *Interior Design in the 20th Century.* New York: Harper and Row.

Interior Designers

Leonard Alvarado
Principal
Contract Office Group
Milpitas, California

Kristen Anderson, ASID, CID, RID
Designer
Sagan Design Group
Tahoe City, California

Naomi Anderson
Publisher
Sources & Design Magazine
Scottsdale, Arizona

Kristine S. Barker, CID
Interior Designer
Hayes, Seay, Mattern & Mattern, Inc.
Virginia Beach, Virginia

Jan Bast, ASID, IIDA, IDEC
Interior Design Program Director
Design Institute of San Diego
San Diego, California

Corky Binggeli, ASID
Principal
Corky Binggeli Interior Design
Arlington, Massachusetts

Rosalyn Cama, FASID
President
CAMA, Inc.
New Haven, Connecticut

Juliana Catlin, FASID
President
Catlin Design Group
Jacksonville, Florida

Stephanie Clemons, PhD, ASID, IDEC
Associate Professor, Interior Design
Colorado State University
Fort Collins, Colorado

Susan Coleman, FIIDA. FIDEC
Orange Coast College
Costa Mesa, California

David F. Cooke, FIIDA, CMG
Principal
Design Collective Incorporated
Columbus, Ohio

Sally Howard D'Angelo, ASID
Principal
S. H. Designs
Windham, New Hampshire

Joy Dohr, PhD, FIDEC, IIDA
Professor and Associate Dean
University of Wisconsin—Madison
Madison, Wisconsin

Theodore Drab, ASID, IIDA, IDEC
Associate Professor
University of Oklahoma
Norman, Oklahoma

Sandra G. Evans, ASID
Principal
Knoell & Quidort Architects
Phoenix, Arizona

Marilyn Farrow, FIIDA
Principal
Farrow Interiors/Consulting
Taos, New Mexico

Neil P. Frankel, FIIDA, FAIA
Design Partner
Frankel + Coleman
Chicago, Illinois

Charles Gandy, FASID, FIIDA
Principal
Charles Gandy, Inc.
Atlanta, Georgia

M. Arthur Gensler Jr., FAIA, FIIDA, RIBA
Chairman
Gensler
San Francisco, California

Cheri R. Gerou, AIA, ASID
Principal
Gerou & Associates, Ltd.
Evergreen, Colorado

Suzan Globus, ASID
Owner
Globus Design Associates
Red Bank, New Jersey

Bruce Goff, ASID
President
Domus Design Group
San Francisco, California

Sari Graven, ASID
Associate Principal
Callison Architecture, Inc.
Seattle, Washington

Greta Guelich, ASID
Principal
Perceptions Interior Design Group LLC
Scottsdale, Arizona

Denise A. Guerin, PhD, FIDEC, ASID, IIDA
Professor
University of Minnesota
St. Paul, Minnesota

Rita Carson Guest, FASID
President
Carson Guest, Inc.
Atlanta, Georgia

Beth Harmon-Vaughn, FIIDA
Senior Associate
HOK Sport + Venue + Event
Kansas City, Kansas

Susan B. Higbee
Director of Interior Design
Group Mackenzie
Portland, Oregon

Debra May Himes, ASID, IIDA
Owner
Debra May Himes Interior Design & Associates LLC
Mesa, Arizona

John Holmes, ASID, IIDA
Interior Consultant
Corporate Express
Phoenix, Arizona

Linda Isley, IIDA
Design Director
Young + Co., Inc.
San Diego, California

Michele King, IIDA
Interior Designer
Dekker/Perich/Sabatini
Albuquerque, New Mexico

Sue Kirkman, ASID, IIDA, IDEC
Dean of Education
Harrington Institute of Interior Design
Chicago, Illinois

**Mary Fisher Knott, CID, RSPI,
Allied member ASID**
Owner
Mary Fisher Designs
Scottsdale, Arizona

Linda Kress, ASID
Director of Interior Design
Lotti Krishan & Short Architects
Tulsa, Oklahoma

Robert J. Krikac, IIDA
Associate Professor
Washington State University
Pullman, Washington

Beth Kuzbek, ASID, IIDA, CMG
National Specification Manager, Healthcare
Omnova Solutions, Inc.
Fairlawn, Ohio

Nila Leiserowitz, FASID
Vice President
Gensler
Santa Monica, California

Janice Carleen Linster, ASID, IIDA, CID
Principal
Ellerbe Becket
Minneapolis, Minnesota

Alicia Loo, CID
Associate
Hirsch Bender & Associates
Santa Monica, California

Jain Malkin, CID
President
Jain Malkin, Inc.
San Diego, California

Terri Maurer, FASID
Principal
Maurer Design Group
Akron, Ohio

Ellen McDowell, ASID
Owner
Historic Perspectives
Baton Rouge, Louisiana

Pat Campbell McLaughlin, ASID
President
Steel Magnolia
Dallas, Texas

John Mclean, RA, CMG
Principal & Design Director
John Mclean Architect/architecture & industrial
design
White Plains, New York

Dennis McNabb, ASID, IDEC
Associate Chair, Fashion and Interior Design
Central College
Houston Community College System
Houston, Texas

M. Joy Meeuwig, IIDA
Owner
Interior Design Consultation
Reno, Nevada

Fred Messner, IIDA
Principal
Phoenix Design One, Inc.
Phoenix, Arizona

Mimi Moore, ASID, CID, IDEC
Professor
San Diego Mesa College
San Diego, California

Sally Nordahl, IIDA
Principal
Group Renaissance Architects
Phoenix, Arizona

Barbara Nugent, FASID
Principal
bnDesigns
Dallas, Texas

Derrell Parker, IIDA, ASID
Partner
Parker Scaggiari
Las Vegas, Nevada

William Peace, ASID
President
Peace Design
Atlanta, Georgia

Jennifer van der Put, BID, IDC, ARIDO, IFMA
Director of Interior Design/Senior Associate
Bregman + Hamann Interior Design
Toronto, Ontario, Canada

Jeffrey Rausch, IIDA
Principal
Exclaim Design
Scottsdale, Arizona

Christy Ryan, IIDA
Designer
DFDCornoyerHedrick
Phoenix, Arizona

Linda Santellanes, ASID
Principal
Santellanes Interiors, Inc.
Tempe, Arizona

Derek B. Schmidt
Project Designer
Design Collective Incorporated
Nashville, Tennessee

Melinda Sechrist, FASID
President
Sechrist Design Associates, Inc
Seattle, Washington

W. Daniel Shelley, AIA, ASID
Vice President/Secretary
James, DuRant, Matthews & Shelley, Inc.
Sumter, South Carolina

Linda Elliott Smith, FASID
President
smith & associates, inc.
Dallas, Texas

Linda Sorrento, ASID, IIDA
Manager, Strategic Workplace Solutions/A&D
Arbee Associates
Gaithersburg, Maryland

Teresa Sowell, ASID, IFMA
Principal Facilities Engineer
Raytheon, Inc.
Tucson, Arizona

David D. Stone, IIDA
Associate
Sasaki Associates, Inc.
Watertown, Massachusetts

Kimberly M. Studzinski, ASID
Project Designer
Buchart Horn/Basco Associates
York, Pennsylvania

Michael A. Thomas, ASID
Principal
The DESIGN Collective Group, Inc.
Jupiter, Florida

Sally Thompson, ASID
President
Personal Interiors by Sally Thompson, Inc.
Gainesville, Florida

Jennifer Tiernan, IIDA
Principal
Geppetto Studios, Inc.
St. Louis, Missouri

Suzanne Urban, ASID, IIDA
Principal
STUDIO4 Interiors Ltd.
Phoenix, Arizona

Donna Vining, FASID
President
Vining Design Associates, Inc.
Houston, Texas

Robin J. Wagner, ASID, IDEC
Principal
RJ Wagner Design Associates
Clifton, Virginia

Lisa M. Whited, IIDA, ASID, IDEC
Program Director, College of Interior Design
Boston Architectural Center
Boston, Massachusetts

Trisha Wilson, ASID
President
Wilson & Associates
Dallas, Texas

Tom Witt, ASID
Associate Professor
Arizona State University
Tempe, Arizona

Robert Wright, ASID
President
Bast/Wright Interiors Inc.
San Diego, California

Index

McNabb, Dennis, 225–227, 250

Medical facilities. *See* Healthcare

Meeuwig, M. Joy, 29, 48, 62, 91, 104, 135, 171, 175, 202, 206, 236–237, 247, 253

Meier, Richard, 6

Merchandise, sale of, 195–197

Merchandising, 94

Messner, Frederick, 14–15, 26, 60, 92, 119, 134, 175, 182, 205, 251

Mies van der Rohe, Ludwig, 6

Model building, 121

Model homes, 121

Moore, Mimi, 221–223, 250

Museum work, 122–123

N

National Council for Interior Design Qualification (NCIDQ), 3, 228, 257
   design phases identified by, 36
   and NCIDQ exam, 214, 220, 228, 229, 242

National Kitchen and Bath Association (NKBA), x, 13, 257

National Society of Interior Designers (NSID), 6

National Trust for Historic Preservation, 258

NCIDQ. *See* National Council for Interior Design Qualification

NCIDQ exam, 214, 220, 228, 229, 242

Negligence, 197

New York School of Applied and Fine Arts, 6, 210

Niches, 65–66

NKBA. *See* National Kitchen and Bath Association

Nordahl, Sally, 27, 62, 119, 130, 132, 175, 184, 205, 247

NSID (National Society of Interior Designers), 6

Nugent, Barbara, 25, 62, 91, 106–107, 165, 171

O

Offices. *See also* Institutional design
   David F. Cooke, 82–83
   corporate and professional, 72, 76
   Bruce Goff, 74–75
   Rita Carson Guest, 77–78
   Susan Higbee, 231–233
   M. Joy Meeuwig, 236–237
   Frederick Messner, 14–15
   Linda Sorrento, 162–163

Office furnishings dealers, jobs with, 160–161

Office systems furniture, 76

Open office furniture, 76

Orthographic projections, 47

P

Parish, Mrs. Henry, II, 6

Parker, Derrell, 28, 62, 92, 134, 174, 184, 202, 206, 254

Parsons School of Design, 6, 210

Partition walls, 58

Peace, William, 30, 63, 80–81, 131, 137, 165, 177, 184, 207, 248, 254

Perspectives, 46, 47, 49

Platner, Warren, 6

Plumbing plans, 49

Portfolios, 119, 150, 164–165

Postgraduate education, 215

Practice acts, 19

Prisons, 105. *See also* Institutional design

Product designers, 121

Professional associations, 10–13
   appellations of, x
   ASID and IIDA membership qualifications, 12
   history of, 6
   NCIDQ exam required by, 242

Professional Interior Designers Institute of Manitoba, 10

Professional-level classes, 214

Professional negligence, 197